remembering reet and shine

remembering

reet
and
shine

two black men,
one struggle

Michael Schwalbe

UNIVERSITY PRESS OF MISSISSIPPI   JACKSON

www.upress.state.ms.us

The University Press of Mississippi is a member of the Association of American University Presses.

12 11 10 09 08 07 06 05 04   4 3 2 1

∞

Library of Congress Cataloging-in-Publication Data

Schwalbe, Michael, 1956–
Remembering Reet and Shine : two black men, one struggle / Michael Schwalbe.
p. cm.
ISBN 1-57806-675-1 (cloth: alk. paper)
1. Mason, Matthew, 1911–2002. 2. Atwater, Anthony, 1933–2000.
3. African American men—Southern States—Biography. 4. African Americans—Southern States—Biography. 5. African American men—Southern States—Social conditions—20th century. 6. African Americans—Southern States—Social conditions—20th century. 7. Southern States—Race relations. 8. Southern States—Biography. 9. Carrboro (N.C.)—Biography. I. Title.
E185.96.S353 2004
975'.00496073'00922—dc22   2004005731

British Library Cataloging-in-Publication Data available

... neither whites nor blacks, for excellent reasons of their own, have the faintest desire to look back; but I think that the past is all that makes the present coherent, and further, that the past will remain horrible for exactly as long as we refuse to assess it honestly.

—James Baldwin, *Notes of a Native Son*

contents

preface

November 6, 1995. Sitting in the passenger seat of my car, Joann slid her index finger down a list of names on a clipboard in her lap, describing each man in a sentence or two. She ran an advocacy group for residents of public housing and had agreed to introduce me to the older black men I wanted to interview for a book about fathers and sons.

We had just pulled into the parking lot at the South Roberson Street complex—two rows of neat one-story apartments, fifteen units in all, many of them fronted by small flower gardens. When Joann came to Anthony Atwater, she tapped her finger on his name and said, "Atwater thinks he's a lover"—she smiled at this—"and there are rumors that people are selling drugs out of his apartment. Be careful with him."

A torn shade was drawn down over the single window that looked into the living room of Atwater's apartment. The rug-sized garden space below the window had been taken over by weeds. Joann knocked on the screen door; the inside door was three inches ajar. "Mr. Atwater, it's Joann with the residents' council," she said. A raspy voice that seemed to strain for volume said, "C'mon in."

The apartment reeked of smoke. A man and a woman sat on the sofa opposite a blaring television, the only source of light in the room. They didn't seem to notice us as we walked past them to where Atwater sat in a threadbare recliner. He wore a burgundy bathrobe over light blue pajamas. At first I thought he was wearing slippers, then I saw that he had stomped down the heels on a pair of worn-out street shoes so he could slip his feet straight into them.

Atwater was thin; the bare ankles that stuck out of his pajama legs looked like bat handles. He was dark-skinned and puffy-eyed, with tightly curled white hair and a few days' growth of beard. An L-shaped

scar ran from the right corner of his mouth down and back along his jaw. I guessed he was about seventy-five.

Joann introduced me as a professor who was studying "how different folks raise their children." I heard a laugh, but I couldn't tell if it came from the TV or the sofa. Joann said, "You have *two* sons, don't you, Mr. Atwater?" "*Four* that I know of," Atwater said, "and maybe some more!" At this he tipped his head back and laughed, flicking his tongue out and opening his legs wide at the knees, flapping them a few times for emphasis.

I smiled at the slapstick, thinking that even if this guy was a joker, he was the liveliest character I'd met in four months of interviewing old men about relationships with their middle-aged sons. When Atwater's laughter trailed off I asked if I could come by the next week to interview him. "Yeah, that's fine," he said. "Come by any time you want." The next week Atwater began telling me about his past exploits as a street-wise stud called Shine, and about the shambles of his present life. It turned out that he was sixty-two, not seventy-five.

Joann also introduced me to Matthew Mason, who lived two doors from Atwater. Mr. Mason was eighty-four and shared the apartment with his seventy-nine-year-old wife Martha. Mr. Mason had three middle-aged sons, and so I arranged to interview him too.

As Mr. Mason later recounted his life, I learned that his paternal grandfather had been born a slave; that his parents had been share-croppers in northeast Chatham County; that he had come to Chapel Hill in 1924; and that in 1934 he began working for an all-white fraternity at the University of North Carolina. I learned that in the course of his fifty-year relationship with the fraternity, Mason had become a figure of legend, known by his nickname, Dr. Reet.

On days I returned to the complex to interview other men, I would drop in on Atwater and Mason to say hello. Both men were congenial— Mason with grace, Atwater with swagger—and liked to talk. As I spent time with them, my interest in writing about fathers and sons waned while my interest in their lives grew.

It mattered that Mason and Atwater were black. What had it been like, I wondered, to be a working-class black man in the South during the Jim Crow era? How did a man deal with the daily threats to his dignity

and to his self-regard as a man? My own social designations—white, from the North, born in 1956, a tenured professor—put me at considerable distance from the lives of men like Mason and Atwater. I was intrigued by what they were telling me about matters I had only read about.

In January of 1996 I asked Mason and Atwater if I could make them the subjects of a dual biography. They agreed, and I shelved the fathers-and-sons study, thinking that I could come back to it later. I hardly knew what I was getting in for. As a sociologist, I had always taken the details of people's lives as bits of data to be lumped together, all flesh and blood and bone disappearing in the process. So what kind of sense could I make of these two men whose lives I was about to enter? I wasn't sure, but I was moving toward something I needed to understand.

remembering reet and shine

room to be human

I knocked once and a male voice said *Come in*. The door scuffed over a hump in some badly laid linoleum. Atwater's thirty-eight-year-old son, Chris, and two younger men were watching television. They glanced up and returned my nodded hello. "He's not ready yet," Chris said, eyes on the tube. "The nurse is still back there with him." This was the home health nurse, giving Atwater his weekly checkup. I flopped into a chair to wait. On the TV screen a trio of sexy black women writhed and rapped in a segment of "Video Soul." The video was followed by an ad urging viewers to get tested for AIDS.

Halfway into the next video the nurse came out and stood in the entryway to the living room, her medical bag hanging in front of her, both hands on the handle. She was thirtyish, white, pleasantly professional. I turned to hear the report she was poised to deliver. She waited for the others to give her their attention. They didn't. It was as if she had just dropped in and was welcome to watch TV, as long as she didn't cause any distraction.

When it became apparent that I was her audience, she turned toward me and said, "He's doing okay. He just needs to be sure to take his medications." She moved past me and opened the door. Facing me again, she said, "I'll be back at the same time next week to check up on him." I nodded. Then, raking her gaze across the faces locked on the tube, she said, "Have a good day," and pulled the door shut behind her. "I'll go see if the old man is ready," I said.

3

Atwater with oxygen tank

"How you doing, Mike?" Atwater rasped, standing up straight and extending his hand for a shake. He was five-eight and 140 pounds, but his hands were larger than mine and his grip surprisingly strong for a sixty-three-year-old man who had been on disability for years. "Not bad," I said. "How're you doing? The nurse said you're hanging in."

"I feel good. This oxygen," he said, holding up the clear plastic tubing that ran from the cannula in his nose to the humming concentrator across the room, "makes a difference. I haven't been getting as short of breath. I'm also feeling more at peace here."

Atwater was staying with his son Chris and Chris's two children in a small house—I guessed seven hundred square feet—at the end of Alabama Avenue in Carrboro. The house had seen better days. A rain gutter in front dangled loose at one end; the roof was tattered; bare wood showed through the faded green paint. "It's been eaten up by termites, too," Atwater had said, adding to the list of problems. "After my father died, no one kept the place up. I hate to see it in this raggedy-assed condition."

Atwater had lived in the house off and on for short periods of time since his parents bought it in 1956. He was back here now after getting evicted from public housing two months earlier. By making it a priority to repay the street lenders who financed his drug purchases, Atwater ended up three months behind on his rent and, by court order, was put out in June 1996. He spent twelve days in detox in Durham, and was set to be discharged to a family-run rehab farm in Roxboro, before Chris agreed, at the last minute, to take him in.

When I'd met Atwater eight months earlier, it seemed likely that he'd be dead by now. One day in early January I'd gone to his apartment for our weekly interview and was met at the door by a white woman— tall, blonde and stocky, about thirty-five years old; not a nurse, but with a nurse's manner. I asked for Mr. Atwater. She said, "Popcorn's sleeping now. He just got back from the hospital. He had a seizure and had to go to the ER. I'm Caroline, a friend. I'm taking care of him." I asked if he— Popcorn?—was going to be okay. "They say he's got about six to eight months to live," she said.

Later Atwater told me what had happened. "My heart stopped," he said. "They had to take me to the hospital and start it up again. I was slap-dead and they brought me back." I asked if they knew what had caused the heart trouble. "Too much 'caine," he said. "I can't handle it anymore. My lungs are shot."

Atwater had made it through the spring and most of the summer without killing himself, but his emphysema had worsened. For a time, Atwater made weekly trips to the ER because of his "breathing attacks," as he called them. "It's like drowning," he would explain—pursing his lips, tilting his head back, and drawing a fraction of a breath to demonstrate what it's like to suffocate in open air. Medicaid had finally agreed to pay for the oxygen machine to which Atwater was now tethered. Neither the emphysema nor the machine kept him from smoking.

"Where to today?" I asked.

"I need to go to the credit union and then to the drug store to get some reading glasses," he said, looking in the mirror and adjusting his black beret. He smoothed his mostly white goatee by drawing a hand across his chin. "We can just go for a drive too. I haven't been out in a while."

Atwater was in his going-out clothes: a white short-sleeved shirt, light gray slacks, and running shoes. For months, when I visited him in his apartment, I'd never seen him in anything but an old burgundy bathrobe that he wore over pale blue pajamas. The first time I'd seen him in pants and a shirt was when he appeared in court to receive his eviction judgment.

We unhooked Atwater's oxygen tube from the machine and connected it to a portable silver and green tank. He set the valve to allow a flow of two liters per minute, the same as the machine. The tank rested in a two-wheeled hand cart that Atwater pushed along in front of him.

"How long do these tanks last?" I asked.

"About six hours, the guy said."

"If it runs out I suppose we could rush you to a scuba shop for an emergency fix."

While Atwater used the bathroom, I told Chris that we were going to the credit union and the drug store and would probably be back in a few hours. "The oxygen tank is supposed to be good for about six hours," I said, in part just to say something and in part to fish for a sign of concern. I wondered how he and his father, who had been largely absent while Chris was growing up, were getting along in these close quarters. Chris nodded and mumbled affirmatively to my comment about the oxygen tank.

Atwater emerged from the hall pushing his tank.

"You all set?" I asked.

"Let's roll," he said.

It took a minute to go thirty feet from the house to the car. Atwater was being careful to pace himself. I opened the passenger door and he lifted his tank in first, then swung himself in and arranged the tank so it rested upright between his knees. I started the car and blasted the air conditioning. It was late August in North Carolina, still a month away from a break in the heat and humidity.

"It'll get comfortable pretty quick," I said.

"Damn!"

"What is it?"

"I forgot my teeth. They're in a cup by my bed."

They laughed in the living room when I went back to fetch Atwater's teeth. It wasn't just the old man's forgetfulness that was

funny. Even funnier, I imagined them thinking, was how he'd conned a white professor into playing chauffeur and teeth retriever.

I wondered about that myself. Why did I think this man, an ex-wino of scurrilous reputation, was worth writing about? Before he'd gotten kicked out of his apartment I'd asked Atwater what sense his friends made of my interest in him. "They don't understand it," he'd said. "I tell them that you just came around one day looking for old black men to talk to, and I was there, ready to talk. Then I tell them that the Lord sent you to take my testimony before I die." If so, I'd told him, I wasn't aware of it. "Doesn't matter. The Boss knows what he's doing," he'd said.

I handed Atwater his teeth. He popped them in and clacked them a few times to make sure they were set right, then laid the cup on the floor at his feet. I was surprised that I hadn't noticed he'd been toothless in the house. "Let's go to the credit union first," he said, his speech crisper now. "I need to draw some green."

We took Main Street through Carrboro and then Franklin Street through downtown Chapel Hill. I asked Atwater how he was getting along with Chris. "So far it's been okay," he said. "He cooks and brings me my meals. Mostly I stay out of the way and watch TV in my bedroom."

"So you're not indulging?" I asked, alluding to the crack he had said, while in detox, he was going to stop using.

"No, I don't touch it," he said. I gave him a skeptical look. "Well, if I want a little piece I go out and get it and bring it back to my room." I couldn't help laughing.

"How do you get it back to your room without touching it?"

"I mean I'm not out there partying all night. I don't *need* the stuff. I'm not ghostbusting pieces off the floor. I just use it sometimes to relax." This was, I would learn, classic Atwater: wrapping himself in contradictions that were, to his mind, not contradictions at all. When it came to self-justification, he was a linguistic Houdini.

"What's Chris think of you living there?"

"He's okay with it. He's getting a piece of my Social Security money."

"I don't suppose it's exactly like a father coming home, is it?"

"It can't be. But maybe I can have a second chance to be a father to him. Now that he's trying to raise his kids, I can tell him things he needs to know."

"You think Chris is going to listen to your advice about fathering?"

"He probably won't, and I can understand that. But it's his own dumb-ass fault if I tell him something and he won't listen."

Atwater traced many of his troubles to his own failures as a father. He had graduated from high school in the spring of 1951, and that fall gotten a girl pregnant. His first son, Bernard, was born the following July. Atwater eventually married the girl in November 1953. At the time Atwater had been in the army for six months and was home on leave before going to quartermaster school. Atwater said that his mother pressured him to get married, so that if anything happened to him in the army his son would get a pension.

After quartermaster school, Atwater shipped out to Korea. He imagined that when he got out he would use the GI Bill to pay for college, perhaps becoming an engineer and realizing a childhood dream to build bridges. He also imagined himself being a father to Bernard, playing ball with him and "teaching him man things."

Atwater's dreams began to unravel when a letter from a friend alleged that his wife was having an affair. "I wanted to go home and check out the situation," Atwater had told me, "but they wouldn't let me go. I begged the chaplain and the psychiatrist to let me go home and put things right, but they wouldn't okay it. That's when I started to go crazy. I was a spit-and-polish soldier until then. But when they wouldn't let me go home and check on my wife, I started drinking and disobeying orders. I didn't care about anything at that point. Everything just went to hell."

Eventually Atwater was court-martialed and sentenced to six months in the stockade. He left the army with a bad conduct discharge in December 1955, having never risen above the rank of private.

Late in the following spring Atwater was back in Chapel Hill, intending to kill his wife. "I planned it for months," Atwater had told me. "I took her out in the woods in my car. I had my pick, my shovel, my liquor, and my pistol. She was down on her knees in front of me, praying. I had my gun at her head. I told her she'd better pray well, because she was about to meet her maker. Then she said, 'I might deserve to die, but if you kill me, Bernard will never be able to love you. He'll hate you all your life.' Those words paralyzed my finger and saved her life. I fell

down on my knees and held her and we ended up making love right there in the dirt."

Atwater was twenty-three at the time. By his account, he felt he had nothing to lose. His army career was ruined and his fantasies of happy family life were shattered. Atwater told it, over and again, as a neatly wrought story in which he was innocent victim, righteous avenger, and merciful lover. Of course, Atwater had had forty years to make the story what he needed it to be.

Atwater and his wife maintained a stormy, off-and-on relationship until 1970, when she finally divorced him. Atwater didn't even realize the divorce had gone through. He was too drunk to know he'd been served papers.

Even before the divorce, Atwater was gone much of time. And when he was in town, he was often drunk and violent. Shortly after Chris was born in 1958, Atwater's wife got a court order to keep him away. "When she did that, when she took my boys away, I told her, 'You have set me free,' and I took off. I told her it would hurt those boys not to have a father, and I knew it wasn't right to leave, but at the time, I didn't care. I felt like all my dreams were ruined and I just wanted to get away," Atwater had told me. He also said, at other times, that the major regret in his life was that he hadn't kept his head together well enough to be a father to his boys. As he figured it, he'd spent only three or four years with them, altogether, as they were growing up.

And now Chris was supposed to take care of him.

We sat quietly at the corner of Franklin and Columbia until the light turned green. Atwater scanned the intersection, taking in the sight of undergraduate women in T-shirts, shorts, and sandals. "Not bad, not bad," he said, turning to me with a grin. He figured I was looking too.

"Hey, is that tape recorder on? I gotta be careful what I say," he said as we turned the corner onto Columbia, heading to the credit union on south Pittsboro.

"No, it's not on. What were you going to say?"

"I got my dick sucked last night."

This was the kind of thing Atwater would say from time to time. Sexual prowess and penis size ("Man, that guy's got a dick the size of a beer can," one of his oddball cousins told me later) were central to

Atwater's sense of manhood. I had to laugh when Atwater got into his dick talk, not so much because what he said was funny, but because of the absurdity of a man in his sixties boasting like a teenage boy.

But what else did Atwater have to stake his manhood on? Not success at work or in raising a family. Once upon a time there was violence: "I didn't take shit from nobody. I didn't play, man. If I had to, I'd cut 'em. I liked to see 'em bleed." But that was in the past; now it was all talk. He could still have shot someone, but not if he had to move fast or far to do it. Even his sexuality was threatened by the emphysema. "I've still got the tool," he would say, "but I ain't got the power to push it."

In the first months I knew him, I took Atwater's sex stories, like all the others, matter-of-factly. I figured that the stories, true or not, were useful revelations of character. Identity talk.

"Who was it?" I asked.

"An old girlfriend. It was about 4:00 A.M. Chris kept coming by the door and saying, 'Dad, you all right?' I told him to go away. Man, I never even had my dick sucked till I was fifty-nine. I got to make up for lost time." Fifty-nine? I gave him another skeptical look.

"Seems kind of foolish for you to have waited so long, considering your condition," I said, giving him the affirmation he wanted. His laughter triggered a coughing fit that lasted until I turned into the driveway for the credit union. I pulled up close to the door to let Atwater out, then parked while he made his withdrawal. I pulled up again when I saw him come out.

"Where to next?" I asked after he got settled in the front seat and caught his breath.

"I'm ready to ride. Wherever you want to go."

"How about lemonade?"

I took Atwater to Foster's, a gourmet grocery store that had a deli counter and indoor seating. Tucked into a corner of Durham, the place was done up to look like an old country store. I thought Atwater might find it interesting. It was the kind of place he'd never get to on his own.

As I drove, Atwater told me about the spiritual experience he'd had in 1970 at the old RCA (Rehabilitation Center for Alcoholics) facility in Occoquan, Virginia. Atwater ended up there after a monthlong binge.

A friendly cabbie had seen Atwater clinging to a street pole in the vicinity of 14th and U in Washington, D.C. Once fancying himself the "best-dressed drunk in Chapel Hill," Atwater had become a wobbling, disheveled street wino. The cabbie pulled over and asked Atwater if he wanted help. At first Atwater thought the cabbie was gay and was hitting on him, but when he realized that the offer of help was genuine, he accepted a free ride to a detox center. After two days he was sent to Occoquan for follow-up treatment.

Atwater was put to work in the supply room and then later asked to stay on as a peer counselor, receiving off-the-record cash wages. "That was one of the best years of my life," Atwater had told me on a previous occasion. "The work I did there meant something. I was trying to help young people avoid the trouble I'd gotten into. I think it made a difference for some of them." Atwater avoided his own troubles for only a year. On a trip to Chapel Hill Atwater got drunk with some old buddies and felt too ashamed to return to his work as a counselor.

Atwater's spiritual experience had come earlier, while he was doing a relaxation exercise at Occoquan. "I was on my back, sinking into the mattress, palms up—just like they taught us. Suddenly it was like I was out of my body, looking back at myself lying there. I was trying to figure out what to do with my life. That's when I heard the Voice." The Voice, Atwater said, told him two things: he would have to go home to Chapel Hill because his father would need help, and that he would "retrieve a fish from the sea," a fish he should not throw back. The fish, the Voice said, would be in the form of a white woman.

"Does that sound crazy to you?" he asked as I parked the car in the Foster's lot.

"It doesn't sound any crazier than what a lot of people might tell," I said, "if they were willing to tell it."

"I didn't tell anyone about the Voice for a long time, because a lot of people might think it's crazy, but it's the truth. I heard it. I heard it again when my other son was born. The Voice said, 'You shall name this child Ansittwa.' I'd never heard that name before and it just came into my head." This child, born fifteen years after Atwater first heard the Voice, was Atwater's son by the white woman who was the fish he was supposed to keep. The child was raised by the woman's parents,

who had obtained legal custody. After a six-year relationship ended, Atwater rarely saw the mother and had not seen the boy in years.

Atwater nudged his cart through the hard-packed gravel of the parking lot. I lifted the tank up the stairs onto the side porch of the store. By the time we got inside, Atwater needed to rest. He steadied himself with one hand on the back of a booth, breathing as slowly and deeply as he could. "Let's sit here," I said, indicating the booth Atwater was leaning on. He slid into the seat with no hesitation.

I got an iced coffee and a lemonade and rejoined Atwater in the booth. "The music sort of fits the place," Atwater said, eyeballing the speaker above our heads. "Kind of countryish." I said it was Dwight Yoakam singing "Long White Cadillac."

"Yeah, man, that's my kind of car," Atwater said. "A convertible."

A smartly dressed black woman in her fifties walked by and Atwater said hello. She smiled and nodded, passing her eyes from Atwater to me, but didn't speak. I imagined her assessing Atwater's class status and wondering how he'd found his way in and what we were doing together. Atwater paid her no more mind as she walked away. Then he turned in the booth, swiveling his head to look around the store. "I wonder . . . ," he began—I expected him to say something about the woman or the other people in the store—"if they sell cigarettes here."

Atwater had smoked since he was six, when a fourteen-year-old baby-sitter played sex games with him and gave him cigarettes to hush him up. "She would say, 'If you tell what I done to you, I'll tell that you smoked cigarettes, and you'll get a whipping,' " Atwater had told me. Though he never told on the baby-sitter, Atwater got the whipping anyway. His father, a short but stocky brick mason, saw the smoke wafting through the airy walls of the outhouse. "My daddy damn near pulled that shithouse door off its hinges," Atwater told the story. "He grabbed me by the front of my overalls and jerked me off the seat. While he was dragging me into the house he must have asked me fifty times where I got that cigarette. I told him I picked it up off the ground. He never believed me, but my mother did."

The beating was interrupted by Atwater's mother. "I don't know what Momma told him, but Daddy was beating my ass half to death and she made him stop. She said she was going to let me smoke cigarettes.

I think she must have threatened him about leaving and taking me with her. I think she did it just to let him know that she was the boss. After that, he never said another word to me about smoking. I'd sit in the house and blow smoke rings and, man, he'd just glare. Shit, that was good. I said to myself, 'you can't hit me now; my momma done told me I could smoke.' "

Atwater's eighty-seven-year-old mother, when I later asked her about this, told it differently. She said it wasn't until her son was fourteen that she bought him cigarettes, because she didn't want him picking butts off the ground. To that account Atwater shook his head no. "When she saw that cigarettes was killing me, she didn't want to have nothing to do with it. She wouldn't admit she gave them to me." Atwater came to wish his mother had let him take the beating. "Maybe if I'd carried that ass-whupping my daddy put on me, I'd have never smoked. Maybe."

It astonished me that Atwater still smoked. Cigarettes had disabled him and nearly killed him with laryngeal cancer in 1993. Atwater had tried to quit many times but couldn't make it stick. When I told him that my father had continued to smoke after a heart attack, despite the doctor's warnings that it would kill him, Atwater understood. "I was a wino for twenty years," he had said, "and I gave up drinking. And I can go for weeks without smoking any 'caine and it don't bother me at all. But I gotta have them cigarettes. They're the worst of all. It's insane."

When I'd visited Atwater in detox after he'd been evicted from his apartment, he told me about his deal with God. "I asked for his help in getting my head together. But I said, 'Boss, I can't quit everything at once. I can't give up the cigarettes right now. I need a little room to be human.' " If God let him smoke to ease his mind, Atwater promised not to fuss and plead when it came time to die. Atwater later admitted that this was crazy: "Now you know you don't be praying like that. That's sick—bargaining with the Boss about dying, just so you can have some cigarettes!" What Atwater was bargaining for, I came to see, was dispensation to hold on to one of the few pleasures left in his life.

Lyle Lovett's voice came through the speaker over our heads. Atwater rambled. He told me that the black beret he wore was his signature headwear and he never went out without it; that he'd discovered the

Discovery Channel and graphic sex on cable TV; and that his favorite meal was pork chops with macaroni and cheese. Atwater abruptly ended his discourse on why he disliked snakes—"they are low and evil"—to ask where the restroom was. "In back and downstairs," I said. "I'll have to help you with the tank."

Going down the long flight of stairs was easy. I carried the tank while Atwater held the railing and took one step at a time. He finished in the restroom and we stood looking up the impossible stairs. For a moment I imagined slinging Atwater over my shoulder, firefighter style, and carrying him up. The kitchen was behind us. I leaned in and saw a door that opened onto another parking lot. "You mind if we use this door?" I asked a dishwasher. "My friend here can't get back up the stairs."

"Go right ahead," she said.

Outside the door Atwater sat on an upturned plastic bucket while I brought the car around. "Man, that's great service," Atwater joked as I got out of the car.

"If you're up to it," I said, "this would be a good spot for some pictures."

"Sure, no problem. Where do you want me to sit?"

I moved Atwater and his tank to a spot about ten feet away where the background was less cluttered. Atwater seemed comfortable in front of the camera. He either ignored me or, if I asked him to, lifted his head and looked into the lens. I'd shot half a roll when he began to sweat profusely and look distressed.

"What's wrong?" I asked, lowering the camera from my face. "Suddenly you don't look so good."

"It's the heat. I can't deal with it like I used to."

"I've got enough shots. Let's get in the car and crank up the AC."

When I got Atwater back in the car I asked him if he wanted to go straight home. "No, I still want to get some glasses. I can't read without 'em. I think I know what number I need."

"What *number*?"

"Yeah, like a magnification number. I think it's two-point-two-five or something like that. I got 'em there once before and they worked fine. Rose's at the mall has them. And they're not far from the door, if you go in from the parking lot."

I parked next to a handicapped slot, which was still about a hundred feet from the entrance. "Is this close enough or do you want me to take you right up to the curb?"

"This is fine," Atwater said. "I can make it, no problem."

As we walked to the door we met a man and a woman, both black, both about Atwater's age. Atwater exchanged greetings with them and talked for a few minutes about people they knew. He didn't introduce me, and I didn't introduce myself. I wondered who they thought I was. Atwater's social worker?

I got used to Atwater running into people. For black folks of his generation, Chapel Hill was still a small town where everyone knew everyone else, or knew of everyone else, or at least knew everyone else's people. Marriage within the black community also meant that most families were linked in their branches, and cousinhood, at some remove, was common. Atwater had sixteen local cousins that he knew of.

The chance meeting seemed to energize Atwater. He walked steadily, almost strode, toward the store. I held the door as he pushed his tank through ahead of him.

We paused about ten feet inside. I thought Atwater was taking his bearings. "Are those the glasses you're looking for?" I asked, pointing to a display carousel on the far side of the cashier's station. Atwater didn't reply. He had turned to the cashier, a young black woman, and was asking, with a sudden urgency in his voice, about the nearest restroom. "We don't have any," she said. "You have to use the ones in the mall."

Atwater glared at her, one hand on the tank cart, the plastic tubing running from his nose to the tank. His expression and posture said, "Bitch, can't you see that I need some extra consideration?" There was a meanness in his eyes that I hadn't seen before. I could imagine him cutting her.

"The restrooms are just down the hall," I said, trying to turn his attention from the cashier. I was also trying to minimize the distance. To get "just down the hall" we had to traverse the store, a hundred feet of mall, and another fifty-foot corridor off the main promenade. "I know where they are," Atwater said. I remembered that he had, about ten years earlier, worked as a janitor at this same mall.

We were halfway down the last stretch to the men's room when I could see that Atwater had gone too fast and was getting short of breath. Sweat beaded on his forehead. He stopped and leaned on the handle of his tank cart, pursing his lips and straining to take a deep suck of air. After a minute he was better and moved forward again. I was relieved when we finally made it to the restroom.

I held the door for him and said I'd wait in the hall. Atwater just nodded. I waited in the corridor, leaning against the opposite wall. It was quiet enough to hear the muffled sounds of Atwater going through the motions on the other side. When he didn't emerge after a few minutes, I pushed the door open to check on him.

"Mr. Atwater?" I said, opening the door slowly. First I heard his labored breathing. Then I saw him leaning on the sink with one hand and trying to pull up his boxer shorts with the other. His pants were around his knees and his ass cheeks touched the outside wall of the toilet stall. There was a dollop of shit on the floor beneath him. I could see that his pants were wet. Atwater turned his head and gave me a pitiful look. A voice from the stall said, "I'll try to hurry up."

"I'll be okay, Mike. I'll be okay," Atwater insisted. The guy came out of the stall and Atwater grabbed his tank and stepped in before the toilet finished flushing. "I'll be okay," he said again from inside the stall. I said I'd go back out and wait. There was nothing else to do. The other guy came out and gave me a quick look that read as a mix of sympathy and embarrassment before hurrying down the corridor.

Two men used the restroom and came out snickering and shaking their heads. I pushed the door open again. "How're you doing?" "I'm okay," Atwater said, still in the stall. His voice was gravelly, as usual, but firm again. It didn't seem, as it had a few minutes earlier, that he was going to have a heart attack. I took a leak myself and then went back into the hall to wait.

Twenty minutes later Atwater came out and explained what had happened. "I had to pee real bad and was almost out of breath when we got here," he said, "so I wanted to use the stall and sit and rest." When he'd found the stall occupied, he tried to rush to the urinal, but his tubing got in the way as he tried to undo his pants. "That's how my pants got wet," he said. "Then I panicked and began to lose control of my

bowels. Oh, man, I half shit my shorts. After I got in the stall I had to take my pants and shoes off to get the shorts off. Then I had to clean myself and wait for my pants to dry. That's why I was in there so long. What a goddamn mess. I'm sorry."

"It wasn't your fault," I said, as forgivingly as I could. "If you'd had a heart attack hurrying to the bathroom, I was thinking I'd sue Rose's for denying you use of a toilet."

"That *did* piss me off," he said.

"So what did you do, flush your shorts?"

"You wouldn't have wanted 'em in your car."

I expected Atwater to want to go home after this episode. I offered to bring the car around to the exit at the far end of the restroom corridor, so that Atwater wouldn't have to go back through the mall in his damp pants. "You don't have to do that," he said. "I still want to get some reading glasses and a few other things." We walked, more slowly than before, back to Rose's, pausing to rest every minute or so.

Atwater tried on several pairs of the $9.99 reading glasses until he found a gold-rimmed pair that seemed to work. He added a Snickers bar, a disposable lighter, and a pack of menthol cigarettes. The cashier was a pretty young black woman. Atwater, old enough to be her grandfather, gave her a line of patter. She gave him a stone face. As she put the change into Atwater's hand, he leaned forward and said, "Thanks for letting me get so close," at which she finally smiled.

On the way to the car Atwater told me that this was the first time he'd been out of the house in two months. It was also his first outing with the oxygen tank. "I learned about how slow I have to go, oxygen or not," he said. I said that the next time we went out we could plan better, anticipating his need for restroom stops. I didn't want Atwater to give up on getting out of the house. Being sedentary had to be as bad for him, I thought, as smoking.

We rode in silence all the way back downtown. Atwater seemed tired. He leaned back in the seat, letting the air conditioning blow over him, both hands on the handle of his tank cart. The faint smell of urine wafted up from his pants. As we drove by campus on Franklin Street, I tried to distract Atwater with a question about the university. Had it made a difference in his life? It was a dull question, but Atwater grabbed it and ran.

"It made a big difference," he said. "My mom worked at the laundry for twenty-six years. The pay wasn't much; she made seven dollars a week when she started. But it was steady income. I had my first job at the university—selling sodas at football games when I was kid. I worked as a janitor there a couple different times. Delivered mail on campus. Did linen supply at the hospital. Even helped build part of the hospital."

He also remembered the university swimming pool. "On hot days we used go by there and the white kids would taunt us because we weren't allowed to use the pool. That really made me hate white people. Uh, no offense," he said, with a short laugh.

I had heard similar accounts from other black people Atwater's age and older. For them, the University of North Carolina was mainly an employer. Going back to the early 1800s, when November Caldwell was slave to the university's first president, Joseph Caldwell, blacks had cooked, cleaned, served, and carried, on campus and in fraternities and sororities, and thereby kept the place running. The university had also been a window to middle-class and elite white society, through which could be seen the moral shallowness of liberal gentility, buttressed as it was by institutional barriers that no one white person had to take responsibility for perpetuating. To black people in Chapel Hill, what the university had not been, for over 160 years after its founding, was a place to get an education or a job that paid white man's wages.

My inquiries about the history of the black community in Chapel Hill had brought me into contact with older whites, some of whom, noting that I was not a southerner, said that it would be hard for me to understand how race relations had been back then. It was never clear exactly when "back then" was, although it seemed to refer to the pre-civil rights era. As one white woman in her late seventies had said to me, in grandmotherly tones, "We got along better back then, before all the trouble of the sixties. There was a lot that needed to be changed, but I think that white folks and black folks had more deep-down affection for each other back then. I don't see that anymore."

When I once mentioned this to Atwater, he said, "What they're talking about is a time when black folks depended on whites for everything and were afraid to speak up, for fear of losing a job, or worse. That's what some of those old white people remember as the good times."

Atwater would have been right in many cases. It wasn't hard to find old white people who spoke wistfully of the interactional ease that had, in their minds, characterized a bygone era, an era when blacks knew their places.

Another time when I told Atwater that a white southerner had questioned my ability to understand race relations in the South, he laid it out for me, with an edge he used rarely in our conversations: "If you were black and saw a sign on the swimming pool fence that said, 'Dogs and Niggers Not Allowed,' could you understand that? If your mother had to pee in the street because a white gas station owner wouldn't let her use the toilet, could you understand that? If you went to college and the only job you could get was as an orderly or a porter, could you understand that? If you were doing the same job as a white man but getting fifty-cents an hour less, could you understand that? Study it, Mike, and I'm sure you'll get a handle on it."

I had said that my sense of what southerners resented was any hint that a northerner was judging them for what race relations in the South had been. "That's right," Atwater said. "They know things were hardly any better up north. Some will even tell you that things were better down here, because people knew where they stood. In some ways that made it easier to deal with. But the whole damn thing was still damn wrong."

What I wanted to understand was how the whole damn thing had shaped Atwater's life, made him what he was.

We passed through downtown and were heading west on Franklin Street, back to Carrboro. "That parking lot there," Atwater said, pointing past my left shoulder to a strip of asphalt squeezed between a restaurant and a car dealership, "I helped put that in when I worked for the city. I helped do the concrete work. If you look there sometime you'll see my Pop Coin installation." He sounded like he was talking about a piece of public art.

"Did you say Pop *Coin*? I thought they called you Popcorn."

"Now they do. But it used to be Pop Coin because I carried two silver dollars and had a way of popping them together between my fingers. I used to be able to keep up a nice rhythm, like playing spoons. If people came into the club and heard them coins popping, they knew I was there."

"So where did 'Popcorn' come from?"

"My grandson. When he was a little boy he said one time, 'You're not the kind of popcorn you eat, you're the kind you love.' Man, that tickled me. He must have heard Pop Coin and thought it was Popcorn. After that, people began calling me Popcorn, so I went with it. To this day, a lot of people don't know my real name. They know me as Shine or Popcorn."

Originally named William, after his father, Atwater changed his name to Anthony in the late 1950s. He changed it, he said, because when he and his father worked for the same construction company there had been confusion, resulting in William Sr. getting William Jr.'s paychecks. Though he never made the change legally, to the outside world he became Anthony. As a child he had been called Burness, his middle name and the name by which people of his parents' generation knew him. When he was a boy, one of Atwater's uncles nicknamed him Shine, the name by which his old cronies knew him. After that came Pop Coin, then Popcorn, or just PC.

"Over there," Atwater said, pointing to the apartment complex on our left before we turned onto Alabama Avenue, "was a dairy farm. When I was a kid, this area was almost out in the country. Now it's all built up. Probably won't be much country left before too long."

At the end of the street I made a Y-turn so that the passenger side of the car faced the door of the house. Like two old men we took slow, short steps from the car to the house. Chris had gone out, leaving the house unlocked. Atwater went straight to his room and sat on the edge of the bed.

"So you're at peace here?" I asked, reconnecting Atwater's tubing to the oxygen machine. I poked the switch and the machine buzzed on.

"In a way. I've got memories here."

"Not all good ones."

"No. This window here—," he said, gesturing past his bedside table, "one time my wife had to crawl out that window when I came at her with a knife. She was buck naked and she climbed right down that tree out there."

"Peaceful place."

"It was, sometimes."

"Didn't your dad die here?"

"In the bedroom across the hall. That's where I found him on a Sunday morning when we were going out to get a taste of liquor."

"Does that spook you?"

"I think he's still here. Sometimes I talk to him."

"If you keep indulging and not taking your medicine, I'll be talking to you the same way."

"I won't go before my time. It's up to the Boss anyway. I just hope he'll let me stick around till this book is done. I want to see how it turns out."

I shook Atwater's hand and said I'd see him next week. He lasted another two months at Chris's place before they nearly came to blows. If he hadn't left, Chris might have killed him, though Atwater, ever the builder of his own mythology, said it would have happened the other way around.

driving mr. mason

r. Mason exited his apartment just as I pulled into the parking lot, as if we'd planned a split-second rendez-vous. He moved with a splay-footed shuffle and a stoop so severe it seemed that only his cane kept him from falling over. He was dressed in his usual summer style: gray slacks with black belt and black Naugahyde oxfords, short-sleeved blue plaid shirt, paisley suspenders, and a white corduroy driver's cap that offset his dark skin. The cap was a nice touch, considering our mission.

I parked at the end of the sidewalk that led to the Masons' apartment. I came around the car and opened the passenger door, holding Mr. Mason's cane while he slowly lowered himself into the seat. "C'mon, Crip," he said, lifting his left leg into the car. "Did I tell you they call me 'Crip' Mason?" he asked, finally getting his right leg in. I said that he didn't get around too badly for an eighty-five-year-old man. "Well," he said, "I *used* to get around a lot better than *this*."

I opened the door to the backseat and pulled out a package wrapped in green butcher paper. "Happy birthday, Mr. Mason," I said, holding the package where he could see it. I could feel the cold through the wrapping. "It's sausage. I got you some sausage."

"Thank you, that's mighty nice."

"You said you liked sausage for breakfast."

"Beef sausage and a fried egg. Coffee and water. *Every* morning."

"Maybe you'll like this kind of sausage. It's the kind we eat in Wisconsin—bratwurst and kielbasa. Have you ever had either of those?"

22

Mason on ramp outside
apartment

"I don't *think* so, but that's mighty nice."

I took the sausage in to Martha, Mr. Mason's wife, so she could put it in the refrigerator. Mr. Mason was humming to himself when I got back in the car. "I might have to come over for breakfast some morning and help you eat that sausage," I said, steering us toward the street.

"Sure enough. You can come over *any*time."

"Of course, I'd still be half asleep. You get up too early for me."

"Five o'clock every morning," he said, drawing out the "i" in five and turning to meet my eyes. "Martha gets up at six and we eat at six-thirty. A little beef sausage and some eggs. Martha, she don't like eggs, but she eats 'em."

As we turned left onto Franklin from Roberson, I said, "There's a mural over there I want to show you when we get back from the driver's license office."

"What's that?"

"A mural," I said, pointing across the street. "A big painting on the side of that building. I think you'll like it." Mr. Mason looked in the direction I was pointing, scanning the street without fixing his gaze on anything.

"I don't see it."

"We'll get up close on the way back. So are you all set for this exam?"

"I'm all set, but I don't believe I'm gonna get no license. Might, though. Can't never tell, can you?"

Mr. Mason's driver's license expired today. He had waited until the last possible day to try to renew it. "That's right, you might do okay," I said with no enthusiasm. I hated to see him lose mobility, but I didn't think he should be driving anymore.

"How are your eyes?" I asked. "Can you see everything when we're driving down the road like this?" The street was full of cars.

"I can see *pretty good*. Not like I *used* to. I can see pretty good, but it's *dim*." I wondered how much he could really see. I'd watched Mr. Mason drive. He drove with the slowness of the elderly, the pace not merely of caution but of fear.

The examiner's office was in a sleepy shopping center on the edge of Carrboro. One end of the L-shaped layout was occupied by an A & P, the other by Kerr Drugs. Between the anchor stores were a branch post office, some specialty shops, and the examiner's office.

"Don't let me forget," Mr. Mason said as we drove by the A & P. "I can't think like I used to. My wife wants some chicken wings, the kind that are already cooked. At the A & P, if you don't mind."

"I'll get 'em for you when we're done at the license office."

"You get old, you know. When I was little I didn't understand it when old folks would say, 'I can't think like I used to.' I didn't believe them. I'd ask my mother, 'Why do those folks act like that? They should know better,' and she'd say, 'Hush, boy! Them folks is *old*. If you get old you'll find out.' I sure found out."

I drove past the examiner's office and made a U-turn, bringing the passenger side of the car up to the curb in front of the door. I was relieved to see that there was no line inside. "You go ahead, Mr. Mason. I'll park the car and be right in."

The examiner's office was a deep rectangular room. A U.S. flag and a North Carolina state flag, both hanging limp on six-foot poles,

flanked the receptionist's desk. Behind her were four larger desks arrayed in two rows. At two of them, blue-uniformed women were giving eye tests. The other desks were empty. At the front of the room were a dozen wooden classroom chairs, the kind built to keep students upright and awake. The room was supervised by a portrait of the governor, Jim Hunt.

Mr. Mason sat in one of the classroom chairs, humming to himself again. The other chairs were unoccupied. I sat down next to him and asked if he'd already checked in with the receptionist. He had. She'd taken his expired license and told him to have a seat and wait.

A pale and gangly young man of about twenty walked past us clutching two sheets of paper and a stubby pencil. As he came by, Mr. Mason said, "Hey, how you doin'?" The young man seemed startled. He stared briefly at Mr. Mason and then glanced at me but didn't say a word. He took a seat two rows away and hunched over his exam.

It irked me that the young man hadn't returned Mr. Mason's greeting. The first time I'd taken Mr. Mason grocery shopping and heard him say hello to everyone he met, I asked him, "Do you know all these people?" He said, "*Some* I do." Only once did he fail to get a friendly reply. A pasty-faced white woman in her mid-twenties was studying canned peaches when Mr. Mason passed by and said, "Hey, how you doin'?" She turned and stared, just like the young man had done. She was surprised, I suppose, to see an old black man, a stranger to her, bent over at the waist and nudging his cart along. Still, I wanted to smack her.

I wondered if Mr. Mason felt stung by the young man's lack of response. "He's probably preoccupied by that test he's got to take," I said, trying to explain away the rudeness. Mr. Mason said, "Who?"

One of the blue-uniformed women walked toward us, stopping at some invisible line that ran parallel to the front of the receptionist's desk. She was white, about thirty, fat, with curly brown hair. She held Mr. Mason's driver's license in her hand. "Mr. Mason," she said, glancing at the photo on the license, "you're next." Mr. Mason put on his glasses, pushed down on the chair to stand up, found his cane where he'd propped it against the wall behind him, and shuffled toward her desk twenty feet away. She was seated before he was halfway there.

"How you doin'?" Mr. Mason said as he sat down in front of her desk.

"Fine, and how are you Mr. Mason?"

"Good. I'm doing fine. Just fine."

"Are you registered to vote, Mr. Mason?"

"What?"

"Are you registered to vote?"

"Yes, ma'am, I'm registered to vote."

"We need to check your eyes today, Mr. Mason. Slide over and put your forehead up against the machine. Keep your glasses on." Mr. Mason leaned over and looked into the machine from about six inches away. "Mash your forehead against the top of the machine and the light will come on." Mr. Mason did as he was told. "That's right. Now read line two."

"What's that?"

"Read line two. Tell me what the signs mean."

"What's that?"

"Start with LINE TWO. The FIRST SIGN ON LINE TWO. Tell me what the signs mean."

"Stop sign. Left turn. Merge. Signal sign."

"It's not a signal light. What's number five?"

"Wheelchair."

"Number six?"

"Left turn."

"Number seven?"

"Crossroad."

"Number eight?"

"Children ahead."

"Number nine?"

"Right turn."

Mr. Mason sounded confident. I wondered if I'd underestimated his eyesight. She asked him to identify more signs.

"Now Mr. Mason we're going to check each of your eyes individually." She leaned forward and turned a big knob on the side of the machine. "I want you to read the numbers on line three."

"Three. Six." Mr. Mason hesitated. "Four. Seven. Two." The confidence was gone.

"Go up to line two and read the numbers."

He read slowly. "Seven. Eight. Five. Two. Three." I remembered the first time I couldn't read the numbers without glasses.

She leaned forward to twist the knob again and said, "Now we're going to check your right eye." She repeated the process. Mr. Mason read off two rows of numbers. "Okay Mr. Mason, that's enough." She switched off the machine and sat up at her desk.

"What's wrong with your left eye, Mr. Mason? Do you have cataracts?"

"Yes, ma'am."

"You did not pass the eye test, Mr. Mason. You missed eight of twelve signs. You can't miss more than three. You won't be able to renew your license today."

"I've had cataracts since 1975. Glaucoma too."

"You can retake the eye test, Mr. Mason, but you'll have to get this form signed by your eye doctor." She held the paper in front of her, moving it up and down as she spoke.

"Dr. Kern over in Durham is my eye doctor. Since 1972." Mr. Mason twisted in his chair and pulled his wallet out of his back pocket. He leaned forward and flipped it open on her desk, extracting a wad of business cards from one compartment. "I have his card in here." Mr. Mason fumbled through the cards in what seemed like slow motion. She waited. "Would you do me a favor?" he finally asked, handing her the cards. "You can find it quicker than I can."

She flipped through the cards. "I don't see one in here for a Dr. Kern." Mr. Mason began probing another compartment in his wallet. "That's all right, Mr. Mason. You don't need to find his card right now. Just make sure that when you see Dr. Kern he signs this form. If you want to retake the eye test, he has to sign this form." She handed him back the wad of cards.

"You also have to study your signs, Mr. Mason," she said as he reassembled his wallet. Study his signs? Mr. Mason was reading road signs forty years before she was born.

"Do you understand what you have to do, Mr. Mason?"

"Yes, ma'am."

"All right, then, maybe we'll see you back here in a few weeks. Have a nice day, Mr. Mason."

"You too."

Mr. Mason stood up slowly and began to walk away from her desk. I got up and moved forward to meet him. He'd left his cane by the chair. "Wait a second, Mr. Mason," I said, stepping past him to retrieve the cane. As I grabbed it the woman behind the desk said, "Are you with him?"

"Yes."

"Do you understand what he needs to do?"

"He needs to have that form signed verifying that he's had an eye exam and some corrective work done before he can retake the test." And then to make sure she didn't have the wrong impression: "He knows what he needs to do."

Mr. Mason was quiet until we got outside. "Well, I figured that," he said with a short laugh.

"Would new glasses make a difference? You could retake the exam."

"No, it's the glaucoma. I can't see much out of my left eye anymore. It's been bad since 1972. Now my right eye's gotten weaker. The other thing is, if you got cataracts *and* glaucoma, you can't have no cataracts taken off." So this was it. Mr. Mason was done driving.

Mr. Mason waited outside the examiner's office while I got the car. We drove a few hundred feet to the A & P. I swung into an empty spot next to the cart-return pen. "A pound of pre-cooked chicken wings, right?"

"Right."

"If you don't mind sitting here, I'll go in and get them."

"That's mighty nice. Here, let me give you some money." I waited while Mr. Mason tried to lean forward far enough to reach behind him and get his wallet out of his back pocket. He couldn't do it. "That's okay," I said. "I'll just get the wings and you can pay me later."

"Okay, I appreciate it."

Mr. Mason was surprised when I returned and told him that the store didn't sell pre-cooked chicken wings by the pound. They were fifty-nine cents each. I'd guessed and bought six. "Will six be enough for Martha's lunch? Six ought to be pretty close to a pound."

"Yeah, that's plenty. Six is fine. Is that a pound? Well, I declare. I thought you could buy them here by the pound, but I don't remember things as good as I used to."

"Stores have been known to change how they sell things," I said. "You probably did buy them here by the pound. But then the store people probably figured they could make more money by selling them for fifty-nine cents apiece."

"Ha! Ain't that the truth. Ain't *that* the truth."

As we waited for the stoplight to let us out of the parking lot, Mr. Mason told me again about Kern being his eye doctor, about the cataracts and glaucoma, and how they can't operate on the cataracts if you have glaucoma. "The glaucoma came on about two years ago," he said. I asked why he didn't have the cataract surgery earlier. "Just didn't do it," he said.

We crossed the intersection and got onto the drab suburban end of Carrboro's Main Street. The houses looked tired, even though they dated only from the mid-1970s. Perhaps it was because they had too little character to fend off age. I asked Mr. Mason how long he'd been driving. "Since I was sixteen," he said. I did the arithmetic. "That would have been 1927," I said, "about three years after you came to Chapel Hill."

"I reckon that's right."

"Did you even *need* a license back then?"

"No. Didn't need no license. Got one when I was eighteen, though."

Mr. Mason bought his first car—a used "T-Model Ford" he thinks it was—when he was sixteen. To buy it, he borrowed $150 from Joe Mason, the son of Tom Mason, who was the son of Wesley Mason, who was the son of John Mason, who was the plantation owner from whom Mr. Mason's great-grandfather Benjamin had taken the Mason name.

"So who taught you to drive?" I asked.

"Didn't nobody teach me nothing about how to drive. I just figured it out by myself. It weren't too hard," he said. I asked if he'd had to take a road test when he'd gotten a license. "Yeah, had to go around the block."

"It was all dirt roads, right?"

"That's right. Even Franklin Street, when I first come to town," he said. When Mr. Mason moved from Durham to Chapel Hill in 1924, the population, not counting the fifteen hundred or so university students, was a little over two thousand. Franklin Street, the main drag, was still a year away from being paved curb to curb.

"Did you teach your kids to drive?" I asked. "Yeah, I taught Tint and Matthew Junior and Allen." The girls—Gloria and Mary—must have learned from someone else. Mr. Mason's youngest son, Thomas, would have taken driver's ed in high school.

"Were you a good teacher?" I asked. Mr. Mason laughed. "I reckon I ought to be," he said, "I drove a cab at night for eight years. Drove for Thurman Adkins. He told me, 'You're the best driver I got. If you can have your toddies and have no wrecks, that's fine with me.' He had one driver who wrecked three cabs in three years. He got fired."

Mr. Mason seemed resigned to the loss of his license. I was relieved, though I wondered how he and Martha were going to get their groceries. Martha hadn't driven since 1966, two years after she and Mr. Mason got married. She'd quit driving because there was too much traffic in Chapel Hill, which even in the mid-1960s was bigger than her native Rockingham.

"Are you gonna get by okay without driving?"

"Oh *yeah*, I can get by without driving. Yeah."

"It's too bad there's no grocery delivery service."

"Hey, that *used* to be here in Chapel Hill. Call to the store and they'd bring it to you. It used to be. But it's not like that now."

I told him about the corner grocery stores that we used to have in my old neighborhood in Milwaukee—two of them just down the block from us, and both of them gone before I'd finished eighth grade in 1970.

"It weren't no surprise," he said with a sigh that surprised me. The only thing Mr. Mason had ever sounded nostalgic about was the homemade corn liquor he drank as a young man and hadn't tasted in years.

"You mean those little stores disappearing?"

"What?"

"The little neighborhood grocery stores."

"My license. It weren't no surprise I didn't get it. New glasses wouldn't make no difference, either." Another sigh. He cared about it more than he let on. "I appreciate you helping me out today," he added, as if to reassure me that his disappointment wasn't my fault.

"I'll tell you the truth, Mr. Mason. I didn't really want you to get it. I worried about you when you'd be out driving. If somebody came at

you from the left side you'd never see them in time to get out of the way." I found out later that he'd had that kind of accident in the early seventies. He hadn't been seriously hurt, but his car got spun around and his nose banged up pretty good.

"That's the truth, I reckon. I been lucky. That's the truth."

We left the chicken wings with Martha and then went to see the mural. It had been commissioned by Barry Jones, owner of the Avid Reader bookshop, to commemorate the history of the west end of Franklin Street, an area that was once predominantly black. We crossed Franklin Street and pulled into the gas station above which the 20-by-30-foot mural freshly loomed. I turned the car so Mr. Mason could see it with his right eye.

"You recognize that, Mr. Mason?" I said, reaching across him to point out a church that was part of the mural.

"That's the old Rock Hill Baptist Church," he said. "It used to be right across the street. That was the *black* folks' church."

"Over there," I said, pointing to a different part of the mural, "is the old Farmer's Dairy Cooperative. Do you remember that?"

"Good gracious! I remember that! Where did they get this? This ain't been here all along has it?"

"No, I just read about it in the paper this morning. The painter is still finishing it."

"Ain't that something. I didn't know this was here. Yeah, that's the old Baptist church. Rock Hill. Why did they do that?"

"The guy who owns the bookstore here wanted to put something on the wall that would remind people of the history of this side of Chapel Hill."

"Well, I declare!"

"The guy who painted this, Michael Brown I think his name is, has done other murals around town. There's one near Bob Page's office."

"Well, that's all right," Mr. Mason said, letting out a laugh. "You showed me something right here in my house that I didn't even know about. Ain't that something?"

"I like stuff like this. He's a good artist too."

"That's the truth. I'm goin' tell you the truth: you all right."

"Let's get your birthday lunch."

Mr. Mason had surprised me when he said he wanted to have lunch at a Middle Eastern restaurant. I'd expected him to opt for something more familiar, like Dip's. "Have you ever had Middle Eastern food?" I'd asked him. "No, I didn't even know that place was there until y'all went," he said. Y'all was me and Thomas, Mr. Mason's son. "But Thomas said it was pretty good, so I thought it would be okay, if you don't mind."

The restaurant was a block away. I turned left onto Franklin Street and immediately realized my mistake. I should have turned right and gone around the block so that I'd be on the same side of the street as the restaurant. As we drove by, I saw an open spot by a fire hydrant about thirty feet from the door. The street was clear so I swung an illegal U-turn and slid into the spot. "You can get out here, Mr. Mason. The restaurant is right there. I'll park the car and be back in a minute."

"Take your time," he said, "I ain't in no hurry." He popped the door open and lifted his right leg out of the car, scolding himself as he moved: "Get out of here, Crip." After he'd extricated himself from the car I handed him his walking stick. "Thank you. I need that," he said.

"I'll be back as soon as I find a place to park."

"Take your time," he repeated.

He pushed the door shut and started toward the restaurant. I *was* in a hurry. I didn't want to leave Mr. Mason standing there for ten minutes while I hunted for a parking spot and hiked back. There were empty tables and chairs outside the restaurant. I wondered if Mr. Mason would feel comfortable sitting there, or if anyone would hassle him if he did.

I parked and was back in a few minutes. Mr. Mason was leaning with his back against the streetside wall of the restaurant, his weight against the building rather than on his cane. His stance struck me as odd for some reason, and then I realized that I'd never seen him fully upright.

We went inside, sat down, and looked at menus. Mr. Mason ordered grilled chicken, which came with couscous, tabouleh, and pita bread. I ordered the mixed grill platter, substituting eggplant for lamb. We each had iced tea.

While we waited for our food Mr. Mason picked up his tea, glanced around, and leaned toward me. He spoke so softly that I had to pull

Mason laughing

in closer to hear what he was saying. His posture and voice implied confession. It took me a second to realize that he was making a bawdy toast—something about a tired old penis. Mr. Mason laughed when he finished. I did, too, though I hadn't heard enough of the toast to get the joke.

"Is that one you used to tell the fraternity boys?" I asked.

"Oh yeah, they liked that one. I used to tell a lot of those."

"Do you remember any others?"

"That's the only one I can think of right now."

Mr. Mason began working for the Phi Delta Theta fraternity on the Monday after Mother's Day in 1934. He cleaned, made beds, served meals, stoked the furnace, tended bar, and roused the brothers for classes. In 1964 he cut back to part-time, then retired fully in 1972,

but still tended bar occasionally well into the 1990s. In the mid-1950s, the Phi's had made Mr. Mason, who could not have joined the all-white fraternity in any other way, an honorary brother.

I'd hoped to get Mr. Mason reminiscing about his life during lunch. I hadn't yet learned that his memory consisted of stories, not answers to questions. "What would you do differently if you could live your eighty-five years over?"

"Not much I *could* do different."

"What would you say you're most proud of in your life?"

"Oh, I don't know."

"Your children maybe?"

"Yeah, my children. They turned out all right."

"What would you say was your best year?"

"They all been pretty good, I reckon. We always had plenty to eat—even during the depression when black folks in Chapel Hill was going hungry, we had food to share."

Mr. Mason declared himself full after eating about a fourth of the food on his plate. "I have to watch my figure," he joked, leaning back and patting his waist.

When we left the restaurant I saw that someone had parked by the hydrant, so I couldn't pull up right in front as I'd done before. I said the car was about a hundred feet away. Mr. Mason said he could manage that. This time as he worked himself into the car I asked, "Is it your *knees* that give you the most trouble?"

"Knees, legs, and back." He laughed. "Knees, legs, and back—they're all wore out. That's what the doctor said: 'Mr. Mason, if you done half the things you said you done, it ain't no wonder you're wore out.' It's okay when I sit, though. It only hurts when I move around." When he got in the car he pulled up his left pant leg to show me the elastic support band he wore on his knee. "I have one on this side too," he said, palming his right knee.

Back at the apartment I asked Mr. Mason if he'd sit in one of the plastic chairs on his front stoop while I took a few pictures. "Right, boy!" he said. This was one of his signature phrases. He used it to convey a mocking eagerness to satisfy whatever request the fraternity boys made of him. He was teasing now, but I got the message that he

was obliging me and would have preferred to go straight to his easy chair rather than sit and stand an extra time.

I took a dozen shots, bracketing my exposures to make sure I got one right. Mr. Mason laughed every time I said, "One more." "I ain't in no hurry," he assured me. I was putting my camera away when Martha stuck her head out the door to see what we were doing. "He'll sit there all day if you keep taking his picture," she said. "C'mon in if you want a piece of cake."

The Masons lived in a one-bedroom apartment in a small, well-kept public housing project. Entering the front door, you entered the living room. Four steps straight ahead brought you to the dining area. Four more steps and you were in the kitchen. Veering right instead of going into the kitchen took you to the bedroom. The walls pressed the outer edges of the furniture, leaving narrow paths for foot traffic. Photographs of family and of fraternity members covered the walls, shelves, and tabletops.

Mr. Mason eased himself into his worn blue recliner, a long-ago gift from the fraternity. Martha hollered from the kitchen, "You got some mail. More birthday cards, it looks like."

Mr. Mason looked toward the coffee table an arm's length away. He skimmed his hand over the cluttered surface of the table, as if the hand could find mail on its own. "I don't see it," he said quietly. I didn't, either. Martha hollered again: "It's by the window, behind Mr. Mike." I turned and saw the envelopes on the small credenza, next to a photograph of Matthew and Martha taken when they were courting. "Here you go," I said, handing the envelopes to Mr. Mason.

Martha joined us, squeezing behind Mr. Mason's chair on her way to the sofa. She was in her usual house attire: a long purple jumper over a long-sleeved white turtleneck, white socks, and soft gray shoes that looked like the kind a nurse might wear. Her white hair was pulled back into two braided pony-tails. When I'd once asked Mr. Mason what first attracted him to Martha, he said, "It was that fine light brown skin." Martha would be eighty in a few months, but she was still spry. She line-dried the wash out back and kept a small tomato garden.

"That one's from Craig's momma," Martha said, indicating the envelope Mr. Mason held in his hands. The other rested in his lap.

Martha Mason

He turned the envelope over, inspecting both sides, then handed it to me. "Would you read it to me, if you don't mind?" he said.

"Dear Dr. Reet," it began, using Mr. Mason's fraternity nickname, "Happy 85th birthday to a truly remarkable person. We hope you will have the happiest birthday ever. You've seen so much happen, so many changes in your 85 years, it's been a privilege to spend time with you. Happy birthday, Mary Ellen and Greg Lowenhagen."

"That's nice. Here read me this one," Mr. Mason said, handing me the second envelope.

"This one says, 'Happy birthday Dr. Reet. Number 85—the first half of 170 years. Give my best to your sugar.' It's signed 'Brother Thurston.'" I gave Mr. Mason the eighty-five-dollar check that came with the card.

"That's mighty nice, too."

I swiveled in my chair and propped the two new cards on the credenza, along with the others.

Martha began an inventory of the gifts that had arrived so far. "He got a shirt, some pants, boxer shorts, and two different kinds of sausage. You brought them sausages."

"And don't let me forget," Mr. Mason interjected, "how much do I owe you for them chicken wings?" I would just as soon have let him forget, but Mr. Mason was determined to square up. I dug the receipt out of my pocket and looked at the amount. "It's three dollars and seventy-one cents." Mr. Mason gave me three dollar bills from his wallet and seventy-one cents from his coin purse. I thanked him and pocketed the money without looking at it. "You'll have to tell me if those sausages are any good," I said.

"He makes me breakfast every morning," Martha said. "He fries my egg. If I make it myself, I poaches it and puts pepper and vinegar on it."

"You put *vinegar* on your eggs?"

"A whole lot of it!" she exclaimed. Martha knew she could surprise me with this sort of information. She'd seen me grimace when she told me to eat sardines and Coke as a cure for a cold. I'd also looked grim while watching her cut up a tomato, drop the pieces into a bowl on her lap, and then douse the pieces with vinegar before eating them one by one. I wanted to amaze her with some culinary oddity of my own, but all I could think to say was that my dad used to eat mustard on pretzels.

"I don't like mustard," Mr. Mason said.

"I loves it," Martha said, "on hot dogs. Or sometimes I'll eat it plain. Yellow mustard."

"Plain?"

"Or when I have gas," Martha went on. "I'll eat two teaspoons of mustard with a cup of hot water behind it. It knocks out the gas."

"I ain't never liked mustard," Mr. Mason said.

"He's a *mayonnaise* man," Martha explained.

"I never met a mayonnaise man," I said to Mr. Mason. "I'll bet you like bacon, lettuce, and tomato sandwiches."

"Oh, yeah, sure do," he said. Mr. Mason was happy to be back in the conversation that had gotten turned to Martha's taste for mustard and vinegar.

"Is your wife coming home today?" he asked.

"Yeah, she'll be back pretty soon. I'm going straight from here to the airport to pick her up."

"How long has she been gone?" Martha asked.

"A little over a week."

"I know you's lonesome and sad," Martha said, teasing me.

I said that I kept busy by working on projects, cleaning the house, and riding my bike. "You could ride a motorcycle too," Martha said, for no reason that I could fathom. I'd never said anything about a motorcycle.

"If I had one, I s'pose I'd ride it. But I haven't had a motorcycle since I was in college, and it seems too dangerous to start riding one again now." I asked Mr. Mason if he'd ever ridden a motorcycle and he lit up like I'd pushed a button.

"They had one one time at the Phi Delt house. I got to feeling like a feather in the breeze and I cranked it up. Oooh! I was gonna *ride* it, you know? Some of the boys saw me and yelled, 'Reet! Reet! Dr. Reet! What are you doing?! Fool, you're about drunk. You'll get killed! Get off that machine!" Mr. Mason laughed, inviting me to laugh along at the preposterous scene he'd conjured.

"What happened then?"

"I don't know. I reckon they got me offen it somehow. Didn't nobody get hurt."

"This must have been a long time ago."

"Oh yeah, it was a *long* time ago."

"The boys came by yesterday and cashed our checks," Martha said, before one pointless drunk story could lead to another.

Though he'd quit drinking in 1972 after being taken to the hospital in an alcohol-induced coma, Mr. Mason's heavy drinking days—decades, actually—with the fraternity remained a sore point with Martha. She'd left him several times because of it. "I prayed to the Lord to take the taste for it out of his mouth," she once told me.

Mr. Mason got Martha's drift. "Would you like a piece of cake?" he asked.

"Sure, if you'll join me."

We moved to the dining area table. A quarter of the unfrosted angel food cake was gone already. I got a knife, three forks, and three small plates from the kitchen. Mr. Mason sat at one end of the table.

"How much do you want?" I asked, poising the knife on top of the cake.

"I can have a *little* piece," Mr. Mason said. "I can't eat too much because I get too full. I also gotta watch my figure."

"When I *found* him he *had* a figure," Martha said from the other end of the table. "He weighed 140 pounds and wore a size-32 waist pants. Now he wears a forty-six."

I said that I used to weigh over two-hundred pounds. "Well, I declare!" Martha said. "But you're tall. You could carry it." I said that I'd lost fifty pounds, ten years ago, after I started riding a bike for fun. "You a *riding* man," she said.

"Your wife's not heavy," Martha said out of the blue. I'd showed Martha and Mr. Mason a picture.

"No," I said, "she's just right," and they both laughed, Martha's laugh bursting through a big grin.

"How big a piece would you like?" I asked Martha.

"I reckon I'll have a piece about like Matthew's," she said.

As I cut, Martha said, "Both of us would like to meet her."

Martha seemed to be hoping for a bond among womenfolk. She knew that Mr. Mason was the focus of my attention, just like he was the one whom most of their visitors came to see. Perhaps she figured that as a woman Sherryl would naturally take more interest in her.

For months I'd been annoyed that Martha was always there during my weekly interviews with Mr. Mason. I wanted to ask him more about his first wife, Fannie, and it seemed that Martha's presence inhibited him. She could also be intrusive. If I asked Mr. Mason about one of his children, Martha might blurt out something about *her* son before Mr. Mason had a chance to answer.

One time Mr. Mason was alone in the living room when I arrived. Martha was in the bedroom taking a nap. I thought this would be a good time to talk to Mr. Mason about his first wife. At some point I asked him how much the rent was on the Eugene Street house where he and

Martha first lived after getting married. While he paused to think, the answer came from the bedroom: "It was forty dollars a month, then it went it up to fifty. That's when we moved to Lindsay."

I came to accept that Martha was going to be part of any conversation that occurred in the apartment. I also came to appreciate that in some ways she knew more about Mr. Mason's life, at least since 1964, than he did. She was also frank about matters that embarrassed Mr. Mason—his heaviest drinking, the obnoxious behavior of the fraternity boys. If I was going to understand Mr. Mason, Martha had to be part of the deal.

I couldn't blame her for craving attention. For over thirty years she'd endured not only relative anonymity as the mere wife of the celebrated Dr. Reet but also a fair piece of misery owing to the drinking culture out of which "Dr. Reet" had emerged. Nor at this time in her life did she have much else to distract her. "Since Matthew got feeble," she said on an earlier occasion, "we don't get out much at all. Sometimes these walls feel like they's closing in on me."

"Your wife's younger?" Martha asked as I cut a piece of cake for myself.

"She's forty-three," I said.

"She's older than you," Mr. Mason said through a mouthful of cake. I was surprised that he remembered.

"How long you been married?" Martha asked.

"Eight years this fall. We met on October 28. That's the day we mark as our anniversary." I worried about that answer sounding strange, since I didn't say anything about actually getting married.

I felt guilty talking about my "wife." Eight months earlier, when I'd begun interviewing Mr. Mason for a different project, he and Martha had asked if I was married. Small talk. Rather than explain about being partnered, or pretend that I was unattached, I just said yes, figuring that would be the end of it. It would have been, too, if I hadn't gotten more enmeshed in Mr. Mason's life.

"We've been married thirty-two years on August the 4th. We got married on August the 4th, 1964," Martha said. "We moved here from Sykes Street in 1972. We were the first ones in here."

Mr. Mason had stopped eating and was staring at the cake left on his plate. "Are you getting tired?" I asked him. "Who? Me?" he said,

coming quickly to attention and looking right at me. "I ain't *getting* tired," he went on. "I *been* tired. It's old age and being worn out. That's all."

"You should probably rest up, then. Aren't the fraternity boys taking you out to dinner tonight?"

"Yeah, they'll be here later. They always take me out for supper on my birthday. Been doing it a *long* time. Always take a picture, too. There's the one from last year." Mr. Mason pointed to the shelf behind him. I leaned over and squinted at a dusty 5-by-7 of a smiling Mr. Mason leaning on his cane, surrounded by a dozen young white faces. "Looks like the alleyway by the Rathskellar," I said.

"Yeah, that's where they usually take me," he said. "But I can't hardly get down the stairs anymore."

I looked again at Mr. Mason's big smile in the picture. "You don't drink liquor with the boys anymore, do you?"

"No, no. Well, maybe a gallon of corn liquor. You ever had any? It is smooooth. Get you high as a Georgia pine." Mr. Mason grinned and winked.

"One taste and he'd be crawling on the floor," Martha said, no humor in her voice.

"But you know, a little toddy never hurt nobody's body," Mr. Mason said.

"As I understand it," I said, "you put too many toddies in your body."

Mr. Mason laughed. "Yeah, that's true, that's true. I drank a lot of liquor with them boys. A lot of liquor. Had some good times too."

"But that's all done now," I said, trying to elicit reassurance for Martha's sake.

"Oh, yeah, all done. That's right. No more toddies," he said.

I looked at my watch. "I need to get going to the airport. If I'm not there when Sherryl gets off the plane, she'll be mighty unhappy." I took my plate and fork to the sink, then came back to the table and pushed my chair in.

"Thank for you everything, you hear? We sure do appreciate it," Mr. Mason said.

"It's your birthday. When you turn eighty-five, you deserve some extra help," I said.

"Makes no difference whether you're young or old," Mr. Mason said, launching another of his sayings that I would eventually hear a hundred times. "Let's get *together* and let the *good* times roll, because—don'tcha know?—when you dead, you done. Ain't that right?"

I allowed as he was right, making a mental note to ask Mr. Mason if he believed in an afterlife where the good times kept rolling. "Get some rest now before your dinner," I said, my hand on the door. "I hope the rest of your birthday is happy and I'll see you next week."

Four days later I was in Centreville, Virginia, interviewing Mr. Mason's youngest daughter, Mary. We'd talked for two hours when Mary startled me by mentioning "what happened to Martha" and expressing hopes that Martha would be all right. Something had happened to Martha? I'd been out of touch with the Masons since I said good-bye on Mr. Mason's birthday. Mary told me that while her father was out with the fraternity boys, Martha had had a stroke.

Shortly after the fraternity boys picked up Mr. Mason, Martha's left foot began to go numb. When Mr. Mason got back an hour later, it seemed to her that she was talking too slowly. "He couldn't tell anything," Martha told me later, "but I knew something was wrong, even though I didn't feel all that bad. *He* thought I was putting on." The next day a neighbor dropped by. She listened to Martha describe her symptoms and said it sounded like she'd had a stroke and ought to go to the hospital.

As it turned out, the stroke was mild. Martha's speech was not permanently impaired, though she lost some control of her legs, necessitating the use of a cane. "We's both feeble now," Martha said, with resignation. Over the next six months her condition remained stable. But by the end of the year she experienced further problems that led to hospitalization and a long stay in a nursing home. Mr. Mason, no longer licensed to drive, found ways to visit her every day.

spoiling for manhood

The old woman and the four-year-old boy stood by the window watching the trees bend in the wind. He leaned into her leg, clutching the hem of her gray dress as rain pounded the tin roof of the little house. Lightning struck a tree in the yard and the force of it cracked the glass in front of the old woman's face. The boy scurried under the kitchen table and crouched there, quivering. The old woman had not flinched. "Come out here, boy," she said. "The Lord made that lightning and that thunder, and if he wants you, he'll get you, even under that table." The boy came out and held his grandmother's hand and was no longer afraid of storms.

Later that year the Lord came for the boy. "He has bronchial pneumonia on both sides," the doctor had said. "There's nothing more I can do for him. It's up to the Lord if he lives." The boy's mother was not ready to relinquish control. And so she took him to her great-aunt, a kind of doctor who knew of roots and other things not made in hospitals and laboratories. The aunt covered the boy in pizzle grease, wrapped him in blankets and laid him by a hot stove. A few hours later the boy's fever broke and he lived to remember the grease, made from the penis of a hog, that smelled like turpentine and ammonia.

The boy also tasted guilt for the first time. He was playing on the floor when his uncle, still a boy himself, yanked him up by his arm and scolded him for messing his diaper. The boy later told his father how his arm had gotten hurt, and the boy's father said the uncle had to go. It was not the first time this had happened, the boy's father said.

Many years later the boy remembered, "My mom was sad when my uncle, her baby brother, was put out. I could see that, and I thought it was my fault. She seemed to change toward me then. I think she liked me less." At four the boy found himself at the center of a pattern of conflict that would largely cancel the promise of his life.

William Atwater and Ella Gattis were married on December 27, 1930. He was twenty-five years old and she was twenty-one. For her, the marriage was a chance to escape her father's Durham County tobacco farm and the responsibility she had borne for raising her younger siblings, a responsibility that befell her at thirteen when her mother died. William was a hard worker, the son of a north Chatham County sharecropper. With some fiscal discipline imposed, William seemed likely to be a good provider. By his lights, Ella was a pretty girl, smart and better educated—eighth grade to his third—and already a fine cook and housekeeper.

Their first and only child, William Burness Atwater Jr., was born on April 3, 1933. At that time the family lived in a two-story plank house on the west side of Merritt Mill Road, near where Carrboro takes Franklin Street from Chapel Hill and calls it Main. Bootleg liquor was available across the street, a convenience for William Sr., who had a taste every day, before and after work. Today a defunct car wash occupies the spot where the plank house stood. The liquor house is gone, too, replaced by an auto lube joint.

Three years after William Jr. was born the family moved to a smaller house in Carrboro, off North Greensboro Street, near Fitch's lumberyard. The house was one of four—three of them occupied by Atwater families—set in a square around a common well. Fifty feet away a Norfolk Southern spur line delivered students, visitors, and coal to the University of North Carolina. None of the houses, renting for two dollars a week, had electricity or indoor plumbing. The address was North Greensboro Street, but that was only where a narrow dirt driveway met the street. White folks lived in the streetside houses.

After two years, the family moved into a larger house in the same cluster. "That second house we lived in by the railroad tracks," as Atwater remembered it, "had three bedrooms, a living room, front and

back porches, and a kitchen off to one end. We had a wood stove to heat the house, but the heat didn't get around to all the rooms very well. The outside of the house looked raw, like the wood hadn't been painted in ninety years. None of those houses was plumb and square. The corners of the rooms sagged, and you could see light through the cracks around the windows. They stood on brick pillars, and some of the bricks was broke. The roof leaked like crazy. My daddy tried to fix the leaks, but he never got all of them. You couldn't count on the landlord to do anything. Those houses were rented to black folks 'as is'—meaning, if you didn't like it, you could leave and try to find someplace else."

The family lived there, occasionally taking in the children of relatives, for almost fifteen years. Atwater's memories of childhood were rooted in that place. "Whenever I dream or think about something from childhood," he would say, "it all comes back to that house and the railroad tracks." The houses are gone now and the site is overgrown with brush and small trees. Among the trees one can find stolen and discarded patio furniture, old clothes and shoes, and empty bottles left by local kids and the homeless. A few trains a week still carry coal to the university's heating plant.

In 1939 there was no public kindergarten for black children, and so Atwater began school in first grade. Like other black children in Chapel Hill, he attended Orange County Training School, which had been built, largely through donations of cash, land, and labor, about fifteen years earlier. At one time the town had drawn its borders to exclude the school, so that there would be no obligation to provide public support. All grades, first through twelfth, were taught under one roof. Atwater's cohort of thirty children, few of whom saw a white face as they walked to school, was considered large.

Atwater enjoyed learning to read, spell, and do arithmetic. He liked to draw and write stories. After school, he did his homework before his chores. A's and B's came easily. His teachers appreciated his nice clothes. One day his second-grade teacher stood him on a table in front of the class. "Now, class," she said, "this is how you should look when when you come to school." It was a mile to school on dirt streets and backyard paths. But on rainy days Atwater took a sidewalk route that was twice as long, so he could keep his shoes and pants

clean. "I used to hate getting dirty," Atwater said. "Even in the summer I didn't go barefoot like the other kids."

He kept his room neat too. "It was just like a girl's bedroom," as his mother described it. Atwater took pride in keeping his shoes and clothes and toys in order. He found satisfaction in control. If anyone moved anything in his room, he knew it.

In these years Atwater enjoyed school and got along well with his teachers and classmates. After school and during the summers there were games to be played (marbles and baseball being the most important), swimming holes to be explored, slingshots to be perfected, Grandpa's stories to be heard, merit badges to be earned, pictures to be drawn, rhymes to be invented, and cowboy and monster movies to be seen for ten cents each. Within the bounds of class, race, and the South, it was, to most appearances, a good childhood. But part of what appeared to be good about it, especially to Atwater as a child, was subtly corrupting.

Among people who knew Atwater as he was coming up, there is agreement that he was spoiled—meaning that he got too much too easily. Though they did not have much money in absolute terms, Atwater's parents both worked, so they could give an only child things that other children didn't have: nice clothes and shoes, toys, bicycles, and, later, a car. By local standards of the time, this was indulgence. "People say I was spoiled," Atwater would admit, "and I suppose I was. For a poor kid, I got pretty much whatever I wanted—bicycles, a nice little scooter, footballs and basketballs. All I had to do was put a little beg on my parents."

When people said that Atwater was spoiled they also meant that he was overly protected, especially by his mother, and, later, not held accountable for his actions. His mother did not want him playing rough, getting dirty, or hanging out with kids she considered coarse. And if her boy was accused of mischief, she took up for him, denied he was responsible, blamed other kids, bailed him out. As one of his boyhood playmates said, "You could never convince Miss Ella that Burness did anything wrong. 'Oh no, not my boy,' she'd say." Atwater not only got what he wanted, he got away with what he wanted, either by his own fibbery or his mother's denial.

Atwater at eight

When he was seven, Atwater asked his mother for a Bible so he could find out "why the Jews killed Christ." For a time, he read a few chapters every night. "I'd go in to wake him in the morning and Burness would be asleep with that Bible under his arm," his mother said. Atwater decided that Christ was killed because he was misunderstood.

Atwater also learned from his reading and from his Sunday school lessons that families were supposed to be places of love and harmony. "But my family wasn't like that," as Atwater saw it. "And for a long time I didn't know why. I never saw my mom and dad hug or kiss. And when I once asked my mom why I didn't have any brothers or sisters, she just said, 'You'll have to talk to your daddy about that.'" What Atwater did know was that conflict could be exploited. "My mom and dad were always pulling against each other, and I took advantage of it." He learned to extract from this conflict not only toys and bicycles but seemingly infinite forgiveness.

The boy walked in single file along a narrow path behind his grand-father, uncles, aunts, and cousins. The boy's mother had walked here when she was a girl. It was August, and at 5:00 A.M. it was already warm and humid. Lush vegetation filled the gaps between the trees on both sides of the path. The scene made him think of an African tribe walk-ing through the jungle. One of his uncles began to sing: "Over my head I hear music in the air/and I really do believe/there's a heaven some-where." One of his aunts joined in, adding a voice so high it seemed like it would scare the birds. At the end of the song and the end of the path lay his grandfather's tobacco field.

The boy would not pick today; the adults would do that. But at ten he was big enough to drive the old mule that pulled the leaf-filled sled from the field to the barn where his cousins would tie the leaves to sticks so the leaves could be hung for curing. Earlier in the year the boy had picked worms off the plants, cut the flowering tops so the plants would grow bigger leaves, and plucked the immature leaf buds called "suckers." As much as he liked coming out to his grandfather's farm and doing important chores, the boy knew that farming was harder work than he ever wanted to do for a living.

Summers on the farm were a mix of work and fun. In the evenings his grandfather and aunts and uncles would sit on the porch and sing and tell stories. His grandfather would talk about how the war in Europe was a sign that the Bible's prophecies were coming true. Sometimes his grand-father would talk about slavery times and how slaves learned to do for themselves and get things for themselves, despite the white man's scheming to keep them down. The boy liked his grandfather's stories, except that once he started talking you had to stay quiet and listen. His grandfather didn't brook any interruptions, especially by children.

The real fun was had with his cousins, most of whom were his age or a bit older. They made up songs, rode the mule, invented games to play in the tobacco barns and the woods, and went fishing and swim-ming. At the swimming hole the boys went naked, making invidious comparisons inevitable. The boy himself was small of body and embar-rassed by his tiny dick. At night he prayed to God to give him a big dick, one that he would not be ashamed of. Years later the grown boy said, "I never prayed for anything I didn't get."

His grandfather's farm, full of aunts and uncles and cousins, was a refuge from the world of town, where it was clear that whites had the upper hand and could, for reasons unclear, create misery out of nothing. One year, near Christmas, the boy wanted a bow-and-arrow set he had seen in the window of a downtown store. The boy waited until payday and then pleaded with his mother to buy it for him. He had already figured out who Santa Claus was. She agreed to take him to the store and make the bow-and-arrow set a special, early present.

On the way there she asked to use the restroom at a gas station and was told, "We don't have a colored rest room here." Her need was urgent and she could not help peeing on herself. She turned the boy around and headed for home. The boy saw her crying and asked why the man had not let her use the restroom. "Because they didn't have one for colored people," she said. The boy asked why he wouldn't let her use the one they did have. "Because white people don't want you to have anything they think is theirs," she said. Why is that? the boy wanted to know. "Because that's the kind of people they are," she said.

There was no bow-and-arrow set that Christmas, though there were other toys, of course. There was also a new idea, one that occurred to the boy as he and his mother walked home from the aborted shopping trip. The idea took shape in disappointment, anger, and perplexity about what had happened: maybe, if the opportunity arose, some white people should be killed. It was an idea the boy would entertain for years.

That spring the boy's mother bought him a baseball glove for his birthday. Sometimes, on Sunday afternoons, the boy would play catch with his father before supper. It was late Sunday afternoon when his father—had he been gone since Friday night?—came into the house and, without a word, began to take off his clothes to clean up. "What you been doing?" the boy's mother demanded of her husband. "I know what *you* been doing," the boy's father replied. The boy, always listening in fascination and fear, had heard these voices before.

This time, when the yelling stopped, his mother was pinned to the floor, the meaty hands of a brick mason around her throat. She twisted beneath him, clawing at his face and gasping for breath. The boy saw himself take the fire poker from beside the stove and swing it into the side of his father's head. His father stopped, as if a switch had been

thrown. Blood began to trickle down a line across the frozen man's temple. Then he looked up at the boy, staggered to his feet, and came for him. The boy ran from the house, still holding the poker, crying.

Atwater was baptized at Hickory Grove Baptist Church, west of Chapel Hill, when he was twelve. "They ask if you're ready to live according to the principles of the church," he explained. "You have to go through some preparation to know what that means. They ask if you understand. Of course a kid is going to say yes, 'cause his momma is sitting right there." Did *you* understand it? "Something of it, but not enough. The doctrines of the church—I wasn't too sure about all that." Did you live up to the principles? "Not for long. I lived my way. That's why I had so much hard luck in my life, and so many good times."

The next summer Atwater worked at a sawmill with his father and uncle. It was a time that marked the beginning of Atwater's break from his mother, who until then had kept him in knickers and dainty clothes. In the all-male world of the sawmill, Atwater learned that to be a man meant drinking, gambling, fighting, and chasing women. Too young to carouse on his own, Atwater nonetheless won praise for his budding aptitudes. As he played cards and took his first burning sips of corn liquor, his father had said to him, "Boy, you gonna grow into a real man someday." The other men teased his uncle because his son, Atwater's cousin John, showed less interest in hell-raising. "Now that boy," Atwater heard his father say, "ain't gonna amount to much of a man."

Atwater might have acquired a work ethic at the sawmill, but he didn't. He remembered being run ragged as he tried to stack planks as fast as they came off the saw. "My daddy put some smoke on my ass! After a while, I couldn't keep up, and I couldn't stand that. When I told my daddy I was going to quit, he didn't argue. He just said go." Atwater took the same lesson from the sawmill that he took from his grandfather's farm: he never wanted to work so hard, if he could avoid it.

School was easier. Biology and geometry were Atwater's favorite subjects—geometry especially, because "you could make everything fit together and prove what was right." Shop class was fun, though he had run-ins with the teacher. "History I didn't care for," Atwater said, "because it was too hard to keep track of facts and dates and stuff."

What Atwater really liked was the good feeling he got from helping other kids with their homework.

In ninth grade Atwater often played hooky and began to get, as he said, "a little wild." Tenth grade was worse. A corrupting influence that year was a sky-blue '49 Plymouth coupe, bought by his parents so that Atwater could drive his grandfather to church. He was the only kid at school with a car, which raised his popularity immensely. At lunchtime he took his buddies and girlfriends cruising, and often didn't make it back for afternoon classes. That year Atwater got credit for only eighty days of school and barely managed, by passing his final exams, to be promoted to the next grade.

Neither sports nor music could keep Atwater engaged with school. "I was too small for football and too short for basketball. At first I wanted to be involved somehow, so I managed equipment. My mom was scared of me playing football. 'You might get killed out there,' she said. She was right too. Some of those guys were twenty, twenty-five years old. They came back to school after being in the service. I wasn't going to go out there and have 'em mess me up. No way." Atwater briefly tried to play the piccolo in the band, but dropped it in favor of the bass drum, which he also later dropped. His only other school activity was with the paper, the *Orange Echo*, for which he did some drawing and once wrote a ghost story.

After getting in trouble one time for spraying the teachers' cars with gravel by spinning the wheels of the Plymouth, Atwater remembered Charles McDougle, the school principal, telling him, "You are a bad influence here, young man. If you don't shape up, you'll never graduate and never make anything of yourself." Atwater shaped up enough to finish on schedule, graduating with his class in June of 1951. His fellow students named him most "kiddish," which he remembered as meaning "fun-loving and unserious," rather than immature.

Once a promising student, Atwater drifted away from school in part because it was more fun to ram around with his buddies and, later, when he got the car, with older guys and girls. The chance to be a big shot was seductive. He used the car to take his buddies to the juke joints that thrived a few miles outside town. In those places he found himself an object of curiosity on the part of the women, God having

Atwater's diploma
and graduation
picture

answered his prayers quite generously. "Word got around about my dick, and them older chicks had to check me out!" he would say with a raspy cackle. He was forming an image of himself as a lover, staking himself on a stereotype.

School, as Atwater began to see it, did not offer escape from the maze of inequalities in which he was caught. "School was interesting until about seventh or eighth grade. Then I started to see that it was just a way to pass time. I also saw that our school was two years behind the white school, with the hand-me-down books they gave us. If I had wanted to study engineering, even at a mediocre school, I would have had to take an extra two years of math just to get in. That put me off. And then I saw kids who had gone to college. They would go to a black college and come out and get the same kind of job they would have gotten anyway—porter, orderly, or some shit like that. So I started to wonder, What's the purpose of that, of going to school, if it wasn't going to get me into something I wanted to do? I knew that whitey was only gonna let me get so far."

His intellectual ability, though, was not in doubt; there was no less consensus about the power of his mind than about his being spoiled. "Burness was smart, really smart, in school," his cousin Lena said. "He could draw beautifully and write poetry that would make you feel like you were on a cloud. He helped other kids get through school, but after a while it was like he didn't care about it himself. His parents gave him

everything they could, and would have been willing to try to help him with college. He could have been anything he wanted to be." Atwater said he had wanted to build long bridges across water. He was always fascinated with how that was done.

In the summer of his seventeenth year the boy had a special girlfriend. She was smart and pretty, a church girl. At fifteen she was still a virgin, with the intention of remaining so until the right time. The two of them talked about getting married and about going to college. She would be a nurse and he an engineer. It was the kind of sweetheart talk that substituted for making riskier kinds of love.

One night that summer they went to a juke joint to listen to music and dance. Pearl Harbor, it was called—a place outside town on the edge of the woods, a place for black folks and, sometimes, white college students who thought themselves hip. That night the joint was set aside for young people. No alcohol was served, and the older, rowdier crowd was supposed to stay away. The boy and his girl walked in, greeting music and friends.

The small cinderblock building was packed with young bodies gyrating and sweating in the residual heat of the summer night. As the boy and girl made their way onto the dance floor, she shrieked and turned to face a man who had grabbed her. "That dude grabbed my girlfriend's butt right in front me," the boy later recounted. "He was older and wasn't even supposed to be there that night. If I'd had my knife I'd a cut him right there. But I pushed that motherfucker back and told him I was going to shoot his sorry ass. He thought I was kidding, but I didn't play around in those days, and man I wasn't going to let nobody grab my girlfriend's butt." The boy ran to his car and got his uncle's ancient single-shot 16 gauge out of the trunk.

"That motherfucker flew when he seen me coming with that shotgun." The older man ran out the side door and jumped down an embankment into a trash pile. "I took a shot at him and missed as he jumped," the boy recalled. "But I caught up with him as he was trying to climb out of that old dump. That's where I hit him upside the head with that gunstock about four or five times. He wasn't gonna play no more grabass that night." But the night was over for the boy.

The sheriff had been called and, because a gun was fired, the boy went to jail. His sweetheart's dreams began to fade.

In an earlier time the incident might have been ignored, the law not caring much about black folks fighting in a juke joint, especially if no one was killed. But times had changed. A complaint was filed and the boy was convicted of assault with a deadly weapon. The judge gave him six months on a road crew. The boy's father hired a lawyer, a fancy white man, to appeal the case in superior court. There was no money for the lawyer, so the boy's father traded a piece of land for services. It wasn't the last piece of land that would be lost in a similar way.

The well-connected lawyer got the boy off. No time would be served, though stories would be told later, stories of manhood and honor. But no land would be recovered, nor would sweetheart dreams be fulfilled. "The best thing they could have done," one of the boy's cousins later said, "would have been to let him serve that time and learn something about accountability." Forty-six years later the girlfriend denied she'd been there, denied the relationship was much to speak of. "He was a flashy guy. A hoodlum. He's lucky he's still alive," she said.

In his teens, Atwater began to resist his mother's control. He felt that she manipulated his father and tried to do the same to him. "For all their troubles, my father loved her," Atwater said. "I don't know why; she just had control over him. He thought she had more powerful mojo than Jesus. I still can't understand it. My father was pitiful—couldn't make up his mind about nothing. Whatever she said was law. And she pulled that on me until I was sixteen. Then I couldn't take it anymore. I told her, 'Momma, I'm gonna try to listen to you and be obedient, but I'm gonna put *my* stuff with it and not do something just because you say so. I'm gonna think about it first and decide what I want to do.' "

Still, Atwater was not inclined to forgo his parents' protection. Throughout high school and beyond he relied on their willingness to bail him out of trouble. There were more fights, wrecked cars, and charges for petty crimes: public drunkenness, lewd conduct, hit-and-run damage to property. Each time, hard-earned family resources, usually a piece of land, were expended to pay fines or lawyers' fees. For all his talk about independence and making his own decisions, Atwater

wasn't learning much about taking responsibility for the consequences of his actions.

Atwater's father didn't know what to do with his son. Scoldings, whippings, and threats, such as he had been able to deliver, had little effect. On at least one occasion he sought the help of a root doctor, a conjure woman, to bring his son under control. That didn't work, either. At the limits of his patience, there were times when Atwater's father showed up, at odd hours, on the doorsteps of relatives, saying that he had to leave the house to avoid killing his son.

As he grew, Atwater saw more clearly that things were not right in his family. He suspected infidelities on the part of both parents, though now, after his summer at the sawmill, his sympathies lay with his father. Men were *supposed* to drink, gamble, and carouse—and women were supposed to be controlled, not controlling. He also continued to exploit the conflict between his parents. "My dad would get on my ass about something, and my mom would say, 'William, who are you to be telling that boy how to behave?' And he'd just shut up and leave me alone. I used her, but she used me to get back at him." Atwater was becoming adept at playing one person off another.

Although Atwater was an only child, he was not the only child his parents cared for. Two of Atwater's cousins lived with the family at times during his teen years. Atwater claimed he shared generously, "right down the middle," when his cousins moved in. His cousins remember him as selfish and jealous of his mother's affections. The latter account is consistent with other reports of Atwater's behavior. Another cousin, one who lived nearby, said, "Yeah, he'd share with us. He'd let us play with his toys. But he was a mean sucker. Mean. If you didn't play the way he wanted, he'd knock you down and take his stuff and go home." If there is a third point of consensus about Atwater, it's that he had to have things his way.

During the summer after finishing high school, Atwater earned money by helping his father with masonry jobs—brickwork and laying sidewalks. Later he worked as an aide in the linen supply room at the university hospital. His wages were fifty cents an hour. He thought about college and about joining the army but not seriously enough to give up the fun he was having as a young man about town. He continued

to cultivate his persona as Shine—a hoodlum, a lover, and a dandy. "Other than earning enough money to keep me going, I was just into my own thing at that time," Atwater said.

The boy was out of school now, old enough to feel grown. He'd been arguing with his mother in the kitchen. He said that what he'd done was right. She said it was wrong. The boy's father heard angry voices and came in from the front yard to see what was going on. "This boy," she told her husband, "is calling me a liar."

"That's enough, boy," he said. "Get on outside."

Now the boy argued with his father on the porch. He felt that his mother had set his father against him and that he wasn't being allowed to explain himself. Words carrying years of anger and frustration flew between them. "I'm gonna give you a chance to cool off," his father said, turning to step off the porch. The boy, misjudging his powers, kicked his father in the back. Before the boy had regained his footing, a razor appeared in his father's hand and the boy fell to the ground with a five-inch gash on the inside of his right knee. "I brought your black ass into this world, boy," his father said, "and if need be I'll take you out of it." The boy looked up, too surprised to speak.

His father's belt was now a tourniquet, his father's shoulder a crutch as the boy hobbled to the old man's pickup truck. They rode in silence to the hospital, where the cut—the result of an accidental encounter with a broken window, it was said—was cleaned and sewn. On the way home the boy stared at his bandaged knee, visible because the pant leg had been cut off at mid-thigh. His father finally spoke: "You've done a lot of bad shit and I've forgiven you every time. But no more. Not for this. You ever come at me again when my back is turned and I will send you to your maker. You hear me, boy?" The boy nodded, turning away to dry his eyes.

The father was dead and now the boy was an old man. "I'll never forget that time I kicked him and he cut me. He was walking away, giving me a break—and I didn't have sense enough to know it. I never did anything like that to him again." But the arguments weren't over. "Yeah, we still argued. One time I called him a dumb old man. That was cruel.

I never forgave myself for saying that. My daddy loved me. He loved the hell out of me. I know he did."

Before things turned sour for him, one of Atwater's good experiences in the army was making friends with a white boy from Okeechobee, Florida. "I had never been friends with a white person before the army," Atwater recalled. "There were some in there who brought all that prejudice shit with them and were as bad as the worst back home. You just avoided them if you could. But a few were all right. They treated you like you was anybody. One I remember was William T. Bass. He was my ace buddy." The friendship was aided by Atwater's ability to write.

Bass, who had gone to Germany after basic training, still remembered Atwater after forty-three years. "Atwater and me was good buddies," Bass told me. "And back in 1953 a nigger and a white man, uh—you know what I mean? It was separate, even though it was the same outfit. But he was my buddy. And I was down in the dumps one day and I said, 'Atwater, c'mere,' and he came over and wrote a love letter for me. To my girlfriend." The girlfriend was impressed. "She wasn't my wife at the time," Bass explained. "But since then I've married her and we been together for forty years next month." Atwater claimed that he wrote great love letters. "I think he might have been writing for a bunch of us in those barracks," Bass said.

Atwater was Bass's first black friend, arrangements not favoring such friendships in Okeechobee County. "I didn't go to school with blacks," Bass said. "They had their school—they stayed on their side of the railroad tracks and we stayed on this side. That's what it was. I didn't associate with them at all." Atwater remembered passing up a chance to go home with Bass on leave. Bass's father had been killed by a black man in a case of mistaken identity, and Atwater feared that Bass's mother still harbored resentment. "No, that wasn't it," Bass said. "It was Okeechobee. Back then there were signs all over that said, 'Nigger, don't let us catch you in this town after dark.' You know, *don't be here*. Back then it was sure enough racial." Bass returned to Florida after the service. He and Atwater did not keep in touch.

Atwater in Korea

The court martial came in June of 1955, while Atwater was sta-
tioned at Camp Schimmelpfennig in Honshu, Japan (after a year in
Korea). It was not the first time Atwater had been in trouble. According
to records of the proceedings, Atwater's priors included three counts
of disrespect to a superior noncommissioned officer; two counts of
disobeying lawful orders of a superior noncommissioned officer; one
count of failure to obey a lawful general order; two counts of being
drunk and disorderly; and one count of failure to go to work-call for-
mation. These offenses had merely gotten Atwater reprimanded and
restricted to base.

Atwater claimed that he was court-martialed for hitting an acting
sergeant with a shovel. "We were on sandbag detail and it was cold as
hell," Atwater said. "One guy shoveled and another guy tied off the bag.
The guy who shoveled kept warm, but the guy who tied—you couldn't
wear gloves, and it was so cold your fingers would get stiff. So I suggested to this acting sergeant, this white boy from Georgia, that we
switch off, tie for a while then shovel for a while. And he says to me,
'Nigger, get your ass back to work.' Man, I went off! Hit him upside the

head with a shovel. Here I am defending my country, wearing the same uniform he is, and this cracker gives me that 'nigger' shit. I'd a killed him if they hadn't pulled me off. The army got me for that one. That's what got me put out."

The record says that Atwater failed to obey the order of Sergeant First Class James Thompson to get a shovel from the supply room and go to the orderly room. There is no mention of assault; the charge is simply "failure to obey a lawful order of a noncommissioned officer." In his defense, Atwater claimed that when the order was given, he was restricted to company area, an area in which there were no shovels. The court didn't buy it, and Atwater was sentenced to six months at hard labor and given a bad conduct discharge. An appeal on procedural grounds failed. Atwater was on his way out, and not, as far as the record shows, for clocking anyone with a shovel.

When Atwater got back to Chapel Hill in the spring of 1956 he was full of anger and alcohol. Although he was dissuaded from killing his wife, the situation remained volatile. "I had to get away," he said, "or I *would* have killed her. There was no way any peace was gonna last between us at the time. So my daddy sent me away to live with my uncle in New York." Atwater went to New York and cooled off, but was back in town by January of 1957. Though Dorothy became pregnant with Atwater's second son, no reconciliation was tenable as long as Atwater was drinking.

The alcohol fueled episodes of violence. "I was still angry with her about what she did," Atwater said. What she had done, to Atwater's mind, was to blight his image of himself as a man. "To go back with her, to be her flunky—I couldn't do that. I had a reputation to maintain. I wasn't gonna be seen as whipped by no woman. Today I can see how stupid all that was. But back then I had no maturity and didn't know how to handle things. All I could think of was getting back at her. At the time, what I did seemed like the right thing to do." The right thing meant trying to reassert himself as a man who would not, unlike his father, be controlled by a woman.

Employment was also a problem. When Atwater returned to Chapel Hill in January of 1957, he was hired as a janitor at the university.

Personnel records show that he was paid 70 cents an hour, or $1,748 per year—not enough, even at that time, to support a family of four. It was also the kind of job into which the university would have locked a black man indefinitely. Not that Atwater gave that possibility a chance: in May of 1957 he was fired. His supervisor noted in the record: "not dependable; laying out without notice; work unsatisfactory in general; would not rehire."

Within a year of his return from New York, Atwater was gone again, this time for a period of hoboing across the country. This pattern repeated itself for the next twenty years. Atwater's local job history during the 1960s and 1970s is an index of his life during that time.

In 1962 he worked again as a janitor at UNC, lasting five months before being fired for drinking on the job. During the winter of 1966–67 he worked as a porter at the UNC pediatrics center, before being fired for drinking on the job. In 1969 he worked off and on as a concrete finisher and plasterer for local construction companies. He lasted one week with the town of Chapel Hill in 1973. And in 1976 he was fired from a job at an apartment complex when his boss saw a six-pack fall off the back of a mower Atwater was riding. During the months and years between these patches of local employment, Atwater lived mostly in New York or D.C., surviving on menial jobs in those places. No job lasted long.

All along, Atwater drank. At his worst he was, as one of his companions during those years put it, "down to a wino." Although Atwater told of supervising construction jobs up north and of living off older women who valued his sexual prowess ("I'd give 'em one stab with old John Henry and they'd say, 'C'mon in the house, Jack!' "), none of the people who knew him in New York or D.C. could verify such exploits. For a time, Atwater maintained his Shine persona around Chapel Hill. "I was the best-dressed drunk in town," Atwater said. "I used to wear a suit and had me a fancy T-handle cane. People would hear that cane a-tappin' or those silver dollars poppin' and they knew *Shine was in the club*! I was sharp!" Shine was a smooth-talking stud who was handy with a knife. It was a hard image for a degenerating alcoholic to uphold.

Although Atwater still liked to dress well when he could, his inability to hold a job and the years of living as a street wino bankrupted his

local reputation. By the late 1960s, Shine had lost much of his luster. Alcohol also continued to poison Atwater's relationships with family and the few friends he had. "He'd be back in town long enough to borrow or steal something, then he'd be gone," Atwater's son Chris once said. Atwater admitted to various petty scams—selling his father's car to a hapless friend, taking money for cement work that was never done—and then ducking out, hoping that matters would be forgotten by the time he returned.

In 1970, Atwater had a chance to dry out during his stay at Occoquan. But his relapse during a visit to Chapel Hill left him feeling too ashamed to return to the work he did there as a peer counselor. "When that happened," he said, "I felt like, how could I go back and tell other people not to drink when I couldn't do it myself?"

Again Atwater was in and out of Chapel Hill, getting and losing a string of low-wage jobs, still drinking. He worked as a cook in a Catskill resort ("them Jews was the eatingest people I ever saw; they could pack it away"); as a janitor in the National Cathedral in D.C. ("I slept there, too, like the Hunchback of Notre Dame"); as a laborer in a Pittsburgh foundry ("I was there only one day—my eyes was burning, and when I saw that red hot steel coming at me, man, I didn't want nothing to do with that shit; it was like working on the edge of hell"); as a stable mucker on a Texas farm that raised Brahma bulls ("those were some mean-ass animals"); and occasionally as a concrete finisher. For all his jobs, Atwater once estimated that, in his entire life, he had probably not worked more than ten years altogether.

It was at Occoquan that Atwater heard the Voice that told him to return to Chapel Hill. He should go home, the Voice said, because his father would need help and because Atwater's destiny was to "retrieve a fish from the sea" in the form of a white woman who would also need help. It took Atwater eight years to heed the advice. In the summer of 1978, a few months past his forty-fifth birthday, Atwater returned to Chapel Hill. This time he was home to stay, though hardly to settle down.

from halves to a piece of earth

fter everything was figured out, it seemed strange that there was ever any confusion. But I was, at first, misguided by Mr. Mason himself. I wanted to see the place where he was born, his grandfather's farm in southwest Durham County. The land had long since gone out of the family, but still I wanted to see what had become of it and try to imagine it as it had been. Where was the farm? I asked. "About ten miles from Chapel Hill," Mr. Mason told me. "Down towards Pittsboro. On the river."

Those were curious directions. From Chapel Hill, Durham County is not "Down toward Pittsboro," and the only river I knew of in that vicinity was the Haw, which Mr. Mason said was not the river he meant. What else was near your grandfather's farm? I asked, seeking a landmark. "Barbee's Chapel," Mr. Mason said. "That's where Effie and I went to first grade." What river is out there? "New Hope Creek. That's what it was. That's what I was baptized in."

I'd been riding my bike through the area for years. On my next ride, I noticed the name *Nunn* on a mailbox that I'd passed hundreds of times. I found the phone number and ended up speaking to James Nunn Jr. He and Mr. Mason shared a grandfather—Richard Nunn. I got directions to the old Nunn homeplace. The land was now owned by a family that ran a construction company.

Two men, one in his early thirties, the other a bit younger, were lounging in the yard on the day I went to look around. The first man's cap bore a Duke University emblem, as did the other man's sweatshirt.

I couldn't help but notice that we were standing near a sawed-off version of the control tower from the old Raleigh-Durham airport. The tower was a relic aquired, I was told, in the course of a construction job.

I explained that I was doing research on a black family that used to live in the area. "I understand that this is the old Richard Nunn place," I said. Neither man recognized the name. For a moment I thought I'd taken a wrong turn. "If this is the right place," I said, recalling what James Nunn had told me, "there should be a cemetery near the house somewhere, and the remains of some old cabins within about a hundred yards."

When I mentioned the cemetery, the older of the two men said, "Okay, yeah, there are some old slave graves on the far side of the pond, down the embankment from that sycamore." He pointed to a tree across the pond. "And back there in the woods"—he pivoted 90 degrees to his left—"are some old slave shacks. Anyhow, you're welcome to look around."

Slave graves? Slave shacks?

I walked around the pond and found the cemetery. The plot was about twenty-five feet square, bordered by rusty chicken wire and grown over with brush. There were two weathered gray headstones, one for Luther (born December 3, 1883, died October 20, 1919) and one for Sampy (born January 30, 1881, died May 19, 1906). Both stones were inscribed "Son of Richard and Marzelia Nunn." I was kneeling on the graves of Matthew Mason's uncles. Several other graves were marked only with fieldstones.

A quarter of a mile away, in a spot thick with pine trees, I found the shacks. All that was left of one was the rusted tin roof, which sat on the ground as if the house had sunk below it. A second had been reduced to a pile of rotted logs. A third, a plank shack about six feet by eight feet inside, was still standing. Between the shacks, in what was once the common yard of this cluster of dwellings, was an old rock-lined well. Mr. Mason must have drunk water from this well twenty years before my parents were born.

I took pictures and sketched a map of the farm. Walking east, I found the waters of New Hope Creek—far sooner than Mr. Mason would have found them as a boy, since the creek had been backed up and turned

into part of Jordan Lake in the early 1980s. When the light began to fade, I headed back to my car, taking what looked like an old wagon road. Local people had told me that years ago the woods were laced with such roads. I tried to imagine Mr. Mason as a boy, perhaps seventy-five years earlier, walking the same road, or riding it in the wagon with his father.

Later I wrote a short article about finding Mr. Mason's birthplace. When I read a draft to Mr. Mason, he listened quietly, smiling and nodding until he heard "slave graves" and "slave shacks." He looked at me, eyes wide, as if I'd made a terrible mistake. "Those weren't no slave graves and no slave shacks," he injected. "Grandpa Dick *owned* that land. That was *his* farm." Mr. Mason was eventually satisfied that the article made his grandfather's ownership clear. It was no small point. Owning land and merely working on it was, once upon a time, the difference between slavery and freedom.

The land on which Matthew Mason was born was once home to the Occaneechi, Eno, and Tuscarora tribes. By the mid-1700s the natives had been forced out and the British crown began to allocate land to colonists. Among the early land-grant recipients was Christopher Barbee, who, along with his relatives, acquired thousands of acres in the area where Durham, Orange, and Chatham Counties now meet. Barbee's great-granddaughter, Mary Hargrave, inherited some of his land and brought it to her marriage to William R. Kenan. Around the turn of the century the Kenans sold off many of these holdings. One buyer was a black man from Chatham County, Richard Nunn, who bought seventy-two acres for $350 in 1902.

Nunn, born in 1854, was a serious, hardworking man who, with the help of his wife and eight children, made the farm thrive. The major cash crops were cotton, corn, and tobacco. Apples and peaches were grown for consumption and for sale. Vegetables from the garden, along with the usual hogs and chickens, made the farm self-sustaining. His economic success and independence made Richard Nunn a prominent member of the black community around Barbee's Chapel. When he went to church, Deacon Nunn rode in a fine buggy, not a clapboard wagon.

Most black families in the area were sharecroppers. A typical arrangement was to "work halves," meaning that half of the cash

netted when a crop was sold went to the landowner, usually white, who provided seed, fertilizer, tools, work animals, and housing. Workers thus bore the risks of drought, pests, plant disease, and glutted markets. Being cash-poor, sharecroppers often borrowed money from landowners to get through the year. Being illiterate, they were also at the mercy of the landowners who sold the crops and kept the books. It was not uncommon for sharecroppers to end a year in debt to a landowner who could insist that they stay on until the debt was paid. This system effectively bound landless workers to the same people who had owned the land, and perhaps owned them, before the Civil War.

The black Masons were a sharecropping family from northeast Chatham, just across the nearby county line from the Nunn farm. It was in this family that Connie, Richard Nunn's oldest daughter, born in 1883, found her husband. In 1908 she married William Arthur "Chain" Mason, born in 1882. Their first child was a girl, Effie. The second child, born June 4, 1911, was a boy. They named him Matthew, after William's father.

As his father—Matthew "Fox" Mason—had done, Chain Mason worked on land owned by Tom Mason, a white man. The common name was, of course, no coincidence. Chain's grandfather, Benjamin (born ca. 1810), had taken the English surname "Mason" from the man who had owned him, John Acree Mason. Generations later, the life of Matthew "Dr. Reet" Mason was shaped by this fact—that he belonged to a category of people who had once been property—and by his family's post-Civil War ties to the white Masons.

The arrival of the white Masons in northeast Chatham County traces to William Mason, who, according to one history of prominent families in the county, was a descendant of Captain George Mason, a former member of British Parliament. William Mason came to North Carolina in the 1790s from Mecklenburg County, Virginia, by way of Bertie County, North Carolina, where he married Nancy Acree. Mason was part of the second wave of white arrivals in the Piedmont.

The land that Mason would make the heart of his plantation was first granted to the Morgans, Mark and John, in the late 1750s. In the following decades there was a flurry of buying and selling and trading of granted land. By the 1780s another early grantee, Pressley George, had acquired

John A. Mason house (built ca. 1850), 1996, before restoration

John A. Mason house, 2001, after restoration

part of the Morgans' holdings in the peninsula formed by Morgan Creek on the west and New Hope Creek on the east. In December of 1797 William Mason paid George £400 (about $39,000 in 2002 dollars) for 671 acres of this land. By 1815 Mason owned 1,100 acres and four slaves. This made him the second wealthiest man in his tax district.

When William Mason died in 1842, his second son, John Acree Mason, inherited a 600-acre tract of land on which he built, around 1850, the "mansion house" (see photos) that would later figure in the

twentieth-century boyhood of Matthew Mason. John Mason eventually extended his landholdings to over 1,000 acres, on which he grew wheat and corn and raised hogs. When he died in 1859, he left an estate valued at about $25,000 ($538,000 in 2002 dollars). A 1974 report written to qualify Mason's house for the historic register characterizes him as "typical of the middle planter class in North Carolina." His estate included twenty slaves. Among those twenty slaves were Benjamin and Isabel, Matthew Mason's great-grandparents.

John Mason's only child, a son named Wesley, had died in 1848, leaving behind a wife and two children, Thomas and Elizabeth, who became wards of the elder Mason. After his death in the spring of 1859, John Mason's widow and grandchildren petitioned the court for permission to divide his property, including the slaves. A drawing was held to see who would get what and whom. His widow drew a lot that included Isabel; his granddaughter drew a lot that included Matthew; his grandson Tom drew a lot that included Benjamin.

Despite the change of ownership, it appears that the black Masons remained together, working on the plantation of John Mason's younger brother Jesse. The 1860 slave census lists, among Jesse Mason's nineteen slaves, a forty-nine-year-old male, a forty-seven-year-old female, and a nine-year-old male. The sexes and ages match Benjamin, Isabel, and Matthew.

Ten years later, after the Civil War, the 1870 census lists Benjamin and Isabel as heading their own household. They are still in northeast Chatham, where he is a renting farmer and she is "keeping house." Both are illiterate. Among their six unschooled children is twenty-year-old Matthew, listed as a farm laborer. This is Matthew "Fox" Mason, who would later marry Fannie and father three sons: first John, and then the twins James and William. Nearly fifty years later the black Masons would still be tied to the white Masons.

John Mason's grandson, Tom, born in 1843, took over the Mason plantation in the "forks of the creek," as the wedge of land between Morgan Creek and New Hope Creek came to be known. In the original division of John Mason's land, Tom got 680 acres, including the mansion house (he acquired another 115 acres when his grandmother died in 1894). It was on this land, handed down through three generations of white Masons, that the black Masons lived as sharecroppers. They

Richard Nunn (Mason's grandfather) and daughter Connie Nunn (Mason's mother)

were probably no worse off than any others. Tom Mason was reputed to be a fair man who treated folks right.

When Matthew Mason was born in 1911, his parents were living on Richard Nunn's farm in Durham County, but his father was working for Tom Mason a few miles south in Chatham. Early in 1914 Chain Mason moved his family—wife Connie, daughter Effie, and toddler Matthew—to the Tom Mason place after a new cabin was built for them. The rest of the children—Charlie, Frances, and David—would be born there. Matthew "Fox" Mason and his second wife, Becky, lived there too, eventually in the big house.

Tom Mason, the last of the major landholding white Masons, died a few years later, in January 1917 (his wife Sarah had died in 1912). His oldest son, Joe, who had largely taken over operation of the farm, had moved off the place in 1916 when he bought his own land a few miles east, across New Hope Creek. Economically, the old plantation was failing. Tom Mason had sold timber rights to the land in the creek bottoms and had mortgaged other parcels. A year after he died, Tom Mason's heirs sold the estate to John Council and Roy McGhee for $1,500 cash and $4,200 worth of notes secured by a deed of trust on the land.

The Masons stayed on, working halves. Fox and Becky were allowed to live in the mansion house—as stipulated, according to local legend, by Tom Mason before he died. This probably mattered little to Council and McGhee, since their interests, by all reports, were in cutting and selling the timber on the land, not in living there or trying to derive income from it as a farm. Fox and Becky both died in 1922. After this, the Masons moved back to Durham County and lived with James Nunn Sr., Connie's brother, who ran a small country store about a mile from Richard Nunn's farm. Matthew Mason, later nicknamed "Dr. Reet," was eleven years old.

Mr. Mason's earliest memories, when it happened that I wished to know them, were already fading. *What he remembered*: riding in the wagon, a two-seater, with his father. "Get up, Rhodie!" his father would say, snapping the reins to put the mule in motion. They hauled caskets—a way to earn a few extra dollars in a time when money was scarce and a worldwide flu epidemic had made death a booming industry. His father hummed as they rode. Did he ever sing? "No, just hummed." Did he tell stories? "No, he was a quiet man."

What he remembered: staying out of the field one morning, claiming to be sick, so he could sample his father's corn liquor. He'd seen where the jug was hidden. At noon they found him, curled up on the floor, moaning. When he passed out they sent for Doc Caldwell, who examined him and told his worried parents, "This boy ain't sick; he's *drunk*." The corn liquor, he remembered, was warm and smooth going down.

What he remembered: "plowing a mule" when he was eight years old, the force of the animal pulling him forward, straining his back. He remembered his father, a patient teacher, encouraging him to hold on and keep the mule moving straight. The fields would later fill with tobacco, cotton, and corn. In the family garden there were peas and potatoes, string beans and turnips. He remembered the smell of greens being cooked in a kitchen detached from the main house.

What he remembered: fishing in the creek with his father. They caught catfish, perch, and eels—and ate them all. He remembered being baptized in the same creek. Who baptized you? "Reverend John Caldwell of New Hope Church. Least I think it was, anyway." He remembered singing, and cold water up to his waist. And thinking about fishing.

Barbee's Chapel School, ca. 1917

What he remembered: going to his mother's church, Barbee's Chapel, every third Sunday; going to his father's church, New Hope, every second Sunday; going, sometimes, on the fourth Sunday, to Mt. Zion. He remembered his mother shushing him, more than once, in church. They went in a wagon—Tom Mason's wagon, pulled by Tom Mason's mule. He remembered staying home one Sunday a month.

What he remembered: first grade at Barbee's Chapel, second grade at New Hope Church. Both schools were one-room plank buildings with cast-iron stoves for heat and outhouses for relief. The school year was October through March, depending on the weather. He remembered walking to and from school with his sister—on dirt roads to get to Barbee's Chapel, and through the woods and across the creek to get to New Hope. He remembered getting through third grade before quitting to go to work.[1] When reminded, he remembered his first-grade teacher, Annie Lyons, and his second-grade teacher, Effie Edwards.

---

1. Mr. Mason was not consistent in reporting how long he'd gone to school. At first he said that he'd gotten through third grade, had been promoted to fourth, and then had to quit school to go to work. Later he told me that he'd not actually gotten all the way through third grade before quitting. Even assuming that he finished third grade, this would amount to less than two years of schooling altogether, since the school year for rural black children, back then, was about six months, from mid-fall to mid-spring, depending on the weather.

What he remembered: working with his father at the sawmill. There were still big trees to cut in the creek bottoms: pine, oak, maple, ash. As a boy, he worked on the green end, hauling away slabs as they were trimmed from the rough logs. He remembered the screaming steam-powered saw and slivers in his hands and being very tired. He worked a ten-hour day and earned ten cents an hour, a man's wage. Who owned the sawmill? "A white man and his son." Council? "That's right. John Council and his son—Hallie, I think. How did you know that?"

What he remembered: living in a frame house on the Tom Mason place; sharing an upstairs room and a double bed with his brother Charlie. He remembered cracks between the planks and waking up some mornings with frost on the wall and snow on the blankets that covered him. He remembered a cotton mattress on a metal spring bed, and oil lamps.

What he remembered: that Grandpa Fox was a happy man, not big, about the same size his namesake grandson grew to be. He remembered that Grandpa Fox didn't drink, but that Grandpa Dick did; that his father drank, buying liquor for a dollar a gallon at the government still down in the forks of the creek. *Who* ran a still there? "The government, they said. Called it Ponto government still. People came from all around to get liquor there. That's all I know."

What he remembered: that he had never seen his "real grandma, Grandma Fannie," who was buried on the Tom Mason place. He remembered two small cemeteries, one white and one black.

What he remembered: that his father was as close to Tom Mason as two fingers on the same hand; that Tom Mason provided whatever they needed. He remembered Tom Mason. "He lived about three years, I think, after we moved there. I don't remember *him* so much as his buggy and his mule." He remembered looking south from the front porch of the big house and seeing a field of corn. He remembered standing in the same spot, later, and seeing lumber stacked for drying and waiting to be taken to the finish mill.

What he remembered: playing games—lotto, bingo, jack rock—though not how to play them. He remembered playing horseshoes and checkers. "Lot of times we'd just make up a game or something to play. That's what we did out in the country." He remembered more work than play. Birthdays were celebrated, meagerly. "Might get a little candy or cake. Maybe a little something for a present. Weren't much."

What he remembered: his Grandpa Fox telling him that the Mason name had come from slavery times, and that Fox's father had taken the name from Tom Mason's grandfather. He remembered that his Grandpa Fox didn't like to talk about slavery times. He didn't remember his great-grandparents on either side. Grandpa Dick's father, he recalled hearing, had Indian and white blood. And Grandma Missy's people? "Pure black, far as I know."

Not long ago there were a few left whose memories were older still. Jesse Lassiter, born in 1907, had sat in the same classroom at New Hope Church school. "A mischievous boy," he said of his younger friend Matthew. "He liked to play hard and he had his own way of doing things, but he never got into fights. He was always good-natured." Even then Matthew walked funny—splay-footed. Rickets? "Maybe. One of his cousins was pigeon-toed. You should've seen the tracks the two of them made in the snow when one was following the other."

"We called Matthew 'Bigboy,'" Georgia Barbee McCallum said, "because he was the oldest boy in his family." She was older by a few months. "He was a lot of fun when we were children. Whatever we played, he was happy if he won, happy if he lost." How was he in school? "I remember that he always sang out of tune and off pitch. The teacher would sing notes—do, ré, mi, fa, and so on—and Matthew would try it and never get it. She'd sing do [high pitch], and he'd sing dow [low pitch]." He worked more than he went to school. "Yes, he always liked to have a job. He was brought up to work for an honest living. It was what he thought he was supposed to do, even as a boy." She remembered something else: that her grandmother, Emerline Purefoy, a self-taught pediatrician who birthed babies for black and white alike, had delivered Matthew Mason.

Times were hard in rural Chatham County in the early 1920s. A university extension study published in 1922 reported that the average annual cash income for black sharecropping families in northeast Chatham was $197. The average daily cash income for black share-croppers was ten cents. On the 329 farms surveyed in Williams and Baldwin townships, the average daily cash income, owners and tenants combined, was twenty-three cents per person. The overall cash poverty

of the area was such that many people struggled to obtain nonfood goods, and there was no surplus to pay for better roads or schools.

Pressed for cash, farmers planted more cotton and tobacco. But this led to market excesses, depressed prices, and reduced cash income, which was needed more than ever because fewer acres were put into food crops. This meant, in consequence, that the farm economy of the North Carolina Piedmont, despite the natural riches of the land, could not support the growing population trying to live on it. Many share-croppers, having no legal ties or rights to the land, moved from country to town, seeking a chance for better lives.

After coming off the old Tom Mason place and living with his Uncle James for about a year, Matthew Mason moved to Durham. Two other uncles had preceded him. His mother's brother, Matthew Nunn, ran a small grocery store on Fayetteville Street. His father's brother, James Mason, or "Uncle Jug" as Matthew knew him, also lived on Fayetteville Street, across from what was then called North Carolina College for Negroes. James Mason worked at Bull City Tobacco and, through friends, was able to get his nephew a job at Liggett & Myers.

The job, unloading raw tobacco, paid seventeen cents an hour. "You were s'posed to be sixteen to work there, but I told a lie. I was only twelve, but I was a big boy—looked older than I was," Matthew Mason confessed. He lived six months with his Uncle James and six months with his Uncle Matthew (who was later locally renowned as an eccentric preacher). A year of factory work was enough. In 1924, the year he turned thirteen, Matthew Mason came to Chapel Hill.

Here, in the college town, the town of Thomas Wolfe and Paul Green, he boarded with Mrs. Callie Durham on South Roberson Street, sharing a room with a friend from Chatham County, P. D. Edwards. P. D. had pre-ceded Matthew and was able to help him get jobs doing yard and domes-tic work. How much did you charge for that? "I didn't *charge* nothing," Matthew Mason said. "I had to work for what they'd give me." Usually it was fifty cents for a half-day's work. A dollar a day was doing well.

Chapel Hill was then a town of 2,146 people—1,411 white, 735 black. The streets were dirt and gravel. Outhouses were still common. In the next town over, a tobacco baron gave six million dollars to Trinity College in exchange for renaming it Duke University. In Chapel Hill,

about twenty thousand dollars was being spent to build a new school for black children. The school's principal, B. L. Bozeman, told the local newspaper, "Agriculture is the base upon which we are building our success."

Early in the twentieth century Chapel Hill was already being touted as a liberal enclave, a place where blacks and whites got along better than in most southern towns and where the well-being of the black community was a widely shared concern. Writing in the April 1914 issue of the *University of North Carolina Magazine*, frequent home to the expression of liberal sentiment in regard to race relations, Stuart Willis explained why whites were committed to the social improvement of blacks:

> We are realizing that our economic and civic life is advanced or retarded by his conditions of living. He washes our clothes in his home. Shall his home be sanitary and free from disease? He prepares our food. Shall he have knowledge of cleanliness and sanitation? He nurses our children. Shall we be concerned about the moral example he sets the child? We have seen the "folly of northern tutelage." His help must come from intelligent southern white people, and the benevolent endeavor of these people is gradually asserting itself. No longer are a few fanatics beating the air and advocating ideal theories and impossibilities. Rather we are coming to have "an enthusiasm for the possible." We are recognizing our social obligations to ourselves thru the negro and our obligation to him for his own sake. (p. 279)

Six years later, in the April 1920 issue of the same magazine, Charles Wiley Phillips described the blessings whites were bestowing on their black neighbors:

> The colored people of Chapel Hill have better manners, more of them know how to live by the principles of Christ than in many other sections of the state and nation. Do you ask why this is so? Do you ask why these negroes are a finer group of negroes than many other groups of like people? It can be laid at the door of the college man who has come here

from year to year working through the channels of the YMCA to give
these people the rudiments of education, the simple stories of the Bible,
and the higher ideal of citizenship and civilization. (p. 213)

No doubt aware that invoking the "higher ideal of citizenship" might
imply, to some readers, a dangerous notion of equality, Phillips took
pains to clarify his meaning:

Do you ask what is being taught them? Not the often misconceived
idea that the negroes are being trained to be the equals of whites. Not
that at all, but it is the effort of the workers to make them have the spirit
of working their very best at all times. They are taught how to write their
names, how to add simple problems, and how to spell a few easy words.
They are catching the idea of trying to be real men and women. (p. 214)

This was an era, as one writer later characterized black-white relations in Chapel Hill, of "affectionate condescension." It was an era
that lasted, some would say, until the protests of the early 1960s,
when young black people in Chapel Hill, including three of Matthew
Mason's children, caught the idea that being real men and women had
to mean, at the very least, an end to legal segregation.

When Matthew Mason came to Chapel Hill, black men were confined to a handful of jobs: porter, waiter, laundry collector, clothes
presser, janitor, delivery boy, gardener, and drayman. "There were," as
one of Matthew Mason's contemporaries, Wayne Durham, put it, "not
many choices. You took what you could get." In 1925, the average
weekly wage for black men in Chapel Hill was $17.78 (for women it was
$7.54). The average workday, according to one survey, was ten and a half
hours. Making, at best, a dollar a day, thirteen-year-old Matthew was
doing less well than he might have. His chance to do better came when
Harry Stern moved from Baltimore to Chapel Hill and opened a small
restaurant to serve the student trade.

Matthew was still doing yard and domestic work when his friends
Wayne Durham and P. D. Edwards started at Harry's Grill. When a job
opened for a dishwasher, they recommended Matthew. The pay was no

improvement—only seven dollars a week—but the work was easier and steadier, and it came with lunch. Matthew washed dishes for a year, then was promoted to waiter—a job that paid nine dollars a week, plus tips. Perhaps more important, it was a job that allowed Matthew Mason to discover his métier. An engaging demeanor, a desire to please, and an uncanny ability to remember names and faces made Matthew Mason the most popular waiter at Harry's.

Matthew's family had stayed in the country. But when his father took sick and was unable to do farm work, there was pressure to move to town. The balance was tipped when Matthew was able to get his sister Effie a job at Harry's. It was 1929.

"That's when I moved my family up to Chapel Hill," as Mr. Mason liked to say. It helped that his great-uncle, Vann Nunn, ran a successful grocery store and owned a house (at the northwest corner of Rosemary Street and Mitchell Lane) where Matthew's family could live until they found a place of their own.

Eventually, Matthew got his younger brother, Charlie, and younger sister, Frances, jobs at Harry's. Chain Mason recovered and, after working most of his life under the open sky, found work as a janitor at the university. Matthew's mother, "Mama Connie" as she was called in the family, took in laundry. And, for the time being, Matthew was happy at Harry's. The family, having found ways to generate sufficient cash income, moved out of Vann Nunn's place and rented a two-story house on North Roberson Street, on the site where, a little over twenty years later, the First Baptist Church would be built.

He didn't remember the first time he met her. Do you remember *where* it was? "The porch at her mother's house, on Rosemary Street, right near us," Matthew Mason said. "P. D. Edwards introduced us." Her people were also from Chatham County, down around Hamlet Chapel, though they had been in town longer. Fannie Lou Strowd, the pretty, petite girl on the porch, the girl who laughed when Matthew joked that the little frame house in which she lived looked like it was going to fall over, would become his wife.

In some ways it was an unlikely match. Her mother had attended Shaw University in Raleigh and later taught school. Her Aunt Daisy was also a teacher, and one of her uncles was a doctor in Virginia.

Fannie herself was quiet, though not unassertive, and liked to read. Although her father, according to local legend, had long ago been run out of town after getting in trouble for bootlegging, Fannie's background and inclinations were more intellectual and, in contemporary terms, more upscale than Matthew's.

He was, however, an attractive young man: handsome, jovial, churchgoing, and, if not exactly ambitious and enterprising, at least hardworking and responsible. And Fannie had perhaps scaled back her own ambitions when the birth of a child led her to drop out of school after the ninth grade. As a young woman with a child, in tough economic times that were going to get tougher before they got better, Matthew Mason's sturdy work ethic and buoyant spirit made him a good catch.

Mr. Mason remembered a great deal. Yet his accounts of his life, long before I asked for them, had been compacted and neatened. One time Mr. Mason, trying to be helpful, offered me what had become a standard summary of his life: "I was born in *Durham* County, on my Grandpa Dick's farm. Then my father moved us back down to *Chatham* County to the Tom Mason place. Tom Mason, he was a white man. We worked halves for him. I was eight years old and was already plowing a mule. Then I worked at the tobacco factory in Durham for a year before I come to Chapel Hill. I was thirteen years old when I got here. Franklin Street wasn't even paved then. I started washing dishes at Harry's Grill and got my sister a job there. That's when I moved my family up from Chatham to Chapel Hill. I started working at the fraternity house on the Monday after Mother's Day in 1934, and I been there ever since. The whole time I ain't never suffered for nothing. We always had enough to eat when a lot of folks didn't. And that's the truth. That's about all I know to tell you." Eighty-four years in fifteen sentences.

As this account was unpacked, it became apparent, by pinning down one date and doing the arithmetic, that years were missing. Did you go right to Durham when your family left the Tom Mason place? Are you sure you didn't stay somewhere else for a while? "I reckon we did stay with my Uncle Jim a while." How long? "Might've been a year, year and a half." Harry's, I found out, didn't open until 1926. What did you do when you *first* got to Chapel Hill? "Yard work, domestic work."

How long did you do that before you started at Harry's? "Couple, three years." How long were you at Harry's before you got Effie a job there? "Couple, three years." Eventually, the numbers added up right.

I doubt that the missing years were truly forgotten. More likely, they were omitted to sharpen an image that later became important when Mr. Mason worked for the fraternity. He was, he wanted it known, a boy from the poorest of backgrounds who, through hard work that began early in life and through natural talents for sociability, ended up rubbing shoulders with elite whites, succeeding well enough to buy his own home and raise a family. The story was true, though incomplete.

Mr. Mason had told me that after he and Fannie got married he moved out of the house he'd been living in with his family and bought a house, with Fannie, at 332 West Rosemary Street. This was the house, he said, where they'd raised their children. When did you buy it? "After Gloria was born. After I started at the fraternity house." That made it after 1934, which again meant that some years were missing. The deeds helped to fill in the blanks.

It turned out that Mr. Mason had bought the house on Rosemary Street in October 1935. But he bought it not with Fannie, but with her mother, Sallie, who loaned him money for a down payment. It was not until 1939 that he paid her back and assumed title to the house. When I checked this with Mr. Mason, he confirmed it. "Yeah, I guess that's right. Now that you remind me. You sure are a finding-out man."

So if you didn't buy the Rosemary Street house until 1935, where did you live right after you married Fannie? "With her mother, about where the cab company is on Rosemary Street. That's where two of my children were born. Miss Minnie Thompson, she was—what do you call it? a midwife?—she delivered my children." A different memory test: How much did she charge? "Eight dollars. Later it went up to ten." Memory, though, can bend.

About his first marriage, Mr. Mason said, "I was eighteen when I got married and my wife was seventeen. I ain't never gonna forget that. Nowadays people don't get married so young." Mr. Mason told me this early on, as we filled in a timeline of his life. Did you get married in Chapel Hill? "No, it was a little town in Virginia, right north of

Hillsborough." He wasn't sure which town. Nor of the exact date. Martha reminded him that the marriage certificate was in an old suitcase in the closet. Mr. Mason dug it out.

Matthew and Fannie were married in Danville, Virginia, on December 8, 1931. When I pointed out that they would have been twenty and nineteen, not eighteen and seventeen, Mr. Mason said, "I guess I kind of got mixed up about that." According to the marriage certificate, Matthew had claimed to be twenty-two, and Fannie twenty-one. Was that so you wouldn't need permission? "Maybe it was. I don't remember." Why'd you go way up to Danville instead of getting married here in town? "I don't know. We just did."

It seemed strange that a man who could remember his wage in the tobacco factory when he was twelve, could remember what he'd paid a midwife to deliver his babies, and could remember the names and faces of fraternity boys going back half a century, didn't remember when he'd gotten married, where, or why he and his bride had driven fifty miles to Danville.

It occurred to me later, after I learned that the oldest boy in Mr. Mason's family was born to Fannie when she was seventeen, that the problem was not one of forgetting. If Matthew and Fannie had gotten married when he was eighteen and she was seventeen, then there was no child born out of wedlock and no stigma to contend with. Perhaps Mr. Mason had told the story of young marriage so many times that he came to believe it himself. The revised story only worked, however, with an audience of outsiders: the fraternity boys. Everyone else, everyone in the black community, knew the truth, which was not hidden at all.

Matthew's job at Harry's allowed a bit of toting—taking home some of the boss's surplus and defining it as part of the wage. In the early 1930s, this was a significant benefit. Were those hard times? "Oh yeah, it was hard times all right," Mr. Mason said. "A whole lot of people was hungry in Chapel Hill. Some black folks used to go begging up and down Franklin Street. But we never did go hungry. We brought leftover food home from Harry's and had some to give our neighbors. A lot of folks was going hungry, but we did all right." According to one survey,

between October 1932 and March 1933, 11 percent of the white population in Chapel Hill was receiving public aid. The figure for the black population was 48 percent.

The other benefit of working at Harry's was that it allowed Matthew to meet people. His congeniality and good service led to offers of jobs doing yard and domestic work. These contacts also helped bring in the laundry that Sallie and Fannie did at home.

Among the students who frequented Harry's were members of the Phi Delta Theta fraternity. In the spring of 1934 the fraternity was looking for someone to clean, serve food, and tend the furnace. Matthew Mason, nearly twenty-three years old, with a wife and three children, saw a chance to do better for himself and his family, and so he took the job, which was, until 1971, called "houseboy." The student who hired him was called the house manager.

Matthew Mason thus joined a long tradition of black men working as menials at the white university. The tradition extended back to November Caldwell, slave to Joseph Caldwell, who was president of UNC-Chapel Hill from from 1799 to 1812. These men cleaned, stoked furnaces, cut grass, gardened, shined shoes, ran errands for students and faculty, and rang bells to mark class hours.

Some of the men had special talents that their employers found endearing. George Horton composed love poems for tongue-tied students. Benny Boothe, nicknamed "Missing Link," charged students five cents to split boards on his skull. Henry Smith, bell ringer in South Building, was revered for his punctuality. At commencement in 1914 he was given an honorary L.L.D.D. degree—"Learned Loyal Ding Donger." The newspaper reported that the degree was bestowed by lowering a rope, with a bell attached, over Henry's head.

There is no doubt that these employer-employee relationships entailed genuine affection. It was a sad day in February 1927 when George McCauley, a janitor in the pharmacy school, died. His death was reported in the *Chapel Hill Weekly* under the headline "Uncle George, Negro Janitor is Beloved by Hundreds of Pharmacy Students." The obituary lauds McCauley's ability to "deliver a beautiful extemporaneous prayer" and says that he "endeared himself to 700 pharmacy students who remember him as a quiet, modest, obliging servant." Grover Beard,

professor of pharmacy, is quoted as saying that McCauley was "a man so white all through that I forget the thin covering of another color."

Jobs at the fraternities and sororities were considered plums, though not because of the pay. Matthew Mason recalled that when he started at the fraternity he was making twelve dollars a week, barely more than he was making at Harry's. So why did you take the job? "Harry was a nice man, but it was more 'back home' at the fraternity house, you know what I mean?" You mean it was less hectic and you had a regular set of chores to do? "Yeah, that's it. That's how it was." There was also the opportunity to tote home more food. And the boys gave tips for extra work, gave castoff shoes and clothes, and paid Fannie to wash and press their shirts.

Back then the fraternity house had a staff of four, not counting the housemother. Matthew Mason had a helper and so did the cook. Matthew arrived early to stoke the furnace and clean the common areas; then he began setting up to serve breakfast. After the breakfast tables were cleared and the boys off to class, he made beds and cleaned bathrooms. Then it was time to set up for lunch. When lunch was over, Matthew went home for a few hours before returning to serve supper and clean again afterward. It was a long day but a predictable one. The job also had the virtue of allowing him to get to know the boys he worked for.

Matthew Mason's warmth and zeal made him a hit at the fraternity. His energy and freshness stood in contrast to the condition of the aging black man he replaced. As one of the oldest of the fraternity members later recalled, "I barely remember Matthew Mason's predecessor. Please understand that that was a very long time ago. The last I had heard, the previous houseboy, the man he replaced—Roby, I believe his name was—had become an alcoholic." When he took over the job, Matthew Mason, it was said, was not known to drink at all, at least not while working. His nickname, in these early years, was "Sunshine."

Home life was good. In the fall of 1935, with his mother-in-law's help, Matthew bought a small three-bedroom house on Rosemary Street, on the south edge of the black neighborhood known as Potter's Field (later called Northside). The houses to the west were owned by black families; to the east, just up the hill, lived whites. Proximity to the white side of town added prestige to the location.

Matthew Mason took pride in making his twenty-five-dollar-a-month mortgage payment. While Fannie and her mother did most of the household chores and childcare, in addition to tending the garden and doing laundry for the fraternity boys, Matthew tried to improve the house. In the afternoons between lunch and supper, he hammered and sawed and painted. Owning a house and a piece of earth mattered a great deal. By virtue of his steady job, his ability to offer food to his hungry neighbors, his good reputation and home ownership, Matthew Mason and his family were among the most respected black folks in Chapel Hill. He had, by the standards of the time, come a long way from life on the old Tom Mason place.

a bubble off center

S oon after his return to Chapel Hill in 1978, Atwater found
the "fish" he was supposed to catch and keep. The fish, the
Voice had told him, would be in the form of a white woman
who needed help. Atwater found her one night after she'd been sexually
used and then abandoned by two men. "She was wandering the streets,"
he said. "She'd been doing drugs and prostituting. I knew she was the
one the Voice told me about. So I took her in, took her away from all
that." What Atwater did was to take her home to his parents' tiny
house, where he expected his mother to do most of the caretaking.
Atwater's mother said she was not about to support a twenty-seven-
year-old white woman dragged in off the street, and so she sent them
packing after a couple days. But then the woman's parents, hoping that
their daughter would be better off living with Atwater than on the
streets, agreed to subsidize an apartment for the two of them.

In January of 1979 Atwater applied for a job as a mason with the
town of Chapel Hill. He was hired in March, at $4.06 an hour, to
help install sidewalks, curbs, and gutters. For a time he did well. By
September he had passed the probationary period, and his boss recommended him for permanent employment and a raise to $4.48 an hour.
But by February of 1980 he began to receive warnings about missed
work. A long string of such warnings, and several for low productivity,
preceded his firing at the end of October. Atwater filed a grievance to
dispute the firing, claiming he'd been a victim of discrimination. A
town appeals board rejected the grievance.

Atwater's domestic situation, as he described it, was more platonic than romantic. "I wasn't interested in sex. That's not why we were living together. It was mostly so I could help her regain self-esteem and get a steady job." In the latter regard, Atwater was an unlikely coach. Although he drank less now than in his worst days, he hadn't stopped, nor had the violence. He moved out and back in several times, claiming that he was driven to do this by the racism of the woman's parents. "They hated this," Atwater said, tapping the dark skin on the back of his hand, "and I just couldn't take it. I had to get away from that."

He didn't go far. Atwater stayed in town, going from one low-wage job to another: janitor at a mall; janitor at an apartment building; stuffer of ad inserts into newspapers; breakfast cook for a food service company on campus. In addition to his drinking interfering with work (Atwater was remanded to detox in 1982 after missing a court date for a DWI charge), Atwater's health was also failing. He was on his way to being, as one doctor later put it, a "pulmonary cripple." There were days when Atwater didn't make it to work because he felt too short of breath to risk leaving the apartment.

Even as his domestic situation deteriorated, it was complicated by an unexpected pregnancy. Atwater said that this created more tension between the woman, her parents, and himself. "They didn't want her to have no child by me. They didn't even think she could have a child; they thought she was sterile. When she got pregnant, they wanted her to have an abortion. But she wouldn't do that. She was too tender-hearted. She wouldn't even kill bugs in the house." The child was born in November 1985, not long before the relationship broke up for good.

The conflict between Atwater, the woman, and her parents now centered on the child. Given Atwater's history of alcoholism, violence, and unstable employment, it wasn't hard for the woman and her parents to have Atwater legally declared an unfit parent, denying him custody and visitation rights. "I could have fought it," he said. "I had a legal right to see my son. I even made sure that he got a piece of my Social Security check when I went on disability. But I didn't have any money to fight it. Her parents had lots of money, and they were white. I couldn't beat that." The boy ended up in the custody of his

grandparents, after the mother proved unable to support herself and provide adequate parental care.

Atwater was aggrieved by all this. He did not want to see the woman he had befriended, perhaps less selflessly than he made out, fall back into street life. And he wanted to have a better relationship with his youngest son than he had had with his older sons. "I was angry and depressed about everything at that time," Atwater said. "*Everything* was fucked up. I was so angry at her [his partner's] mother for taking my boy that I could have killed her. That's all I thought about some days. I'd get drunk and pass out and wake up the next day worried that I *had* killed her and didn't remember it. Other days I just wanted to kill myself. That's how sick I was."

Atwater was also troubled by the death of his father.

The Voice had told Atwater that he should go home to help his father, and indeed his father needed help. Himself a lifelong drinker, now in his seventies, Atwater's father was suffering from senile dementia. On at least two occasions after his return to Chapel Hill, Atwater had gotten his father out of psychiatric wards to which he'd been sent for evaluation after becoming disoriented and violent. After the second incident, Atwater's mother moved out and Atwater moved in to take care of his father. "That's when we became buddies," Atwater said. "We talked and got to know each other better during those months than during all the time before that. It was also a chance for me to make up for all the shit I put him through."

On a Sunday morning in late September 1985, Atwater and his father planned to go out for a taste of tax-free liquor. That morning Atwater found his father, fully dressed, lying across his bed, barely conscious. "At first I thought it was a seizure, but when I saw his face I knew it was something worse. His eyes were open but he couldn't talk. All he could do was squeeze my hand a little." Before the rescue squad got Atwater's father to the hospital, he was dead from a heart attack. Atwater was too distraught to go to the hospital, preferring to go drink by himself. "At the funeral," he said, "I couldn't stand by the grave when they put dirt on him. I was too tore up inside to watch that. We had just become friends and now he was gone."

A year after his father's death, Atwater lost the last job he ever held. He was working as a breakfast cook in a dining hall on campus. Atwater's transportation at the time was an unreliable moped.

"I was running late and that damn scooter wouldn't start," Atwater said. "Then on the way to campus I had to pee so bad I couldn't hold it. When I got there I opened the oven door and tried to use the heat to dry my pants. The supervisor came in and saw me like that—in my shorts, holding my pants up to the cookie oven—and that was it. He fired me on the spot." After that, Atwater applied for and received disability payments because of his emphysema. Now he was officially defined as unable to work. His income, including a small disability payment from the Veterans' Administration, was about six hundred dollars a month.

About this same time, Atwater moved into the public housing apartment of Lula Mae Perry, a friend of Atwater's uncle. Miss Perry, who was about Atwater's mother's age, was paraplegic and in need of live-in help with cooking and cleaning. Atwater was out of work, on disability, and unable to do much else. It seemed a convenient arrangement for both of them. "I did for her all those things she couldn't do for herself anymore," Atwater said. "I was like a God-sent son to her, and she was just like a mom to me."

Atwater was, in fact, a dubious caretaker. Miss Perry also had daily help from a series of home health aides, all of whom reported to Orange County Social Services that they felt uneasy in the apartment because of the naked bodies, bottles, and drug paraphernalia they saw there. Atwater admitted that Miss Perry disapproved of his guests and partying. Nonetheless, the arrangement lasted for several years, until Miss Perry was hospitalized for surgery and then placed by her family in a nursing home.

When Atwater heard that Miss Perry was not coming back, he expected to be evicted. He had never properly applied for public housing; he had simply moved in. And even if he was eligible, was he entitled, as a single person, to a scarce two-bedroom apartment? There was also the matter of his behavior, which had provoked complaints from other residents. Atwater wanted desperately to stay in the apartment, because he knew it was his cheapest option in Chapel Hill, and because it was easily accessible to his stream of walk-in guests.

Atwater considered suicide. One evening he topped off a couple lines of coke with half a quart of whiskey, turned on the oven, and knelt down with his head on the open door. "That didn't last but a few minutes," Atwater said. "I had forgotten to blow out the pilot light, so the oven came on and all I was doing was burning my hair." He decided to finish the bottle and take a cab to the hospital emergency room, where he was able to say, before passing out, that he had tried to kill himself. "They put me in South Wing, the nuthouse, for a few weeks after that. I was depressed all right, but I didn't really want to kill myself. I just needed time to get my head together and think about the apartment thing."

In the hospital, Atwater built his case. He would claim that his eligibility for public housing was established by the facts that he had been put on the lease and had paid part of the rent. Atwater also persuaded a doctor to testify that, because of his emphysema, he would soon need live-in help himself, and was thus entitled to a second bedroom. For once, Atwater won. "There was an uproar when we let him stay in the apartment," said Harold Wolfe, director of public housing. "We were aware of the allegations about him. We knew he had issues with drugs and alcohol, and we told him he was going to have to knock it off. In view of everything, I felt he deserved a chance."

For a while Atwater was a model resident. "I knew I had to straighten up, 'cause the Wolfeman was on my trail," he said, referring to the public housing director. Atwater cooled the partying and insisted that his guests be quiet as they came and went. He even picked up litter in the parking lot and around the grounds. But the peace and good behavior did not last long.

In 1993, shortly after he had managed to hold on to the apartment, Atwater was diagnosed with cancer. The doctors advised surgery to remove the marble-sized lump on his vocal chords. But surgery meant the loss of normal speech.

"It was the morning of the day they were gonna cut me," Atwater told me, "and I said, 'Doc, isn't there something else you can do?' He said they could try radiation, but that it probably wouldn't work and I'd need surgery later anyway. I told 'em to try the radiation first, 'cause I didn't want to lose my voice." The doctors were surprised, Atwater said, when, after six weeks of radiation, the tumor was gone and no

cancer cells could be found in Atwater's body. "I spit that damn cancer out," was Atwater's summation.

Still, the doctors were not optimistic. "The doc told me that even though he couldn't find any more cancer in me, I had only two years to live," Atwater said. "That's when I decided that in the time I had left, I was gonna squeeze in as much as I could of whatever I wanted more of, and *pussy* was at the top of my list." Atwater said he had about five thousand dollars saved at that time, and he planned to spend it on partying, which meant, in large part, spending it on women, liquor, and drugs. "I did it, too. I went through all that damn money. Did everything I wanted to—women, smoke. Man, if that apartment could talk, I'd a had to burn it down."

Atwater had already outlived his two-year death sentence when I found myself in his apartment listening to his stories. It occurred to me that he might be nothing but a charming bullshitter, and not worth writing about solely because of that talent. So before proposing the biography, I checked a few public records (birth, death, and marriage certificates, arrest records, and job history as reported in old city directories) and found, to my surprise, a fair correspondence to Atwater's accounts. If he wasn't lying about the outlines of his life, I thought, then perhaps the details would bear looking into as well. What I didn't appreciate at the time was Atwater's ability to sculpt the truth, or why he needed to do it in the ways he did.

Visiting Atwater's apartment gave me another basis from which to judge his stories. I never knew who or what I'd find there when I came by. One day in late March 1996, I came by at 1:00 P.M., the usual time for our interview. Atwater's meals-on-wheels tinfoil lunchbox, which was delivered at noon, was on the stoop outside his door, untouched. I knocked hard several times and got no answer. Though it seemed unlikely, I thought maybe Atwater was out, so I ran errands and came back at 2:30. This time a woman's voice answered my knock.

"Who is it?"

"Mike Schwalbe," I said. I heard the deadbolt click, then the door opened about six inches and stopped. A young black woman with matted hair looked at me for a second, then pulled the door open and said

Atwater with beret

"come in" as she walked away. She wore jeans, a wrinkled white t-shirt, and no shoes.

I stepped inside and saw two other young women sitting on the sofa. One, razor thin and tall, with dark skin and braided hair, got up and went to the kitchen. "He'll be out in a minute," she said. The other woman, also dark but shorter and plump by comparison to the first, stayed on the sofa, lying down now and pulling a blanket up to her chin. She stared at a cartoon show on the muted TV. Since conversation did not seem in the offing, I stood by the door and watched along with her.

The first woman had disappeared into the back bedroom. The other two said nothing to me or to each other. It dawned on me that they'd all been in the apartment earlier when I'd knocked on the door.

I heard Atwater's cough before I saw him. He came out of the bedroom in his pajamas and bathrobe. He had forgotten, or hadn't bothered, to put in his dentures. He looked rougher than I'd ever seen him

as he took short stiff steps to get across the living room. He barely got out "Hello, Mike" before starting another coughing fit, one that doubled him over. When he stopped coughing he took a couple more steps, then reached out to the open door and held onto it for support.

"Mike, I'm sorry. I'm awfully tired. It seems like I can't get enough sleep," he said, with a lispy rasp. No wonder you can't sleep, I thought, thinking of his company.

"You don't look so good," I said.

"Yeah, I was up all night. Just got to sleep a little while ago. I was watching TV and I got to thinking about old times and my mind got all tangled up on that shit and I couldn't sleep."

"If you're not up for talking today, let's make sure we do something special for your birthday next week. How about lunch? We can probably find pork chops and macaroni and cheese if we look hard enough. At Dip's, maybe."

"That would be nice. I'd like that. Pork chops and macaroni and cheese—that's my favorite. Right now I'd better take my meds so I'll be around next week." He stepped back to the coffee table and bent down to open a day-by-day pillbox. He plucked three pills from one compartment. "Sweetheart, would you bring me some water?" he said to the tall woman in the kitchen. She brought him a glass and he took each pill separately. Three tilts of the head and three swallows.

"You know, Mike, I hate to miss our meetings," he said, setting the glass down on the coffee table. "Talking to you makes me feel better than talking to my psychiatrist." He laughed at this and then turned to recross the living room to get to his ancient recliner. He flopped down and took as deep a breath as he could. I followed and stood in front of him.

"Let me get a few puffs here, Mike," he said, pulling an inhaler out of his pocket and giving it three snappy shakes. He inhaled and held the mist for a few seconds, then repeated the procedure twice. His face eased after the third puff.

"That's better," he finally said. "Whew! Without these inhalers, I'd be dead." Atwater was not yet on oxygen.

"This is obviously not a good day to talk," I said. "You're tired and you've got company, so let's just figure on next week. I'll come by at noon instead of one. That'll give us some extra time for lunch."

"Yeah, Mike, that'll be nice. I'd like to do that. Call me ahead of time to remind me and I'll be ready." I said good-bye and left, wondering what would transpire after the door closed behind me. The next week, on Atwater's sixty-third birthday, I tried to call to remind him about lunch, but his phone had been disconnected. He was at the apartment when I got there, though my knock woke him and he wasn't feeling up to going out. That day we had the place to ourselves.

Atwater bolstered his credibility by giving me names of people to talk to about him—relatives, friends, bosses, doctors, social workers. He also eagerly signed releases and forms so that I could get access to his employment, medical, military, and social service records. If his stories weren't true, I thought, would he be so eager to have me check them out? He knew that it mattered to me that his stories were not a crock, and it seemed that he was trying hard, in good faith, to prove they were not.

The first anomaly cropped up in Atwater's story of the events that led up to his eviction from public housing. In March 1996, Atwater told me that he had borrowed money from street lenders to buy drugs and that because he had to pay them back first ("they'll kill your ass if you don't"), he had been late in paying his rent. He said that the housing people had begun pestering him about the late rent, because "they're looking for any excuse to put me out." What he said about the drugs, the street loan, and the late-rent notice was all true. He was also right, most likely, about the housing authorities being glad to have an excuse to get rid of him.

Two months later Atwater was still telling me that the housing people were out to get rid of him because of a late rent payment. "They're on my case about that," he said. "Man, that's bullshit, Mike. They know that poor-ass people sometimes get behind on rent, and they don't put 'em out." In May, Atwater showed me a letter from the housing authority saying that they were going to court to get an eviction order. According to the letter, Atwater had not paid his rent for the last three months.

"This says you haven't paid your rent for three months," I pointed out.

"That's bullshit. I paid them for that first month."

"Okay, so you're *two* months behind."

"That's bullshit, too," he said. "They have a funny way of figuring when the month begins and ends. It's not three months yet. It's barely two, and that makes it only one, 'cause I back-paid that first one." I almost laughed.

"So why haven't you paid your rent? You've got money."

"I guess I'm just not a good budget man."

"From this," I said, glancing down at the letter, "it looks like they intend to put you out."

"Naw, they have to take you to court three times before they can put you out. This is just like a court warning. This is the first step if you get behind."

Atwater later admitted that he had failed to pay his rent because he spent most of his money on crack. "It's easy to go through five hundred dollars in a weekend, if you put your mind to it," he once told me. He was right about not being a good budget man, but he was wrong about eviction. In a hearing that took less than five minutes, a judge ordered him out. Yet for years afterward Atwater told of being unfairly evicted from public housing for being "a little behind on one month's rent." It was as if he could make this claim true by repeating it often enough.

When I talked to people who figured in Atwater's stories, they invariably contradicted him in some significant way. Atwater urged me to talk to Rebecca Clark, a former town council member and leader in the black community, who had been on the board that heard his appeal after being fired. Atwater claimed that he had been fired because his racist bosses resented his assertiveness and his involvement with a white woman—and thus conspired to make him look like a bad worker. "Clark, she supported me," Atwater said. "She knew what was really going on. If she voted against me, it was only because she had to get along with the whites on the board."

Fifteen years later, Clark remembered the case. "He was a very angry man," she told me. "He wanted to do the work his own way, to be the judge, but he didn't complete jobs properly and didn't come to work on time. He also refused to do some work he should have." In Chapel Hill's tight-knit black community, she had known Atwater all his life. "He's always been a schemer. He's that kind of person." When I mentioned

that Atwater lived in public housing, she said, "And he's going to get thrown out, too, if he doesn't get off drugs." She was indeed a knowledgeable reference, though hardly the kind Atwater led me to expect.

Atwater told of the time he fought the Orange County Department of Social Services ("I took them all the way to the damn state level!") when, as he saw it, they unfairly stopped providing home health services for Miss Perry. Atwater said I should talk to Kim Lassiter, a social worker whom Atwater believed supported his complaint. Lassiter, an adult services social worker with Orange County, told me that services had not been withdrawn. The problem, rather, was that the department could no longer find aides willing to go into the apartment. "Aides would go in and find broken glass on the floor, drug paraphernalia lying around, people sleeping naked on the couch, eight or nine guys drinking. Eventually, the health agency said they wouldn't send their aides in there anymore," Lassiter said.

Lassiter knew about Atwater. She had once intervened with Duke Power to get Atwater's electricity turned back on when he didn't pay his bill. On another occasion she took him to apply for food stamps and Medicaid, neither of which he qualified for at the time. Her exasperation was plain when she said, "Mr. Atwater is not typical of the people we work with. His income is sufficient to meet his needs. In his case, the problem is self-neglect." She also told me that at the hearing convened because of Atwater's complaint, he wore a three-piece suit and carried a briefcase. "He seemed to think he was Perry Mason." The complaint was dismissed after being reviewed at several levels. "I've found Mr. Atwater to be very interesting," Lassiter summed up, "but I'm afraid he's not a very moral person."

In his stories, Atwater's ex-wife was the villain whose misdeeds got his life untracked. This was, of course, a matter about which I expected perceptions to vary greatly. The great variation, however, was between Atwater and everyone else.

Atwater had suggested I talk to Howard Baldwin, a man with whom he had hung out years before. "You're writing about Shine Atwater?" Baldwin said, surprised, when I found him. "Shine was something else. He was wild! He's been through it all. If he don't live another day, he's lived his life." Atwater's wildness was not in doubt. When I asked

about Atwater's marriage, which he had described as a huge mistake, Baldwin laughed. "Dot was a good person," he said. "If it was a mistake, it was a mistake on *her* part. Shine seemed to think she was going to take care of him the way his parents did, and that just wasn't going to happen."

The consensus, even among those who liked Atwater, was that he had few legitimate grievances. If his ex-wife had once sought attention outside the marriage, no one who knew Atwater blamed her for it. "Dot worked two and three jobs to support her children," one of Atwater's old friends told me, "and Popcorn would come home drunk and he would beat her and he couldn't hold a job, so he wasn't supporting the family. Under those conditions no love feelings are going to last. Anything Dot did, she did because she had to to survive and take care of her children." The worst anyone would say was that she had been "out in the world" for a while when she was much younger, "like most of us."

Another glaring discrepancy arose when I obtained Atwater's military records. Atwater had told me several times about being court-martialed for hitting an acting sergeant with a shovel, in retaliation for a racist slur. The record told of failure to obey an order to get a shovel and report with it to the orderly room. Atwater had been charged before with failure to obey orders, but there was no mention anywhere of assault. When I reviewed the record with Atwater, he was quiet, almost sullen. "That's bullshit. That's all twisted up," he finally said. When I asked how there could be such a difference between his account and the record, he said, "I was drunk a lot in those days, and it was hard to keep things straight. It must have happened some other time." A few months later, Atwater was back to telling the same old story, as if we had never had a conversation with the court record between us.

In seeking information about Atwater's time at Occoquan, I spoke with Chris Walsh, a probation supervisor with the city of Washington, D.C. Although the Rehabilitation Center for Alcoholics had closed in the 1970s when the facility became part of the Lorton Reformatory Complex, Walsh was familiar with the old RCA and had worked with alcoholics for years.

When I mentioned the mix of fact and fiction in Atwater's stories, Walsh said, "I can tell you from dealing with many, many probationers that the way they portray their lives is often just way off. If a guy dropped out of tenth grade, a few years later he had graduated from high school. If he worked at McDonald's for six months, according to him, it turned out to be six weeks, according to McDonald's. That's typical. I don't think these are conscious lies; it's just their perception of life. Six weeks at McDonald's probably felt like six months. This was especially true with the old alcoholics. Sometimes you couldn't get anything out of them that made any sense at all. They wouldn't know how many kids they had, or they didn't know their parents' names, or they weren't sure where they lived. It could be very strange." If this was how badly memory could be damaged by alcohol and life on the street, then Atwater was doing well, I thought, to be as accurate as he was.

Atwater also lacked middle-class memory aids: ties to schools and employers that can be used to retrospectively track one's life year by year. After the army, Atwater was never in school again. He did not make "career moves" after five years with one firm and six years with another. He never owned a home. And so Atwater struggled to piece together his past as we tried to determine where he had been, what he'd been doing, and when. By using national events ("They were looting all around me in D.C. after King was killed"—April 1968) and the records I dug up, we eventually created a time line with most of the blanks filled-in.

I also attributed some of Atwater's departures from the record to a habit of fictionalizing formed during his down-and-out days. One way that street people maintain a sense of dignity is by telling outlandish stories about past exploits and improbable futures. On the street, such stories are seldom challenged; people allow each other to fashion respectable selves using the main resource they possess: talk.[1] Perhaps Atwater, in telling his stories, was merely doing what he had routinely done, as a matter of psychological necessity, for a third of his life.

1. David Snow and Leon Anderson describe this kind of cooperative self-fabrication in "Identity Work Among the Homeless: The Verbal Construction and Avowal of Personal Identities" (*American Journal of Sociology*, 1987, vol. 92, pp. 1336–71).

Even when my interviews yielded a stream of contradictory accounts, Atwater still urged me to talk to others about him. I took this as a sign that his professed interest in the truth was genuine. But when I would try to resolve the discrepancies, Atwater impugned his own witnesses: "he's a little slack in the reasoning department," "she's always been a bubble off," "that lying-ass fool never could get anything straight," and "that's just what she had to say because of her job." No one else, it seemed, was able or willing to tell the truth. I began to joke about it. When I would tell Atwater that I had talked to an old crony of his who told a different story, I would preempt Atwater's response and say, "Let me guess. He's a 'bubble off center,' right?" At which Atwater would laugh and say, "Man, that dude is *two* bubbles off!"

Beyond these token protests, Atwater did not say much to defend himself. At first I thought this was because he expected me to believe him, regardless of what others said. But surely he could see that I was doing no such thing, that I was trying to find out, by checking records and talking to others, what had actually happened in his life. He knew that I was not simply taking him at his word. What I finally realized, as we began to joke about the divergent stories, was that Atwater wanted me to talk to others not because he expected them to affirm what he told me; what mattered to Atwater was that people knew he was the subject of a book.

As Atwater's special audience, I was his accomplice. Atwater was astute at discerning what people wanted to hear, and the stories he told about himself were shaped to meet my expectations, as he perceived them. Why would a white professor listen to the stories of an old, ne'er-do-well black man? What did I want? A bigger story, of course. A story of a black man beaten down by racism—and not just any black man, but one whose intellect and promise made the injustice all the worse.

My political sympathies were obvious, and Atwater could see that I was especially interested in his stories of confronting racism. Asking to write his biography also affirmed a notion in Atwater's mind that I saw him as a kind of hard-luck hero: a good man, a bit of a rogue, who'd fought, suffered, and lost, but nonetheless survived with spirit intact, and who had acquired valuable wisdom for having gone through it all. He was partly right about what I wanted him to be, and so he obliged.

Yet there was still the odd matter of Atwater dissembling about events that I had witnessed myself. The eviction was one example; others arose later. At first I was annoyed by this behavior and would remind him of what had actually happened ("As I recall, it wasn't *one* late payment; you hadn't paid your rent for *three months* by the time they kicked you out"). Atwater would accept the correction, rescind the fable, and then, weeks or months later, repeat the version he preferred. It was his tenacity in this regard that led me to see what Atwater was up to.

The version of himself that Atwater created in his stories was not simply the version he could comfortably share with me. Most of the stories I heard were parts of his standard repertoire; everyone who knew Atwater for long had heard them. These were, then, the stories that Atwater could accept about himself.

I still wanted to know how the stories departed from fact, for without *that* knowledge, part of the meaning of the stories was lost. But I also saw that Atwater's stories—in their form, content, and omissions— did reveal who he was. The task of understanding Atwater thus became less a matter of uncovering facts than a matter of seeing how he wove a select set of facts, twisted though they might be, into stories about his life. After months of worrying about discrepancies, I realized that most of what I needed to see was in front of my nose.

Atwater once told me, "I've been *two* legends in my time: Shine and Popcorn," revealing his concern for dramatic self-characterization. Shine, the slick badass, was dead. "Shine died a long time ago," Atwater told me early on. "I'm Popcorn now, or just PC. I'm more laid back, like an old man should be. When I was Shine, I was wide open and out for myself. Now I'm like a father figure to young people who are going through what I went through. They know they can talk to me and I'll listen and not judge them, 'cause I been on the street. I give them advice they can trust, 'cause I know what they're dealing with, with drugs and all. They come through my apartment and when they leave they say, 'No one can take advantage of me, 'cause I been to the School of the PC.' It gives me satisfaction to see them get confidence and get their lives under control." This was Popcorn: the compassionate, streetwise sage who had risen from the ashes of Shine.

But how could it be that the suave, aggressive Shine and the wise, tender Popcorn had ended up broke, disabled, and largely bereft of family and friends? Many of Atwater's stories served to account for this incongruity. His mother let him get hooked on cigarettes. She hadn't let his hapless father properly discipline him. Whites thwarted his desire to use school as a means to upward mobility. His ex-wife had messed up his mind, ruined his army career, and turned him into a drunk. Whites locked him into lousy jobs. When he lost jobs, it was for exposing corrupt bosses, who then fired him. His ex-wife had turned his sons against him. And if he was broke and about to be evicted, that was because his doctors had told him he had only two years to live, and so he had tried to party his way out of despair.

Here, then, was the pattern, or the core of it, in Atwater's self-representation—no part of which was implausible on the face. In his stories he was a victim of injustice, a man who tried to do the right thing and got slapped down. His stories were told to sustain these images. Facts were just flexible raw materials. Atwater used them to turn himself into the kind of man he wanted to be, and the kind of man he wanted others to see him as being.

Atwater's ideas of what it meant to be a man were not idiosyncratic. They were, in fact, close to a cultural ideal. He wanted to be seen as honest, generous, hardworking, chivalrous, and wise. He was also invested, like many men in Western culture, in brash toughness and sexuality as signs of masculinity—hence the macho Shine and the lusty Popcorn. If Atwater could think of himself in these terms, and get periodic affirmation from others, he could live with himself.

In one of our earliest conversations, Atwater told me this story. "One time we were on a job, and this white supervisor came up behind and grabbed me. He had a nephew out there, a teenager. The kid was not a concrete finisher; he didn't even work on the job. He came around, this kid, and started to tell me what to do. And I said, 'Look son, I wish you'd step aside 'cause I got some steel I got to put down here. You don't know what you're talking about. I'm not going nowhere and do nothing else right now.' He'd told me to go somewhere and change something. This is the supervisor's nephew.

"I told him, 'I'm not going *anywhere* right now, 'cause I'm trying to get these steel rods in here. And if I go anywhere, I can't get 'em in here.

You tell whoever sent you that I'll be there in a few minutes.' Oh, he started raising hell! Then his uncle came over and grabbed me from behind. I liked to beat that man to death with one of those steel rods before my daddy could get to me! That supervisor wore a neck brace for two months. I didn't get fired, either, 'cause I told 'em, when somebody came up behind me like that—I'd been in the service and it was kind of a reflex—I told 'em I just couldn't help it. I started wailing on him, I did. I didn't know he was coming, see?

"But after I turned around and hit him the first time, I knew who he was. Then I hit him four more times. My daddy told me I was wrong to do that. He said that if I'd hit him one time, that would have been enough. They couldn't fire me for it, though, because the superintendent wouldn't allow it. The supervisor shouldn't have had his nephew telling me nothing, and he shouldn't have grabbed me. That was the kind of shit we had to go through [with white people].

"My daddy would scratch his head. He used to tell me, 'Don't ever let the white man get ahead of you mentally. If you think you gotta scratch your head, scratch it. Appease him. Satisfy him. Because he's in a position where he can make it so hard on you that you can't live or can't feed your children. You got to do what the man say do, because if you don't, he can take your job.' That's what my father told me. But I couldn't handle that shit. When I got grown, I said the hell with it. My daddy would scratch his head. But I wouldn't."

This is a story from the Shine era. Atwater portrays himself, in contrast to his father, as unwilling to bow down to the white man. Atwater's hero is unfailingly polite but takes no shit from anyone. It is a story much like that of hitting the sergeant with a shovel. It is also nearly identical in form to several others Atwater told me. Is it true? I was never able to verify it (Atwater could not remember names in this case). But I suspect that as with the army story, this one, if it grew from a grain of truth, was greatly embellished. To note the obvious: it is improbable that a black man who beat a white boss with a steel rod, in the late 1950s in the South, would be forgiven for his lapse of self-control and, with no further consequence, go back to work the next day.

It is nonetheless possible to see other truths in this story and the others like it, truths about racism, manhood, dignity, and Atwater himself. He lived in a time and place where it was not unusual for a

white boy, related to the boss, to rob a black man of his dignity by telling him what to do. And Atwater, like any proud man, would have *liked* to strike back. A reckless few probably did, though most did not—for exactly the reasons cited by Atwater's father. To be unable to respond as pride and justice demand is wounding. It is hardly surprising, then, that many men in Atwater's shoes, lacking other resources to heal these wounds, would numb the pain with alcohol and later try to rewrite their lives.

In his storytelling Atwater showed himself to be an ordinary man. We all selectively remember and forget, weaving what we are willing to remember into stories that make sense of what we have become and where we have arrived. Like Atwater, we use stories to create the versions of ourselves we can live with and can bear to have seen by others. As much as the stories themselves, *how* we do this reveals who we are. Atwater's stories were of a man who wanted to be a good man. They were stories told by a man who knew what a good man should be and how the world could unfairly trip him up.

Atwater was ordinary too in using stories to reconcile his mistakes and failures with the version of himself he needed to believe in and have others believe in. Here again the boat is full; we all narrate our lives, or at least parts of them, to make bad choices and bad results seem like fate. If men have an especially strong need to do this, it is perhaps because of the difficulty, in a viciously unequal world, of being what we are told we should be—in control, admired for our vast doings, potent. As a black man, the struggle for Atwater was all the harder. Circumstances and his own weaknesses conspired to wither him. Stories pumped him back up.

the making of dr. reet

At a public university of about three thousand students, freshmen (all of whom were, literally, fresh*men*) attended chapel twice a week. Upon graduation each received a Bible from the governor. Room and board cost $30 a month. Tuition was $370 a year. In the fraternities, young southern gentlemen wore jackets and ties to dinner. Housemothers and preceptors kept order and exerted what was optimistically called a "positive influence." Matthew Mason, houseboy, addressed his young employers as *Mister*.

Originally hired to stoke the furnace, clean, and serve meals, Matthew "Sunshine" Mason gradually expanded his job. He washed cars, shined shoes, ran errands, and packed suitcases. In the morning after the boys left for class, he folded their hastily doffed pajamas. He took out the garbage, mowed the lawn, and did minor repairs around the fraternity house. When they found out he could read, they began to leave notes on their doors: "Matthew: get me up for my 8:00 class." Sometimes a note added, "Use water if necessary."

The wake-up requests created an opening for the relationship between Matthew and the fraternity boys to evolve. Because the boys did not always spring up gratefully when he rapped on their doors in the morning, Matthew would sometimes have to pull off covers, tickle feet, or pull a leg. The boys grumbled, but they enjoyed the play and were later grateful for Matthew's persistence.

Matthew was inventive too. He recalled a phrase his father had used: "Off the bed and on the floor. It's time to get to work, boy." But that had

to be adapted. College wasn't really *work* as Matthew Mason knew it. Nor in the mid-1930s could he have barked "boy" to his white employers. So he improvised: "Off the bed and on the floor. It's time to go back now." Sometimes he added a note about the weather, letting the boys know if it was going to be cool—"sweater weather"—or hot—"shirtsleeve weather."

The ease and familiarity that grew out of the wake-ups carried over into what became, by the end of the 1930s, a regular part of Matthew Mason's job: greeting guests and bartending at parties.

At house parties Matthew, in black slacks and white blazer, greeted the boys on the portico as they arrived with their dates. "Good evening, Brother Winston," he would say. There were about forty-five boys living in the house and another twenty-five living off campus, and Matthew knew them all. If he didn't know the name of a boy's date, he addressed her in a way that the boys found charming and sometimes profitable. If the boy was Brother Winston, his date became Mrs. Winston.

Inside, behind the makeshift bar, Matthew dispensed drinks and good cheer. He never failed to ask the boys and their dates how they were doing and how their families were doing. "He always gave the impression that he was interested in you and genuinely liked you," one of those boys said many years later. Here again Matthew was able to do more than clean and wait tables. He could be the generous, affable man he was—and receive in return far more appreciation than he would ever receive for his best janitorial work.

By 1940 Matthew knew over a hundred boys who had come through the fraternity and graduated. When they returned for a football game or a reunion, Matthew greeted them by name and made them feel glad to be back. "He created an atmosphere of warmth," as one boy, long since a grown man, remembered. Matthew also introduced the older members to the new ones, at first bridging a gap across a few years, and then later across generations. He did something else too: he told stories of the hijinks perpetrated by older members.

The new boys loved to hear these tales. They anticipated similar exploits of their own and imagined some day being the heroes of stories Matthew would tell new cohorts of Phi Delts. The alums loved the stories too. They enjoyed reliving, if sometimes with chagrin, their days of reckless youth.

Compared to what would come later, these were subdued times. The nation was still in the grip of depression, and parties were, by modern standards, few and modest. Young women were not yet allowed above the first floor of the fraternity house. And Matthew Mason, despite the comfort he had developed with his employers, was still cautious enough to avoid drinking when he tended bar. It was a context in which he, as a black man, needed to keep his wits about him.

Campus life was largely untroubled by the war that had already embroiled Europe, though there was anxious talk about whether the United States would get involved. When the Japanese attacked Pearl Harbor in December 1941, the question of U.S. involvement was settled. In the spring of 1942, thirty-year-old Matthew Mason, like millions of other American men, volunteered for service. Matthew and nine of his friends went to Fort Bragg for preenlistment physicals.

"They were all going, so I wanted to go too," Mr. Mason told me. "They had us in T-shirt and shorts and we had to walk a straight line, about a hundred feet. They had one man on each end watching us. I was all knock-kneed and slue-footed, and I got about halfway down the line and the man started hollering for me to go back. I pretended not to hear him and kept walking. I tried to straighten my legs out but I couldn't, and finally he hollered at me, 'Go back, dammit! Go back!' That was it. I didn't get in. I was the only one that didn't get in. My buddies kidded me, laughing and everything all the way home."

Several of those buddies did not make it home from the war. And while Matthew Mason's bad legs and flat feet saved him from that fate, part of him did not make it home from the failed exam. Were you disappointed about being turned down? "Yeah, like a fool I wanted to go, wanted to do like my buddies were doing, you understand? I got crazy when they turned me away." What did you do? "Got high for two or three days. High on liquor." When he sobered up, he went back to work as a houseboy.

Campus life changed as the war escalated. The number of civilian male students dwindled, though the number of men did not, as the university became home to a naval preflight training school. The preflight students were put up in the dorms, and those displaced were moved to the largely vacant frat houses. Matthew Mason's duties at the Phi Delt house now required only a few hours a day, and so he took a job delivering campus mail. He was, as he recalled, the only black man left

on campus who could read well enough to tell where the mail was supposed to go. He could deliver all the mail in an afternoon, by bicycle.

The economic upswing and labor shortage caused by the war created other opportunities. In addition to light work at the fraternity house and delivering campus mail, Matthew Mason alternately drove a taxi or waited tables at night. Fannie worried that he was running himself ragged, but he had five (soon to be six) children, and he would do anything to make sure they were well fed, had decent clothes to wear, and got an occasional treat. He also needed money to renovate the house that was now all his, having repaid the loan from his mother-in-law.

By 1944 young men who were combat veterans began to trickle back to campus. They brought with them a new attitude. They were no longer naive, excitable boys. The war had grown them up fast and instilled harder tastes. In later years, the veterans who returned to campus after the war were sometimes referred to, collectively, as "the wild WWII crowd."

The fraternities had always nurtured a cult of masculinity. Before the war, this cult vaunted prowess in sports, academic achievement, involvement in campus affairs, gentlemanly poise, and career ambition. A young man's status was also enhanced by popularity with women, a willingness to take a few risks, and by a capacity to hold his liquor, if he chose to indulge. This was the manhood ideal for white fraternity boys. But after the war it was military service, especially in combat, that became the mark of manhood for a whole generation.

For returning veterans, campus life seemed tame and the old rules infantilizing. Having survived the war, these young men intended to live it up, on their own terms. One of the first things many of them did, upon returning to campus, was to drink in celebration of victory and reunion. In their cups, these young men sought to rekindle the feelings of brotherhood they had known in the service. Even those who had not served were drawn into this ritual of manly comradeship. Failing to join in was an affront, or an aspersion upon one's own manhood.

The young men who returned to the fraternity house were delighted to see Matthew Mason, who had acquired a new nickname. One of the boys had dubbed him "Reeter Skeeter," after a floorshow comedian he'd seen in New York in the late 1930s. The name had stuck, first being

shortened to Reet and then later becoming *Doctor* Reet, when another young man "promoted" him.[1] Matthew welcomed the returning members by name. In a spirit of exuberance and equality they invited Matthew to join them for a drink. He was too polite to refuse. Sharing a drink with them made his employers happy and, more important, allowed Matthew Mason, who had sat out the war, to feel like one of the boys.

By its charter at that time, membership in Phi Delta Theta was limited to white Christian gentlemen. Similar restrictions would have kept Matthew Mason out of nearly every fraternity on campus. But of course he could not have been a student either. It was not until 1955, by which time Matthew Mason's oldest child was already past college age, that the university would, after losing a court battle, admit four black undergraduates.

I wondered what it had been like for Mr. Mason in those days of Jim Crow, days still openly bearing the cultural and economic legacies of slavery. What had it been like for him as a black man from a sharecropping family to work for white college boys, most of whom were from privileged backgrounds? By Mr. Mason's accounts the fraternity boys had always treated him well.

Mr. Mason told me that the boys had helped him out of many financial scrapes over the years. He said they had given him cars; paid for all his children to attend college; paid a hospital bill when Martha had cataracts removed; and had, since he retired, paid the rent on the apartment he shared with Martha. He said the boys had even found the apartment for him. Some of the older members, he said, having become doctors and lawyers, provided free medical and legal services. The older

---

1. Matthew Mason picked up the "Reet" nickname between 1938 and 1941. The story about the name deriving from a floorshow comedian was questioned by several fraternity members who graduated during this era. They thought the nickname derived from Mr. Mason's use of the jazz expression "that's all *reet* [right]." It's possible that both stories are true. Mr. Mason adapted pieces of his shtick from the culture of jazz and blues, and the unnamed New York entertainer might have been Cab Calloway, who popularized the use of "reet" and other hepcat slang. Mr. Mason himself told the story related in the text. The fraternity brother who had allegedly first bestowed the "Reeter Skeeter" nickname was deceased.

Mason, ca. 1956

members often gave him money on holidays and birthdays or when they stopped to visit while in town for a football game or alumni event. And the younger boys still brought supper from the fraternity kitchen two days a week.

There was no doubt about Mr. Mason's gratitude. Nor any doubt about the many kinds and instances of extra help the fraternity members provided. Nor about the genuineness of affection motivating their actions. But the real story was more complicated.

Why did he so often get in financial jams? The simplest answer is that he wasn't paid enough. At twelve dollars a week (raised to fourteen dollars a week a few years later), Matthew Mason was paid less than the average black man in Chapel Hill at that time. Being able to tote home food and clothing compensated somewhat for the low wages, but not enough. Which is why he needed to drive a cab at night, wait tables in restaurants, and do domestic work on the side. "If they had paid him an adequate wage," his daughter Mary said, "he wouldn't have had to go to them so often to be bailed out."

Matthew Mason's lack of education was perhaps a liability when it came to budgeting, but Fannie was no slouch in this regard, and neither were they profligate spenders. On the contrary, by necessity theirs was a frugal household that relied on gardening, canning, sewing, and do-it-yourself repair. Mr. Mason's real weakness as a money man, according to his friends and neighbors, was his desire to provide as much as he could for his children—six of them after 1944—and his uncautious generosity. Mr. Mason was known as a man who would give his last dollar to someone in need.

In view of the collective wealth of its membership, it seemed to me that Mr. Mason overestimated the sacrifice represented by the extras that came from the fraternity. The cars they had given him were used and sometimes in need of repair. Martha's onetime hospital bill of $3,500 was paid in lieu of providing health insurance. The rent on the publicly subsidized apartment was less than $150 a month (in 1996). The two weekly meals the boys brought, irregularly (and later not at all), were no more than the leftovers that Matthew had once carried home himself. And while Mr. Mason could, if a need arose, ask for a special dispensation of funds, the fraternity provided him no regular pension.

I was impressed, however, when Mr. Mason told me that the fraternity had paid for his children to attend college. If so, this would have been a truly generous and progressive benefit. I imagined them saying, "Send the bills for tuition and books to us. We'll write the checks." Which is not at all what happened.

"Mary was the only one who got any money out of them for college," Mr. Mason's oldest daughter, Gloria, told me. "And that was because she pestered them for it, after all their years of promising." The oldest son, John Lee, went to college on a football scholarship. Matthew Jr. worked full-time and used the G. I. Bill. Gloria worked and paid her way through business school. Allen had joined the army. Mary affirmed what Gloria told me. "I complained that they hadn't lived up to their promises to send Papa's children to college, and they ended up contributing to one semester," Mary said. The youngest son, Thomas, relied on the G. I. Bill and worked to pay for school.

Mr. Mason's claim that the fraternity had found the apartment in which he and Martha lived also turned out to be fanciful. When I mentioned this claim to Mary, she said, "Gloria would be livid to hear that.

She got them the opportunity to choose that apartment before anyone else moved into the complex. Some of those boys might have helped Papa and Martha *move*, but Gloria found the apartment." Gloria, who had a long career in social services and as a community activist, confirmed that she had, through local connections, gotten her father first dibs on the apartment. No one I talked to thought it plausible that it had happened any other way.

The issue of what the fraternity could or ought to have done for Mr. Mason is distinct from his representation of the fraternity. He clearly exaggerated their generosity, sometimes inventing good deeds they had not done. This was attributable, I supposed, to his wanting to underscore, for his benefit and mine, the esteem in which the fraternity held him. It was also, as I came to see later, a matter of habit. Mr. Mason had learned the importance of showing gratitude to a benefactor, no matter how small the boon. No doubt he had seen what happened to other black men of his generation who failed to do so.

In 1987 two of the younger fraternity members, undergrads at the time, produced a thirty-minute video, "Right, Boy! The Matthew Mason Story," featuring older members telling their favorite Dr. Reet stories. After watching the video with Mr. Mason, I remarked that it looked like he'd had some good times at the fraternity. "Oh, yeah," he said, laughing. "I had some *real* good times with them boys. Drinking liquor. Cutting up. Letting the good times roll." Sounds like they teased you and played tricks on you sometimes. "Yeah, they teased me. All the time." How did they tease you? "You know, 'Dr. Reet, do this, do that,' you know. Just teased me." Did it ever bother you, what the boys said? "No, never," again with a laugh.

Months later, when I interviewed dozens of older fraternity members, many admitted that the teasing had been racially tinged. "Someone might say, 'Dr. Reet, get your black ass in here and clean up,' " as one brother recounted. "But it never seemed to bother him. He'd just say, 'I ain't black, I'm chocolate.' Or if someone said, 'Reet, you dumb ass,' he'd just say, 'I ain't got a dumb ass, I got a sweet ass.' " And the teasing never seemed to bother him? "Not that I could tell. I think it just rolled off his back." As another brother explained, "The teasing

was incessant, but it was all in fun. It was never ugly. It was teasing with love, on both sides."

The same point was made by brothers who graduated during the years between World War II and the mid-1960s. There was, they stressed, no intent to degrade, and the racial content was innocuous. "Back then the word 'nigger' didn't mean what it means today," I was told. "He sometimes used that word to refer to himself." Several brothers from this era said that the teasing had perhaps gone too far on occasion, though all agreed that Dr. Reet appeared unruffled by it. "Looking back at it today," one brother said, "some of what was said would make your hair stand up." But as Dr. Reet himself had told me, it never bothered him.

Then again, there were a few ugly incidents over the years, as I first learned from Gloria and Thomas. In one case, some boys had hung a sheet out the window so that Mr. Mason would see it when he got to the fraternity house in the morning. On the sheet they had written, "Just wanted you to know, Dr. Reet, that we're KKK." The culprits had disappeared, and so Mr. Mason found a marking pen and wrote on the back side, "I don't care what you are. If you're KKK, you can kiss my ass."

Another time, as Mr. Mason made his wake-up rounds, a boy who had seen Mr. Mason's daughter Mary picketing one of the segregated theaters on Franklin Street told him that he ought to keep his daughter at home. His response was to pull the boy out of bed and tell him that his daughter could do as she damn pleased and, what's more, *he* was going to join the picketing. On still another occasion, a fraternity boy who was helping tend bar bristled at Mr. Mason ordering him about. When the boy made it plain that, being from *Mississippi*, he didn't like taking orders from a black man, Mason said, "I don't care where you're from or what you don't like. Get busy and *pour!*"

When I asked Mr. Mason about these incidents, he was not happy. "I don't like digging up that mess, all that bad old stuff," he said. "I like to let bygones *be* gone. You know what I mean?" He could have let it drop, but instead he retold the stories with verve, confirming what Gloria and Thomas had told me.

Mr. Mason seemed surprised that I found these incidents of special interest. It was as if I should have known, without bringing them up

for painful reinspection, that of course such things had happened. How
could it have been otherwise? Didn't I understand the time and place
in which he lived? Martha listened to his retelling and added a few
incidents he didn't mention. Pranks, mostly. Scaring him with stuffed
alligators and with a live snake. Pranks that she, like Fannie before her,
thought were mean.

Mr. Mason's reluctance to go into the "bad old stuff" was partly
a matter of avoiding unpleasant memories. The equanimity he had
achieved in his old age depended on selectivity in revisiting his past,
and some of my questions tugged him back to places he preferred not to
go. His real fear, however, was not of being disturbed by memories of
the past but of consequences in the present. "I hope you won't go down
to the fraternity house and tell those young boys about all this old *shit*,"
he said (the only time I heard him use the expletive). "They don't know
anything about it, and that's how I'd like to leave it, you understand?"
I assured him that the brothers I wanted to talk to were the older ones,
the ones who had graduated years ago, and that I had no plans to interview the younger boys. This seemed to put him at ease.

I wondered, though, why he cared so much about the younger boys,
the current undergraduates. Shouldn't he have worried more about the
older members, the ones who were closer to the bad old stuff? The
answer struck me later: he depended on the younger boys—they brought
him checks for his rent, brought meals twice a week, and occasionally
gave other forms of help—and if they took those old stories in the wrong
way, Dr. Reet might be seen as another black man "with an attitude."
After sixty years of service to the fraternity, their support of him still
required, he believed, cultivating the image of a happy, grateful Dr. Reet.

Mr. Mason could see that I was unsettled by his strong reaction to
the prospect of the younger boys hearing stories of racist incidents in
the past. Now he tried to put me at ease. "Look here, it's like this," he
began, as if helping a sorry pupil get back on track. "Slavery times was
hard times. I wasn't *in* slavery times, but I know *about* it. And something like that, you see, it stays on. Even now, a whole lot of white people hate niggers. You know what I mean? Right now. And there were
some Phi Delts like that. I don't know how it is *now*, but back then
there were some that just didn't care about a black fella. And I had to

let them know who I was, that I wasn't scared of them. Once they found it out, they treated me nice."

What continued to fascinate me about the relationship between Mr. Mason and the fraternity boys was the paradox of the affection they felt for him and the demeaning social arrangements—Jim Crow segregation—within which this relationship existed. "Those boys loved him and he loved those boys," his daughter Gloria told me. Her brother Matthew Jr. and sister Mary said the same. The fraternity members, young and old, professed their love and respect for Dr. Reet. I wondered, then, about the fruition of this feeling. Had it translated, for instance, into support for the civil rights struggles that shook Chapel Hill in the early 1960s?

The consensus was that it had not. Most of the Phi Delts were, at best, passively sympathetic to the antisegregation marches and sit-ins. None of the members I spoke to recalled much conversation among themselves about the issue. One member who participated in the protests, James Reston Jr., was teased for it. "The guys called me 'Crusader Rabbit,'" he said. Another member tried to explain why it was possible to love Mr. Mason but largely ignore the civil rights movement:

> Maybe it's a cliché, but we much more readily accepted the person than the race. I know from my experience—and a lot of us were middle class and some upper-middle, but most of us had the experience of black people working for the family. I was raised, when I was small, by a black nanny. So maybe that's why I could bond to, relate to, Reet so quickly and easily one-on-one. But my philosophy regarding the civil rights movement—rights for the race—was certainly not as tolerant and as warm as for Reet individually. I don't want to speak for others, but I suspect that if you dig around, that's what you'd find. I think everybody was very fond of Reet *personally*, but without that being a springboard to becoming socially active. And that's probably because of how most of us were raised.

That is in fact what I found—a kind of compartmentalizing that made it possible to like individual black people, and even treat them very well,

without liking the idea of equality for black people as a group. Looking back, some of the members regretted their abstention from the civil rights movement. "It was like the dark ages," as one member put it. "We weren't smart enough to challenge segregation. We weren't making the connections we should have been making."

Matthew Mason's work and personality helped to make the fraternity the place it was. For this, and for who he was and all he did, he was deeply appreciated, even loved. And so the "race problem" was not one of malicious intent but of unjust social arrangements enforced by law and custom—arrangements that were as taken for granted by most of the fraternity members as by Matthew Mason. Hiring an adult black man to be house*boy* and answer to undergraduate white males was normal. Just as it was perfectly unthinkable to put an adult white man in the same position.

It may be a true report of experience to say, as one member put it, "To us, Reet wasn't black; he was just Reet." Yet this seemingly humane color-blindness is also blindness to the social realities that shaped Matthew Mason's life. He held the jobs he did, earned what he did, interacted with the boys as he did, endured what he did, faced the limitations he did, and *felt* what he did, in part because he was a black man in a society organized to privilege whites. Interpersonal affection might have made those facts more bearable, but it did not and could not make them go away.

As a black man of his times, Matthew Mason took for granted that the teasing, including its racial content, came with the territory. And it seems that, on the whole, he enjoyed the banter and joshing, giving him as it did a feeling of being one of the boys—an equal, almost, to his aristocratic white bosses. Perhaps part of the appreciation the members showed for Dr. Reet, especially after they graduated and gained perspective on their adolescent behavior, came from recognizing how much he had suffered. As one member said:

> I think Reet recognized that young rich white boys can be vulgar and mean, but it didn't bother him. If people made prejudiced remarks, he just disregarded it. Despite all that, if he'd see you, he'd sort of try to help you unwind. He was just really generous toward us over a long

period of time. He knew something that we didn't know. All I can say is that he was a remarkable human being to make the brothers remember him and be the *kind* person he was, despite our relatively little effort to make him feel better in *his* life. I mean, he took a lot of verbal abuse. Everybody cared a lot for him, but it was still a very difficult relationship for him. So I admire him for having put up with us.

However Mr. Mason might have felt when he was with the fraternity boys, this was not the whole of his life. There was the matter of his life as husband and father. What happened in one realm affected the other, sometimes for the good, though often not.

Fraternity members returning after the war not only drank more among themselves but also wanted to tip a few with Dr. Reet. Now he joined in, finding it possible to negate some of the stigma of sitting out the war by showing that he could hold his own with other men when the bottle was passed. Parties became more frequent and raucous. Matthew Mason, amiable, accommodating bartender, had plenty of liquor at hand, chances to consume it, and lots of invitations to do so.

Matthew Mason's playful spirit was, at first, set loose by the drinking. With a few drinks and some encouragement, he would offer bawdy toasts and risqué jokes. This delighted the boys, and Matthew delighted in pleasing them. With a few more drinks and some egging on, he could be gotten out from behind the bar to do a little shuffle-step dancing. Or, even better, gotten up to the microphone to sing with the band. The boys rewarded his impromptu performances with laughs and more drinks.

At first the consequences at home were minor. If Papa was a bit tipsy after working a party, it just made him livelier, more fun. After drinking, he was as playful with his children as he had been with the fraternity boys. It was Fannie who disapproved. But if her husband occasionally overdid it and gave himself a headache the next day, she saw it as a small cost to bear, considering the other benefits that the job provided. After all, Matthew often came home from tending bar with a pocketful of badly needed tip money.

But before long there were times when he didn't come home after working a party. He would be too drunk to walk, let alone drive. And

so the boys would let Matthew sleep on a sofa, or on a cot in the basement. The next morning, mouth dry and head throbbing, Matthew would make his wake-up rounds, serve breakfast, clean, and then go home to sleep. By the early 1950s this pattern of behavior was becoming part of Dr. Reet's legend.

Still, family life was good. The emphasis that Fannie and her mother placed on education was paying off. The two oldest boys were in college and the other children were coming up through school and doing well. (Matthew and Fannie would produce one school body president, two class presidents, and two valedictorians.) On weekends the family took driving trips, sometimes short ones to Durham or Raleigh, and sometimes longer ones to Virginia Beach or Danville. Once a year they enacted the middle-class ritual of a two-week vacation.

In the nearly twenty years that he owned it, Matthew Mason worked hard to improve his small house. He built a new indoor bathroom with tub and sink and undertook other small renovations. He was, as one of his nieces put it, "always fixing up *something* on that house." Despite these efforts, the structure was cheap and the soil beneath it was soft, and eventually the foundation needed repair. It was not the kind of work Mr. Mason could do himself, so he took a second mortgage to pay to have it done.

He was also trying to help his sons with college expenses and to repay loans he'd taken to make earlier home improvements. Soon he fell behind on payments of the second mortgage. By the time he asked some of the older fraternity members for help, it was too late. He was $4,300 in debt and had no prospects for pulling himself out. In October of 1954 he had to sell the house, the first and last he would ever own.

Mr. Mason moved his family—Fannie and the two youngest children, Mary and Thomas—into a smaller, rented cinderblock house on Eugene Street in Carrboro. The loss of his home and the move to a shabbier neighborhood crushed Mr. Mason's pride. His status in the community had been staked in part on being a homeowner. But more than this, being a homeowner, husband, and breadwinner had given him a status edge relative to the fraternity boys. When it came to these aspects of manhood, he had been able to stand above his late-adolescent employers.

Matthew Mason now fell into a cycle of spending more time with the fraternity boys to avoid the tension he felt at home, tension that arose in part because of all the time he spent with the boys. The drinking became more frequent, no longer confined to parties. Now it might be any night of the week. After supper the phone would ring and a boy at the fraternity house would say, "Dr. Reet, we need you to help out down here tonight," and, ignoring Fannie's wishes, Matthew would go. Hours later, early in the morning, the boys would bring him home, staggering.

If the boys brought the besotted Dr. Reet to the door, they would often see him get chewed out by Fannie, or be scolded themselves by Mary, who was in no mood to be gentle with boys she felt were abusing her father. One night, seeking to avoid a confrontation, the boys left Matthew at the curb. He made it halfway to the house before pitching head first into the concrete walk. Mary and Fannie found him there, unconscious and bleeding. At the hospital he was diagnosed with a fractured skull. He suffered headaches and impaired vision for days.

Fannie was not only angry about the drinking, she was disappointed that Matthew seemed to have given up. She urged him to bounce back, to muster the spirit he'd shown as a younger man. But he could never manage it for long. Perhaps he couldn't bear having failed her and so was afraid to reassert himself and risk failing again. Perhaps it was too easy and seductive to play Dr. Reet, a role in which he was not a failure but a hero.

Things got worse. Drinking with the fraternity boys kept Matthew from working steadily at the second and third jobs—waiting tables, driving a cab, or working as a dispatcher—that had once bolstered his earnings. There were also nagging debts left over from days of taking small loans to fix the Rosemary Street house. And now Matthew was no longer consuming only the alcohol freely provided by the fraternity boys. He was spending a good share of his wages at local liquor houses.

After several years on Eugene Street, the family was forced to move to a cheap, tiny apartment in the same neighborhood. It was a further step down, underscoring Matthew Mason's sense of failure. "Rock bottom" was how Mary described it later. She was then nearly through college and vowed that she would, as soon as possible, get her mother out of that

place. In less than two years, having graduated and gotten a job in a medical lab at Duke University, she was able to do exactly that.

It wasn't as if the boys were oblivious to Dr. Reet's problem. There were, of course, those who fed it, prodding him to drink and finding sport in his drunken antics. But others saw the damage being done. At one point in the early 1960s several of them formed the "Rehabilitate Reet Committee" to purge his booze stashes and try to get him professional help. The task was more than the boys could handle. "That committee was more good intentions than fact," said one of the brothers involved. "Reet was a middle-aged man and we were twenty-something undergraduates. His drinking problem was far more complicated than we were equipped to deal with back then."

Within the fraternity subculture, Dr. Reet's alcoholic behavior did seem genuinely funny at times. Telling off-color jokes, making bawdy toasts, and singing and dancing at parties were only parts of it. The boys laughed when they found the beer he'd hidden in the soda machine. They laughed when his moonshine concoction—he called it "charge"— blew up in the basement and scared the daylights out of the housemother, who thought the furnace was exploding. They laughed about how he used his scotch-tinged breath to wake them up in the morning.

It was less funny when he was found filthy and passed out in the coal bin; less funny when he didn't show up to work for days; less funny when he had seizures caused by alcohol poisoning. Though there was plenty of behavior that wasn't funny at all, still it was hard to know what to do about it. One proposal was to fire him if he didn't straighten up. The idea was that the threat of losing his job would force Matthew Mason to pull himself together. When word of this proposal got out, several older, influential members nixed it. Firing Dr. Reet, they told the young brothers, was not an option.

Opinions varied as to the overall drinking climate in the fraternity. A few members used the term "Animal House" to conjure the image they had in mind. "Yes, it was clear that Matthew had a drinking problem," one member said. "But then, well, there was a time when that whole *house* had a drinking problem." Or as another said, "Reet was a raging alcoholic. No doubt about it. But the sad truth is that by some standards we were probably all certifiable ourselves."

On the other hand, there was agreement that, as drinkers, the Phi Delts were far from the worst. "If there were ten fraternities on campus," as one member put it, "we would probably have ranked ninth or tenth in drinking." Indeed, on the UNC campus the Phi Delts were better known as high achievers than as hard partiers. The climate was, in any case, sufficiently conducive to drinking to pull Matthew Mason into a downward spiral.

Matthew Mason's tie to the fraternity brought more than wages, food, clothes, cars, and bailing-out when he was overwhelmed by bills. There was also the aura of protection he and his family received by virtue of being favored by elite whites. More than once a member intervened when a cop found Matthew Mason behind the wheel with a snootful, or when one of his sons got in trouble for small mischief. Such protection was part of the paternalistic arrangement. "It was common," as Mr. Mason's daughter Gloria described it, "for an affluent white family in Chapel Hill to 'adopt' a black family and look after them, extend their protection to them. Because of Papa, we were 'adopted' by the fraternity."

It even seemed, as Gloria recalled, that association with the fraternity shielded the family from many of the day-to-day blows of racism and poverty. "It was like we were in our own little world with the Phi Delts," she said. "Being like their adopted family, we got food, clothes; it felt like plenty. But I was a child then and I wasn't facing reality. It was later, when I went into my professional work and saw statistics on poverty, that I realized how poor we had been." Do you think your father knew how much money those boys' families had, or how much they went on to make? "No, he thought of them as 'rich,' but I don't think he ever grasped what that really meant."

The overlap with the world of the fraternity brought an additional, inadvertent benefit for Mr. Mason's children. This came in the form of a sense of possibility that took root when the boys dropped off laundry and then stayed for supper. "It seemed like there were always a few of them around, or we'd go with Papa to the fraternity house," Gloria said. "He would show deference to them—say 'yessir' and all that—but I'd talk to them and argue with them just like they were anybody." Her siblings reported similar experiences. It was clear to the Mason children

Mason working at a fraternity event in the late 1970s

that these boys had a lot of desirable things. It was also clear that they were nothing special.

This perception, combined with Fannie's (and Grandma Sallie's) stress on education, led the Mason children to suppose that they too could have the good things that the fraternity boys had. In effect, the boys became a reference group for Mr. Mason's children. "Because of how we interacted with them," Gloria said, "we just took for granted that they weren't any better than we were and that we could do anything they could." Mr. Mason's other children remembered it the same way. The advantages these white boys enjoyed, the Mason children could see, did not stem from any intellectual or moral superiority.

If not for the relationship Mr. Mason established with the fraternity boys, his children might not have seen their own potential so clearly. And if the boys had not been so privileged, and thus unthreatened, and if they had not so loved their Dr. Reet, they might not have treated his children as equals, or at least as interlocutors worthy of respectful response around the supper table. The unfortunate cost of the familiarity that helped to instill a sense of possibility in Mr. Mason's children was, later, the drinking.

Family efforts to curb the drinking were no more effective than those of the Rehabilitate Reet Committee. Fannie's doorway scoldings provoked shouting matches, about which Matthew would claim to remember nothing the next day. When sober, he listened politely when friends and family members urged him to stop drinking. "He would listen to you," his son Matthew Jr. said, "but then he'd do what he darn well pleased." One time Mary and Thomas tried to cut off their father's supply by telling the bootleggers in town not to sell to him, under threat of being turned in to the police. "Did he holler at us about that! He was furious," Mary said. In the end, it did little good. He found other sources outside the sphere of his children's influence.

Mary's job at Duke paid enough for her to afford a house in a nicer part of Carrboro. She was thus able to get her mother out of the apartment in which the family had been squeezed for several years. Tension between her parents was running high, and so Mary offered Fannie a chance to move into the new house and leave Matthew behind. Fannie refused, saying that she loved her husband and would not abandon him. And so Mary, her parents, and younger brother moved into her house.

It was a nicer place, but the move did nothing to reinflate Matthew Mason's pride. Indeed, he now felt as if he'd become his daughter's tenant. Though Mary asked only that he help pay the utility bills, even that he managed to do only sporadically. Over thirty years later, when he first told me about moving out of the apartment, he said that he and Mary had bought the house together. It was clear, when Mary told me what had really been the case, that Mr. Mason was still embarrassed about the condition of dependence into which he had fallen.

Already at that time Matthew Mason could have said that his children had done well. Five of the six had finished high school. Three had gone to college and two had graduated. One had gone to business school. Another was building a career in the army. The youngest would finish high school soon. All were hardworking and responsible; none had been in any serious trouble. Mr. Mason had reason to be proud of them all, and at some level he surely was.

Under other conditions he might have basked in their achievements. But alcohol and his sense of failure fueled thoughts that his children looked down on him. These thoughts in turn bred resentment

that he vented on the family members around him. "I think he *was* proud of us, especially of how we did in school. But he probably also felt bad that he wasn't able to help us pay for it, those of us who went on to college," Mary speculated. Her hypothesis was consistent with other pieces of her father's behavior: he did not attend her graduation from college or Thomas's from high school.

An emblematic blow-up occurred one time when Mr. Mason called the office at Lincoln High School and asked that Thomas be let out early to help at the fraternity house. Over the years, Mr. Mason's sons had often helped to serve food and tend bar at parties and special events. But calling Thomas out of school was extraordinary. When he stopped at home to change clothes before going to the fraternity house, Fannie was outraged. She was not going to have her youngest child follow in Dr. Reet's footsteps. She sent Thomas marching back to school.

Mr. Mason was outraged too. His fatherly authority had been challenged. Worse, when Fannie sent Thomas back to school, she implicitly rebuked her husband for being foolishly overdedicated to the fraternity. In the spat that followed, Mr. Mason declared that he had worked all his life, from the time he plowed a mule when he was eight years old, and if *working* was good enough for him, it was good enough for his children. He perhaps felt that he couldn't win. He was trying to do the work he had done so well for so long, the work that had supported his family, and now it seemed that his family betrayed him.

By reputation among family and friends, Matthew Mason was an irrepressibly upbeat man. Such a reputation did not come from readily sharing his troubles with others. His inclinations were to the contrary: to make others feel better, to avoid burdening them. When he did finally ask for help, the situation was often desperate. And even then, when it was necessary to importune others, whatever embarrassment or shame or anger he might have felt, he kept inside.

I once asked Mr. Mason if he had a best friend. He said no, that he had many friends. But was there someone—maybe someone around your own age, someone from your church or your neighborhood or your lodge—that you especially liked to hang out with and talk to? He said he couldn't think of anyone like that; he'd just had a lot of friends. But among all your friends, I insisted, there must have been one that you

were closer to, like a special buddy, that you would tell how you were feeling about things. "What do you mean?" he said.

Between debt, feelings of failure, conflict in the family, and—exacerbating all of these—the drinking, these were Mr. Mason's worst years. He talked easily of his early life with Fannie, up to the time of selling the Rosemary Street house, and easily too of his life with Martha. But the decade between 1954 and 1964 was full of pain and trouble. He was always willing to tell of his adventures as Dr. Reet but reluctant to revisit his home life during that period. Though Mary had called the years in the tiny apartment "rock bottom," true bottom was just around the corner.

a fine man in his right mind

Twenty chairs were arranged in a circle in what could have passed, if not for the faint smell of cigarette smoke and perfume, for a Sunday school classroom. A large banner hanging from the ceiling over one corner of the room said BUT FOR THE GRACE OF GOD. Smaller signs urging FIRST THINGS FIRST, EASY DOES IT, ONE DAY AT A TIME, and THINK were tacked to the walls. We waited, eighteen of us, for the orientation session to begin. The half-hour session, offered every Sunday afternoon, was mandatory for visitors to the drug rehab facility.

I was there to see Atwater. One day, about three weeks after his eviction hearing, I had come by his apartment and found him gone. His neighbor and party buddy, JC, told me that Atwater had been put out. After a few calls, I located Atwater in the psych ward of UNC Hospital. He had put his crazy-as-a-bat plan into motion. Shortly after a sheriff's deputy taped an ejection notice to his apartment door, Atwater called the rescue squad to take him to the hospital because of shortness of breath.

At the hospital, Atwater reported drug use, severe depression, and thoughts of suicide. They kept him for a standard seventy-two-hour evaluation. A social worker reviewed his case and got him into rehab. It was the second time in seven months.

On the prior occasion, Atwater had told me that he didn't really need treatment, that he used drugs only to help him understand their effects on the people who visited his apartment. "I appreciate my experience with drugs," he'd told me. "Ain't nobody can tell me about drugs. I been

there. I was only going to that program to bring back knowledge for my young people. Users will only listen to other users, and I was there to get knowledge that my people would listen to." Others who had seen Atwater go in and out of such programs had a different take. "He goes in to rest and build up his strength and then comes out ready to party again," his buddy JC told me.

After the orientation, patients began trickling in and huddling with their visitors, pulling off to corners of the room in a futile effort to gain privacy. Most of the space had been staked out by the time Atwater arrived a few minutes later. I suggested that we sit at a table I'd found near some vending machines, just outside the visiting room. We had the spot to ourselves, and no one seemed to mind.

Atwater was in a good mood. In a week he had gained weight and looked healthier than I'd ever seen him. He told me that he was getting rest and eating well, and that they were getting his medications adjusted. The counselor who had led the orientation session stopped at the table on her way to the vending machines. She saw me taking notes. "Are you the one who's writing a book about Mr. Atwater?" she asked. I confessed.

"Well, he is certainly a character," she said.

"What kind?" I asked.

"A dirty old man, for one thing," she said. Atwater was eating this up. A big grin spread across his face.

He said, "I told her to come on by when the lights are out and jump on for a little ride."

"I told him I would, but it would kill him," she said.

"Yeah, but I'd die happy and it'd take three weeks for the undertaker to get the smile off my face!" This was Atwater's shtick. She'd heard it all before, too, but she played along and let him have his moment.

After she left, Atwater reminded me that he didn't really need to be there. "I'm not like these other people," he said, referring to his fellow patients. "These people are addicts. I'm in control of it. Crack's not important to me. It doesn't make me happy. It's a social thing. It's really about young women. That's what I'm addicted to. They cook and clean and do whatever I want, if I pay 'em off in crack. I say, 'I'll do something nice for you, if you do something nice for me,' and man, I've learned

more about sex since I was fifty-five than in all my prior life. You talk about one old nigger having a good time! Whooo! I had some *times* in that old crib of mine!"

He was done with his apartment. He had yet to get his stuff out of there, but it was not his crib anymore. I asked what he was going to do when his stay in rehab ended in a few days. He said they had arranged for him to live in a family care home in Roxboro, a small town about forty miles from Chapel Hill. "It's nice. I've seen pictures of it. It's kind of farmish and quiet. I need that," he said, just a minute after speaking wistfully of life in his old apartment. Somehow it didn't fit. I couldn't picture Atwater retiring to a clean life in the country.

When I left, we agreed that he would call me and let me know how to reach him in Roxboro. Atwater called the next day and left the name of the place and a phone number on my answering machine. It seemed set to happen. When I later tried to call him in Roxboro, I was told that he didn't go, that "his family took him somewhere else at the last minute." By now Atwater's disappearances and abrupt changes of plan didn't surprise me. I'd make a few calls and find him again soon enough. What surprised me was finding him back in his apartment.

It was July 3, 1996, and I had stopped to see Mr. Mason, who told me that Atwater was in his apartment. Astounded, I excused myself to go see. Atwater was there, watching a muted TV. The shades were drawn and the lights were off. He was hiding.

"I was all set to go to that place in Roxboro," he explained. "Then at the last minute John and Chris said I should live with him [Chris]. They said I could help Chris make his house payment, and I thought maybe it would be a good thing to do, to help Chris out. So when those folks from Roxboro came to get me, I said I wasn't going, that I was going to live with my son. I could tell that the rehab docs were pissed off about that, after getting me in to that other place." He was going to stay in the apartment over the weekend, until Chris had a bed ready for him.

At first, after Atwater moved in with his son, he told me that he was "at peace" and things were going well. But in a few weeks he began to complain about what Chris wasn't doing for him and about how Chris was spending his money. Chris chafed under his father's demands to be waited on, and by mid-October the situation had grown tense. Chris

wanted him out and Atwater was ready to go. The arrangement lasted less than four months.

In addition to his emphysema and earlier bout with laryngeal cancer, Atwater had a host of past and present ailments. Pyorrhea caused his teeth to begin falling out when he was in his twenties. By his mid-thirties he wore dentures. He had had surgery to remove warts on his penis, to remove hemorrhoids, and to repair a punctured eardrum ("I couldn't hear out of that ear for twenty years, and after they fixed it I stayed awake all night listening to the air conditioner with one ear and the TV with the other"). He had peptic ulcers and high blood pressure. His lower right eyelid was inverted, causing the hairs of the lid to irritate his eye. He kept nitroglycerin pills handy for when his angina bothered him.

Emphysema was Atwater's most debilitating problem. Years of smoking had destroyed the elasticity of his lungs, which now functioned at about one-third their normal capacity. "My lungs don't blow out the way they should," Atwater said. "The doctor told me my lungs are like a hard old sponge." What Atwater's lungs could no longer do was to keep his muscles—most critically his heart—properly oxygenated if he exerted himself. By walking across the room too quickly, Atwater could get desperately short of breath. When he did, he panicked, sometimes losing control of his bladder and bowel.

Soon after he moved in with his son, Atwater was put on oxygen. Medicare paid for a machine and several refillable tanks. The round-the-clock oxygen allowed Atwater to sleep better and, if he was careful, to avoid getting short of breath. When he first introduced me to the machine, he said it was a blessing and he wished he'd been able to get it sooner. The machine was indeed a blessing, but Atwater knew what else it meant. "By the time you get one of these," he said, pointing at the machine, "you're standing at St. Peter's gate. A strong wind will blow you in."

Not that Atwater quit smoking. He claimed that a doctor had once told him that his lungs were in such bad shape that a little more smoking wouldn't make much difference. When I said that that sounded like a Doctor *Atwater* prescription, he said, "Well, I've studied my own disease more than any of those people."

Atwater insisted, from one week to the next, that he could quit smoking *any time he wanted to*; that he *couldn't* quit, because nicotine was more addictive than heroin, cocaine, or alcohol; that it *wouldn't make any difference* if he quit; that he *should* quit; that he was *going to* quit; that he *had* quit; and that—upon starting up again—he was *damn well going to smoke as long as he enjoyed it*. One day he noticed me laugh and shake my head as he lit up. "Are you going to alternate puffs?" I asked, nodding toward his hands. Atwater looked down. "Lord, have mercy! A cigarette in one hand and an inhaler in the other! That's insane!" He took one more draw on the cigarette and stubbed it out.

At UNC Hospital alone, Atwater's medical history was voluminous. One day, about a month after I'd filed the requisite paperwork, I received a call from Heather in the records department. "It's taken us a while to pull it all together," she said, apologetically, "and I think I should tell you before we put in this order that it's fifteen hundred pages." The service that copied and sent out records charged fifty cents a page, she told me. I asked about options. "We could send just the abstracts and summaries; that's only about fifty pages," she said. I said I'd try that route first.

I wondered how Atwater had managed to get medical care, since he had never (as far as he could remember) had health insurance. One day in early October 1996, while he was still living with Chris, I went to see Atwater and found him sitting on the sofa, oxygen tank at his side, dressed and ready to go out. No one else was around. Atwater said he wasn't feeling well because he had run out of medicine and needed to go to the hospital to get his prescriptions refilled. I thought it odd that he wanted to go to the ER, but then I figured that Atwater knew his own business.

At the check-in desk Atwater said nothing about needing medicine. He reported being short of breath and having chest pains. They put Atwater in a wheelchair and took him to an ER cubicle, where he was hooked up to oxygen and to the usual monitoring devices. When the initial flurry of activity died down and we had a minute to ourselves, I asked him about the chest pains. "Mostly it's just stress. I can't get comfortable. Once I get back on my meds I'll be all right," he said. Citing chest pains, Atwater knew, was the way to get seen fast in ER.

During the next hour a series of doctors, nurses, and technicians fussed over Atwater. One technician hooked him to a portable computer for a cardiogram. Another gave him a nebulizer breathing treatment, measuring Atwater's lung volume before and after. A nurse took a blood sample while Atwater joked with her about being "vampired." Another nurse set him up for a chest x-ray. Atwater told her that they usually had to take two pictures, "because my lungs are so long." She smiled sweetly and took one shot. Ten minutes later she was back to take another. "I guess you were right," she said. A boy doctor who had overdosed on cologne and mousse came in and poked through Atwater's bag of empty pill bottles. "This is interesting," he said, then left and never returned. At one point in that first hour, Atwater commanded the attention of two doctors, four nurses, two x-ray technicians, and one respiratory technician.

About two hours later a doctor-and-nurse team came in and told Atwater that the x-rays and cardiogram checked out okay and that he could go home. The doctor said he had authorized refills for Atwater's prescriptions. I used a wheelchair to take Atwater to the pharmacy, where he handed the plastic grocery bag full of empty bottles to a woman behind the counter. In fifteen minutes Atwater's pharmacopoeia was replenished and I wheeled him out. It had taken three hours in the ER, but Atwater hadn't paid a cent for the checkup or the fresh meds.

In the car I asked Atwater if he ever got billed for his trips to the ER. "They sometimes send me bills, but if you go through the emergency room, Medicaid pays for the prescriptions. Then you can get them refilled within thirty days," he said. "The important thing is that you got 'em when you need 'em. Without those inhalers, I'd be dead." I asked how he paid the bills. "I don't worry much about that, since I don't have anything to pay 'em with. How do they expect poor-ass people to pay those bills anyway? It's damn crazy."

When Atwater first intimated that he wasn't getting along with Chris and might need to move, I asked where he would go. He said that a social worker was looking into rest home placement for him. He also mentioned an old friend who might take him in. "I let her stay in my

apartment a couple times when she was put out, so she'd be paying me back for the help I gave her," he said. I asked if her place was going to give him the peace he claimed to want. "Oh, yeah. It's quiet. It's just Cat and her husband. She's been straight now for a couple years."

When I came to see him at the Alabama Avenue house on October 25, 1996, Atwater was gone. Chris told me that his father had moved out earlier in the week and was living with Cat in Durham. Atwater had left no forwarding address or phone number. I'd cut him a lot of slack before, but now I was miffed. It was Friday and Atwater had left on Monday. He could have called to let me know where he was.

I had Cat's last name, so I tried the phone book and found no listing. I called a few people in Chapel Hill who I thought might know where she lived but had no luck. A week went by and Atwater hadn't called. Finally, I tried the reference desk at the Durham County Library, hoping they would have a city directory. They did, though it was a few years old. It gave an address on South Roxboro. I knew I had the right place when I spotted the NO SMOKING, OXYGEN IN USE sign on the apartment door.

It was no one's idea of a lovely neighborhood. On the south side of Roxboro Road was a large public housing project built in the 1960s. On the north side of the road was a string of four-unit brick apartment buildings that had seen better days. The buildings were bordered by mangy lawns in front and gravel parking lots in back. Despite thirty-five years of de jure integration, the neighborhood was still almost entirely black, though as one resident told me later, the area's downhill slide was being hastened by "all the Mexicans moving in."

No one answered my knock. The ground-level apartment opened to the front yard, so I was visible to anyone on the street. I was glad to have found Atwater, but less glad to be standing there looking lost. As I was about to leave, a car pulled up and parked behind the building. I waited to see who got out.

She was a black woman, somewhere in her fifties I guessed, with a body that had filled out in middle age but hadn't lost all its curves. My impression was of a waitress who had just gotten off work after a double shift of fending off grabby male customers. The scowl she wore said that the last thing she needed right then was to see a strange white guy standing outside her door.

"I'm Mike Schwalbe," I said. "I was looking for Anthony." The scowl gave way to a smile and her face turned sweet. We were both relieved.

"He's been trying to call you," she said. "He went next door one time—we don't have a phone yet—and tried, but your line was busy."

"How's he doing?"

"His breath is getting shorter. Other than that he's doing okay. His son put him out, you know." It didn't seem like the time to suggest that Atwater's behavior as a tenant might have had something to do with his need to move.

"I'd like to see him, if you don't mind."

"Sure, c'mon in. He's probably sleeping."

It was a small two-bedroom apartment. The living room flowed into the cul-de-sac of a kitchen. A short hallway led to two bedrooms and a bathroom. A sofa, two chairs, a coffee table, and an end table made the living room crowded enough to require care in squeezing through. "He's up. C'mon back," Cat hollered. Seven paces got me to Atwater's bedroom.

Atwater sat on the edge of the bed, wearing his pajamas inside out. I said I was glad to see that he was still alive, hinting that he could have done more to let me know where he was alive. He explained his arrangement with Cat. He was going to pay a third of the rent and utilities, and would pay for a phone, which was supposed to be installed soon. In return, Cat would fix his meals, wash his clothes, help him clean his room, and keep his meds stocked. If anyone asked, she would say that he was her uncle.

The bedroom was eight by ten, with a closet. Atwater had an old recliner parked in the center of the room, facing a color TV. One window looked out onto the gravel parking lot. "This is the best retirement plan a poor man like me can expect. I got my oxygen, my meals, entertainment, just about any kind of help I need. Once I get a phone and cable, I'll be all set." Before I left, I told Cat that I'd like to visit Anthony once a week. "That's fine," she said. "Popcorn told me about you."

Later I asked one of my students, an ambitious young black man who had grown up in Durham, what came to mind when he thought of South Roxboro. "What comes to mind," he said, "is 'don't go there.'" Mr. Mason's son Thomas, when I told him where Atwater was living,

advised that I stop seeing Atwater. "Durham isn't like Chapel Hill," Thomas said. "They'll kill you over there." The next time I saw Atwater, I asked about the neighborhood. "It's not bad during the day," Atwater said. "Some fucked-up crackhead might shoot your ass for two dollars, but don't worry, no one will mess with you." They won't? "No, they'll leave you alone. You look like a social worker."

Atwater's life began to change after he left his apartment. In the hospital, in rehab, at Chris's, and now at Cat's, Atwater was cut off from the flow of guests looking for a good time or a place to flop. The all-hours partying was over, though Atwater continued to indulge. And while Cat's apartment was quieter than Chris's house, it was not quite the health spa that Atwater had made it out to be.

When I visited Atwater on the day after his sixty-fourth birthday, about five months after he'd moved to Cat's apartment, it was clear that there was tension between them. Cat was not happy, and her unhappiness was aimed at Atwater. He told me that she was angry because he had sneaked a little smoke (crack) from a guy next door, and had downed several of her beers. As Atwater told it, Cat's complaint was that he hadn't invited her to party with him and hadn't asked if he could drink her beer.

Cat told a different story.

"It was Popcorn's birthday, and he decided he was going to party," she said. She told me how he'd smoked crack next door, then came back and drank all the beer in the fridge. But that wasn't the problem. "He could hardly breathe 'cause of that smoking, and then that alcohol was making him mean and he got to talking bad to me—saying ugly things. At one time I'd a beat him to death for talking to me like that, but I just told him, 'Popcorn, you aren't gonna live in my house and talk to me like that, and I'm not gonna be taking you to the hospital every time you smoke and get out of breath, so you can either straighten up or I'm putting you out.' And he did. He knew I wasn't kidding."

Cat felt bound by her own ultimatum. "I realized," she said, "that I couldn't tell Popcorn to quit if I was doing something. And I wasn't going to put up with him getting mean and ugly. So that was it, Mike. I just said no more drugs or anything was coming into that apartment."

It was only later that I heard Cat's side of the story. But I knew that something had changed after that episode. Atwater was reliably alert when I visited him, and Cat began a transformation that was remarkable. What didn't change was Atwater's characteristic frame of interpretation. A year later he told me, referring to Cat, "She's like a different person now. She's really got her shit together. I did that. It makes me feel good to make that kind of thing happen."

By the spring of 1997 I had known Atwater for over a year. He had seen me follow him from place to place and keep coming back week after week. His need to perform, to invoke Shine or Popcorn, abated somewhat once he trusted me not to abandon him if the truth of his life didn't match his stories. His mind was also clearer now that Cat had put a lid on his partying. At Cat's we had time to talk, with no distractions, and I tried to use the time to go deeper into the roots of Atwater's behavior.

When I asked Atwater why he dealt so badly with his marriage after getting out of the army, he attributed it to an adolescent male ego that wouldn't let him forgive and reconcile, or forgive and move on. He said that at the time he felt he had to lash back and exact revenge, to reassert himself as a man and avoid being seen as his wife's flunky. "Now I can see how foolish I was. Maybe with a grown mind I could handle that sort of thing different today, but back then I couldn't, and that's what fucked me up." Didn't anyone try to help you sort it out and pull yourself together? "Sure they did. My dad. My uncle in New York. They talked and talked. But I wouldn't listen. Young men don't know enough to listen, especially if they're hurting and drinking."

How much Atwater had grown up was an open question. But he was at least willing to be critical of himself as a younger man.

Why, in all the years after his marriage fell apart, had he never found anyone else to settle down with? His first answer was the usual blustery one: "After my mother's domineering ways and what my wife done to me, I decided I was never gonna let no woman born of woman dominate me." I said that, as a grown man, he could have negotiated a better relationship. This seemed to cut through the act. "I suppose," he said, speaking slowly, the bluster gone, "that it's because I never got in

love again. After my marriage was ruined, women were just a convenience to me. Use 'em and be done. That's not gonna get you much love on either side." He then asked if I was in love. I said yes. "That's good, Mike. That's wonderful. You do whatever you need to to hold on to it."

Alcohol played a big part in keeping Atwater from rebuilding his life. When we first talked about this, Atwater gave me a sound bite: "My wife fucked up my mind and turned me into a drunk." I pointed out that he drank *before* he went into the army (though not as heavily), and that his drinking had wrecked whatever chance he might have had to reconcile with his wife. He was willing, then, to revise his story. Yes, he drank before the service. "When I was in [high] school I was too small to do much dukin'. That's why I carried a knife. And when I'd get some liquor in me, man, I didn't take shit from nobody," he said. His early drinking, he acknowledged, if not in so many words, was an essential aid to his manhood act.

By all accounts, Atwater was genuinely distraught over his situation after he got out of the army. He'd fouled his nest in the service, his marriage was in trouble, and he had no good prospects for school or work. Nor did he have the kind of coping skills or support network, to use the modern jargon, that could have steered him away from alcohol as a form of manly self-medication.

So drinking was a way to ease the pain and to forget? "That's for damn sure," Atwater said when I started putting the pieces together. Then, while drunk, he'd disgrace himself or hurt people he loved. "Lots of times that happened," he said. "More than I like to admit." When he sobered up and realized what he'd done, the guilt and shame hit him hard. "Then I'd damn sure have to get drunk again." And in the long run? "After a while everything is fucked up and you don't feel like you've got anything to live for, and you don't care about nothing. I didn't have any family to work for, so why put up with the man's bullshit? Why not stay drunk?"

One time when we talked about his drinking, Atwater put it in a nutshell: "Alcohol and drugs allow you to accept yourself as you are, or to escape the shame and dissatisfaction of being who you are." This sounded like it might have come from a pamphlet Atwater had read in rehab, but it seemed to me then, and still does, that he chose this

language because it fit his experience. Recalling what Atwater had said about never remarrying, it occurred to me that he was a man who fancied himself a lover, without believing in his own lovability.

Making sense of Atwater's drinking was easier than making sense of his bitterness toward his mother. Atwater portrayed her, along with his ex-wife, as one of the major villains in his life. He often referred to his mother's "evil-assed ways." At times he obsessed about her, knotting up his mind and losing a night's sleep. I didn't get it. Taken individually, the mother-son conflicts Atwater described in his stories did not, it seemed to me, justify his feelings.

One time I made a list of his mother's alleged sins against him. I wanted to review the list with Atwater to see if I could understand where his feelings were coming from. "Let me see if I've got this straight," I said. "One reason you're angry at your mother is because you think she betrayed your father, and that's what created the situation when you hit him with the stove iron. You regretted that later because you thought your father was justified in going after her."

"Yeah, that's part of it," Atwater said. "When I found out why he was choking her, I regretted hitting him. All my life I regretted that, and it was her damn fault."

"You also resented how she controlled you, or tried to, when you were a boy," I continued. "And you think she sided with your ex-wife when your marriage broke up. And you think your mother 'worried your father to death.'"

Atwater nodded. "That's it, Mike. You got it."

A piece seemed to be missing. Atwater was usually eager to go off on bad-mother riffs whenever she was mentioned. This time he just followed along, checking off the boxes. I was skeptical of his calm. Perhaps I hadn't hit the right button. "What about your children?" I asked, recalling something Atwater had once said.

"She took control of my children," he said, snappishly. I'd found the button. "She was on Dot's side. She'd tell the kids to do what *she* said, because it was *her* house. If I tried to discipline them, she'd say, 'You're *drunk*—you don't know what you're saying.' She wouldn't let me be a man. That was like pouring gasoline on fire. It just made me want to

drink more." This was the missing piece. Atwater's anger, once again, arose from a feeling that his mother had denied him his manhood—which in turn led him to drink and mess himself up even further.

Of course, this was only part of a complex relationship between Atwater and his mother. She had loved him dearly, generously provided for him, and protected him during his boyhood. She had forgiven him time and again for his misbehavior. Her concern was evident when I spoke with her in the fall of 1996. "God knows I did the best I could with him as he was coming up," she said. "But after the army he went backwards. I couldn't do anything with him then. I said, 'Jesus, you take him,' and I believe he will take care of Burness in his own way. As long as Burness can draw breath, there's hope."

I was surprised, then, when Atwater told me that his mother had once said to him that she wished he had never been born. Atwater was in his teens at the time. What was *that* about? I asked. "She was mad because I'd accused her of messing around on my father, and she didn't like it that I knew about that." So it was just a cruel thing she said in a fit of anger? "I think it was more than that. I think she never meant to stay with my father, and when she got pregnant with me, she felt she couldn't leave. I think she blamed me for that, for being stuck with him." If Atwater was right, it brought other pieces together.

"The other thing she used to say to me when she got mad," Atwater had told me, "was, 'You're just like your daddy.' This was when I was up to a teenager and getting into my own ways. Oh, man, she hated that, me being like my father." I had heard enough from his mother and from others in the family to believe this was true. If there was anything Atwater's mother did not want her son to become, it was a replica of her drinking, gambling, carousing husband.

Although it was not uncommon in the 1930s for mothers to dress little boys in dainty clothes, Atwater's mother did this until he was twelve. It seems she was trying to delay his entry into manhood as long as possible.

In describing what a good boy her Burness had once been, she told me, "He was like a girl. Up until he finished high school, he kept his bedroom clean and neat like a girl's. He always hung up his clothes and dusted." She spoke as if recalling the golden days of motherhood.

And when Burness got older? She sighed and shook her head. "It's hard to keep up with a boy when he gets some size on him. I didn't know what he was doing or the company he was keeping." Her tone now suggested a mother who had lost a child to illness or accident. Her little boy, beautiful and lovable when he was still "like a girl," had gone away.

If Atwater was right about his mother feeling that he was the reason she had stayed in an unhappy marriage, then behaving like his father would have come as a painful betrayal to her. For years she had sacrificed and suffered for her son, only to have him reject her by emulating William Sr. It would be understandable, then, if she had tried, past an appropriate time, to control her son, to pull him off the path he was taking. It would be understandable, too, if her son rebelled, as most boys do. And finally it would be understandable if the conflict persisted as long as her son tried to assert this manhood in ways noxious to her—ways that evoked the anger she felt toward her husband and the sadness she felt at the loss of her sweet little boy.

Later, when real trouble came, adult trouble, and there was no one to bail him out, Atwater was ill-equipped to deal with it. He had learned to plead and evade, or to lash out, and, when those tactics didn't work, to escape trouble by leaving or drinking. Drinking worked, though only for hours at a time, and it also led to the cycle of drinking, shame, and more drinking. When Atwater got trapped in this, he became to his mother a living sign of her failure to make him into what he could have been. He became the great unfulfilled promise of her life. No doubt Atwater perceived this, and thus had to bear his mother's disappointment—resenting it all the while—on top of his own.

In July 1997, Atwater's mother had a stroke. She was hospitalized briefly and then discharged to a nursing home. I offered several times to take Atwater to visit her. Cat offered too. He never felt up to it, claiming that he "couldn't get in the right mood to see her," and in fact he never saw her before she died that September. When she was gone, I thought perhaps Atwater would experience a release of feelings. If he did, he hid it well.

"I didn't shed a tear when she passed," he told me. "I thought about her but couldn't get the sorrow I should have. I'll miss her, but I'm relieved that I won't have to fight any more battles with her. Won't have

to spend any more mental energy figuring out how to counter her moves. It's over now. Mommy gone. Daddy gone. My family's done too. If we can't be together in peace, at least we'll be separated in peace."

His mood shifted when he told me how he'd caused a ruckus by proposing to have his mother cremated. No one else in the family wanted this, and Atwater had taken some glee in holding this prospect over people's heads. Eventually he relented. After the funeral, when I asked if his mother would have wanted to be cremated, he said, "Hell, no! If she thought I was gonna cremate her, she wouldn't have died."

Atwater was fraught with contradictions. He could be generous and kind, insightful and self-deprecating, but also selfish and cruel, childish and grandiose. His volatility was well known. His cousin Joby told me, "Shine was up and down. Sometimes he'd do good, and sometimes he'd do bad. It's like he had two personalities. He'd be playful and tease you sometimes, then if you teased him back he'd fly off the handle. You never knew how he'd react."

His cousin John told me, "He's like a Doctor Jekyll with a Mr. Hyde as his internal man. But when Burness is in his right mind, he's a fine man. I mean fine. Even now, when he's got his act together he's a fine man." One time Cat told me, "You're lucky you never seen him drunk, Mike. It's like you wouldn't even know he was Popcorn. It's like he's another man."

I had indeed seen mostly the better sides of Atwater, only glimpsing, or hearing about, what else was there, deeper still than Shine, waiting to come out when alcohol or other drugs fogged his right mind. But other contradictions were plain to see. So many, in fact, that it would be fair to say that Atwater was not merely afflicted by contradictions but defined by them.

One time, in remarking on a federal policy of kicking drug users out of public housing, Atwater said that he would go further and "cut off all government aid for drug users." When I pointed out how such a policy would come back to haunt him, he thought about it for a moment and said, "You're right. I guess it would. Maybe that's not such a good idea." Sometime after Atwater told me that he had never liked to work and had worked only ten years altogether in his life, he said, "I don't feel

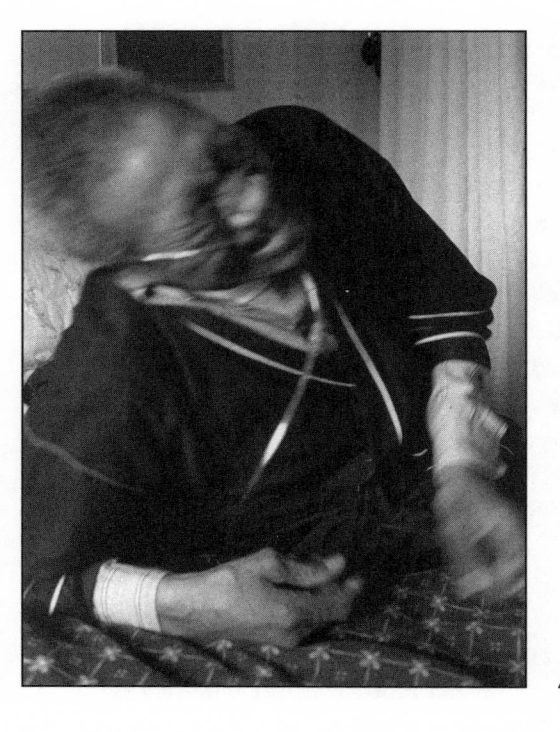

Atwater laughing

guilty taking Social Security money. I worked hard for many years and made my contribution." When I reminded him of his previous account of his work life, he said, "Yeah, but I made a contribution when I *did* work. Besides, we never got those forty acres and a mule."

Atwater could not only entertain inconsistent thoughts, he could put them in adjacent sentences. Speaking of his son, he said, "I have no animosity toward Chris, none at all. But I won't talk to him until he apologizes for putting me out." Of the effects of the moral lessons he received as a boy: "My daddy beat my ass for stealing, and so I never stole again. Well, a few things. But I was never a thief." Elaborating on the latter theme, he said, "I'd go into a store and eat stuff, but not steal. If I got caught, I was always willing to work it off by sweeping up or whatever." My favorites were the most succinct: "It wasn't the real me that done all that bad shit years ago; it's just what I chose to do"; "I get into trouble because I can't say no to people and because I only do what I want to do"; and "I don't believe in roots; I'm scared to fuck with that shit."

These things he said actually made sense, within Atwater's system of logic. If he was not angry at someone at the moment he was speaking, then he could honestly say that he felt no animosity toward that person. If he didn't make a living as a thief, then he wasn't a thief, because "thief" was an occupational identity. If he worked off the value of some purloined fruit or lunch meat, then it wasn't stealing, because stealing meant getting away with the goods. If his true self was good at the core, then a few bad choices did not make him a bad person. He did get into trouble, sometimes, for not saying no to people and, sometimes, for doing what he wanted to do. As for roots and conjuring, what he didn't believe in was messing with stuff that could, if it took hold of one's mind, produce nasty effects.

Where Atwater truly tangled himself up was in the rhetoric of responsibility. At times, he claimed to have courted his own fate. "I drank because I chose to drink. I smoked because I chose to smoke. Whatever came into my mind that was gonna make me happy, I did it. Now all those chickens have come home to roost in my life. I got nobody to blame for my circumstances but me." Other times his troubles were everyone else's fault: his mother, his ex-wife, his estranged sons, the corrupt and racist bosses he worked for, greedy nursing home operators, whitey. What struck me was that his rhetoric was polar; his troubles were, alternatingly, either all his own doing or all the doing of others. He never seemed to arrive at a balanced assessment of the internal and external forces that had shaped the course of his life.

One time when Atwater was going on about how he had no one to blame but himself for the mess he'd made of his life, I interrupted and said that he often blamed other people. "That's true," he said. "My mother and my ex-wife twisted up my mind and put so much shit on me that I could never get myself straightened out. That's why I did what I did and been doing things my way all my life. I can't change shit about all that. I just have to accept it." Atwater could see that I was puzzled. "I don't mean to sound all mixed up about this, Mike," he said, apologetically. "I wish I could get it good and tight and explain it to you, but I'm mixed up about it myself. That's how come I ended up in South Wing so many times."

Atwater joked about his confusion, but there was a tinge of fear in his voice, as if he knew that being unable to get his self-understandings

"good and tight" meant that he was vulnerable to coming apart. The inner contradictions that created this vulnerability mirrored his outer world. He was a spoiled child with a sense of entitlement in a world that wasn't going to hand him anything. He wanted his family to be a place of harmony, as the Bible promised, yet he found advantage in exploiting conflict between his parents. He had been told he was smart and could be anything he wanted to be, even an engineer, yet he knew that his chances did not equal those of white kids who were less smart.

Atwater learned that he should be a man. At the sawmill, as a boy eager to cut his mother's apron strings, he learned a working-class masculinity that emphasized drinking, gambling, fighting, and chasing women. Atwater learned well and was rewarded for his performance. Even so, he knew he had the potential to do more, to be a different kind of man than his father. But how could he realize that potential without the head-scratching that he was loath to do? He never found a way. It was easier to be Shine—easier, except that Atwater would forever carry inside him the contradiction between the man he knew he could be and wanted to be and the only kind of man he thought the world would let him be.

home again

Fannie was cooking sausage for breakfast. A headache came on suddenly, bringing with it a wave of nausea. She felt woozy and weak, and made her way to the kitchen table to sit for a minute. Perhaps it was the flu, she thought. When the spell didn't pass and her vision blurred, her husband and children helped her to the car and took her to the hospital. The doctors, recognizing the symptoms of cerebral hemorrhage, were not hopeful. At noon the next day, July 7, 1963, Fannie Lou Strowd Mason died, having just seen her last child graduate from high school.

If Matthew Mason had been overwrought at times before Fannie's death, he was now at the edge of despair. He woke at night and cried out for her, and then, remembering that his wife was gone, he reached for the bottle of liquor on his bedside table. For months he was inconsolable, insisting that no one could understand his loss. And for all the late-night scoldings when he had come home drunk, for all the tension caused by Dr. Reet's dedication to the fraternity boys, she had been what he needed to come home to. What now, without her, was home?

About four months later, in Carthage, North Carolina, a man named George Thompson died of a heart attack. His widow, Martha, moved to Chapel Hill in January 1964 to live with her cousin Aggie and do domestic work. Martha was in her late forties, with a grown son from a previous marriage. Martha's cousin was a friend of Matthew Mason's daughter Gloria, who thought that Martha would make a good girlfriend for her father. She knew her father needed someone, or he would

surely drink himself to death in his misery. Martha, she found out, needed someone too.

The courtship got off to a shaky start. Gloria suggested that Papa pay a visit to Miss Martha after church. "And don't you stop for a drink first," she warned him. A still-handsome man in his early fifties, sporting his best Sunday clothes and a heart-melting smile, Matthew Mason made a generally favorable impression that day. But he had not precisely followed Gloria's advice, and when he turned to leave after introducing himself to Martha, he fell off the porch and into the hedges. As she helped him up, Martha wondered what she might be getting herself into.

Friends and family saw that it was a good match, and so Matthew and Martha found themselves being pushed together. "Let's give Mr. Mason a ride home," Martha's cousin said after church the next Sunday, "and you two can sit together in back." "When are you going to see Miss Martha again?" Gloria asked her father, nudging things along. Martha and Matthew understood each other's losses. They also shared a desire for companionship and for reestablishing their independence. Martha did not want to live with her cousin forever, and Matthew was ready to get out from under his daughter's roof.

"When he fell off the porch into the bushes," Martha recalled, "he was so embarrassed he said he weren't never coming back. But he did. I couldn't keep him away. He'd come to see me every day, walking down the railroad tracks whistling like a rooster. I thought for sure he'd get killed by a train." For his part, Matthew had decided that he didn't want to let anyone else get a chance to call on Martha. "If you see something you want," he said, explaining why he'd moved so quickly, "you gotta get it before someone else does."

As his sorrow eased, Matthew Mason again showed the warmth and good humor that had appealed to Fannie. Martha could see, too, that he was loyal and had a kind of stubbornness that might, under her influence, be turned into a resolve to get his life back together. He likewise knew that two could pull harder than one, and that as partners they could make a better life than either could alone. "He kept coming back to see me, so I figured I'd better marry him," Martha said. On August 4, 1964, she did.

It was the drinking that gave Martha pause. "We went to Salisbury on our honeymoon," she recounted, "and Matthew was so drunk he could barely stand up. I had to drive." Martha was a nondrinker ("I couldn't stand it; drinking made me swimmy-headed") and was determined to dry him out. "I prayed to the Lord to take the taste out of his mouth," she said. "I used to put notes in the church money basket asking the preacher to say a prayer for Matthew to quit drinking."

Under Martha's influence, Matthew eased up a bit, reducing his intake during the day. But still he drank hard when he was in his Dr. Reet persona with the boys. And after the honeymoon period was over and Martha's admonitions grew sterner, he reacted by raging at her the way he had raged at Fannie. He would not be bossed, not outside the fraternity house, and even there he had made himself largely unfit to be bossed.

Despite his long service and his place in local Phi Delt history, Matthew Mason still struggled to make ends meet. In 1964 the fraternity was paying him, as he recalled, about sixty-five dollars a week. The nights of cab driving and waiting tables were over, and so he joined Martha in doing domestic work in the afternoons after serving lunch at the fraternity house. "We were a *team*," Martha said. "We could clean a place up just as fast as you like, and then go do another one." With no children and two small incomes, things stabilized. Old debts were resolved, and Martha made sure that the rent and other bills were paid on time.

Martha's temperance lobbying had a modest effect, but still there were the binges, which several times led to seizures and trips to the emergency room. One time when Dr. Reet collapsed on the front lawn of the fraternity house, the panicked boys rushed him to the hospital, certain that he'd had a heart attack. He hadn't, as it turned out. But the doctors could see the trend and told Mr. Mason that if he didn't stop drinking and smoking, a heart attack or a stroke was likely. They gave him medicine to lower his blood pressure and advice to change his ways.

Matthew seemed to heed the wake-up call. He stopped drinking during the day, and with the boys and alums he invoked "doctor's orders" to fend off exhortations to imbibe. He also cut back to four days a week at the fraternity house and cleaned only on the first floor

(so he wouldn't have to lug the vacuum cleaner upstairs). By the late 1960s it was clear that Matthew Mason and Dr. Reet were winding down. "It was time," Matthew said, "to begin to take it easy and *cool it.*"

Yet he remained vulnerable. As Fannie had once been, Martha was now his only confidant, and if he wrangled with her, there was nowhere else to turn for support. There were also unresolved issues with Thomas, who had hoped to reconnect with his father, to close the gap that had grown between them in the time around Fannie's death. But now it seemed to Thomas that Martha treated him as an intruder, wanting Matthew all for herself. The tension between Thomas and Martha was obvious, but Matthew, caught in the middle, didn't know how to deal with it. The sudden death of his oldest son, John Lee, in December 1970, struck another blow.

In the time that I knew him, Mr. Mason always denied that he was a worrying man. "Worrying don't do no good, does it?" he would ask rhetorically. Usually I gave the congenial reply, allowing that worry itself was of little use. One time I asked how he made worry go away. The answer, without hesitation: "Liquor." And so, when worry and confusion weighed on him, Matthew Mason resorted again to the coping strategy he knew best.

It was as bad as before—drinking during the day, binges, rages, blackouts. This time Martha left him, fleeing to the cinderblock cottage they'd bought in Hamlet, warning him to stay away until he got himself together. It was 1972, and not long before Martha left they had moved into the apartment on South Roberson Street. When Dr. Reet didn't show up to work for several days, one of the boys stopped by to see if he was okay. The boy found him passed out, head down on the table, an empty quart bottle on the floor at his feet. Failing to rouse him, the boy carried Dr. Reet to the hospital.

Two days later, the doctors told Matthew Mason that he had not merely passed out but that he had been in an alcohol-induced coma. His brain, the doctors said, had nearly shut down under the burden of poison, and, if not for the young man who brought him to the hospital, he might have died. Now, as he approached his sixty-first birthday, the second wake-up call sank in. He called Martha and told her that he was going to quit drinking. She'd heard that before, but this time seemed

different. "There was something in his voice that told me I could believe him," Martha said.

When Matthew came to see her in Hamlet, to try to make amends, Martha took him to church. "I put a note in the basket and asked the preacher to pray over Matthew. He did too. It was Reverend Asbury from Albermarle. Matthew went up to the front of the church and the preacher prayed over him. He didn't drink no more after that."

"Just quit," was Mr. Mason's version of the story. Was it hard? "Yeah, it was hard, but you know, I weren't no alcoholic." No? "No. I drank a lot of liquor—a *lot* of liquor—but an *alcoholic*, that's someone who drinks on the street and ain't got no job and no home. I wasn't *never* like that." And you quit because you didn't want to end up like that? "That's right." And because you had Martha and other people you cared about and who cared about you? "Yeah, that's right. You said it exactly right."

The fraternity brothers, once they realized that Dr. Reet was serious about going dry, and why he had to, supported him. A few who didn't know better—those who returned for a ballgame or reunion and felt nostalgic for an alcoholically animated Dr. Reet—urged him to drink. But he held fast, and other brothers backed him up.

Matthew Mason never got to the point of not caring whether he lived or died. Drinking had been about easing pain and having a good time, and when the opposite results were no longer deniable, he quit. It was crucial that he had the support of people who liked him sober and wanted him to stay that way. On the other hand, "just quit" was not a lie. "That's how he did it," Thomas said. "Same thing with smoking. One day he decided to quit, and that was it."

In the fall of 1972 Mr. Mason retired more fully, limiting his work to playing host at the fraternity house during special events. He stayed in close touch with the boys, eating dinner at the house two nights a week and helping with pledge training every fall. The boys still visited Dr. Reet often, and made sure that all new pledges got to hear the old jokes and stories. Every year on his birthday, the boys would take Dr. Reet out for dinner and spend hours tapping his memory.

In June 1996, while Mr. Mason was out having his birthday dinner with the boys, Martha suffered a mild stroke. The main consequence

was a loss of some control over her legs. Before the stroke, she had been spry by comparison to her husband. Now she struggled to get around with a cane. She refused to use a walker.

In the two weeks before Christmas in 1996, Martha fell three times. Each time, Mr. Mason called the rescue squad to get Martha off the floor and to the hospital. Luckily, she broke no bones, though the third fall left one arm badly bruised. When I saw the Masons on December 20, Martha said she was feeling better, that her strength was returning. I was skeptical as I watched her rock back and forth in her recliner, trying to build enough momentum to stand.

The fraternity boys had brought the Masons a Christmas tree, a perfectly conical fir about seven feet tall. Suited to a bigger house, the tree took up nearly a fourth of the Mason's living room, making it impossible to get to the sofa. The tree was conspicuously naked, as if it had grown up through the floor and had no particular reason for being there. "The boys said they'd come back and decorate it for us," Martha told me.

At 4:00 P.M. on December 24, Sherryl and I went to see the Masons. I'd found an ornament I thought Mr. Mason would appreciate: a tiny wooden rocking chair, which I intended to say was symbolic of his state of retirement. The apartment was dark and no one answered the door. Peering between the gap in the blinds, I could see that the tree remained undecorated, save for one string of lights. Where were the Masons?

I saw that Rosetta Barbee's inside door was open. Rosetta lived in the next apartment over. Although she was only two years younger than Matthew, she got around much better ("I had to quit climbing trees when I was seventy-five," she once told me) and did what she could to look out for the Masons.

Rosetta told me that Martha had fallen again and that the rescue squad had taken the Masons to the emergency room about an hour earlier. We talked about how Martha seemed to be getting weaker. I showed her the ornament I'd brought to put on the Masons' Christmas tree. "Those boys never came back to decorate the tree," she said, then leaned out the door and spit a stream of tobacco juice into a dormant flower patch. Rosetta was Atwater's aunt.

Thomas was pacing in front of the emergency room entrance when we got there. I asked what the situation was. He raised his eyebrows

and shook his head. "I told Papa it can't go on this way—calling the rescue squad every other day," he said. "These aren't real emergencies, and at some point the rescue squad is not going to come. Then what are they going to do? Rosetta is old herself. She can't take care of them." Thomas said his father got angry if the possibility of placing Martha in a nursing home was even mentioned.

I'd hoped to see Mr. Mason on Christmas Eve, but, under the circumstances, it didn't seem that there was much chance for a pleasant visit. I told Thomas to tell his father that we'd been there and that I'd check in again tomorrow. "If you'd like to see him, I can sneak you in," he said. It didn't require much sneaking; we just walked in with Thomas. Mr. Mason sat in a wheelchair in one of the curtained emergency room cubicles. Martha was off being x-rayed.

Mr. Mason, not expecting visitors, didn't recognize us at first. When he did, his usual cordial greeting lasted only a moment before Martha's plight refilled his mind. "I'm eighty-five years old," he said, urgently, "and I'm not gonna let 'em take my wife to no nursing home. My mother died in a nursing home. They didn't take care of her there, and we had to go and clean her up. Do you follow me?" His eyes were wide and watery, as he pleaded for our understanding. I'd never seen him so upset.

I had nothing to offer but platitudes: better to wait and see how Martha's doing before deciding what comes next; yes, it might be hard to make a decision, but you and Thomas will figure out what's best for Martha; no, we won't let Martha be neglected in a nursing home; we'll keep an eye on her. I felt awkward saying these things, knowing that it was Thomas, not me, who had to deal with the situation, make decisions, and live with the consequences.

Mr. Mason continued his plea. "If we *have* to go to a nursing home, I will," he said. "But I don't *want* to. We can stay where we are right now, if we can get some help." Thomas reiterated the point that they couldn't keep calling the rescue squad and coming to the emergency room. "Now that's not right, is it?" Mr. Mason said, trying to enlist us on his side of the argument. "They're *supposed* to come and help if you call." Thomas sighed and stepped outside the cubicle.

It turned out that Martha was okay, or at least she hadn't broken anything. A hospital social worker was going to arrange for the Masons

Mason alone in
apartment

to get a temporary health aide and to receive lunches from meals-on-wheels. Martha resigned herself to using a walker.

When I visited the Masons on December 27, the fir tree was on the ground outside their apartment. Martha told me that the fraternity boys had come by yesterday—too late, as far as she was concerned—to decorate it. Though Martha was steadier using the walker, she was not getting around well. Two days later she woke up feeling weak and disoriented, and, fearing another fall, went back to the hospital.

On January 3 Martha was still in the hospital and Mr. Mason was home alone. I noticed for the first time how he was daunted by simple tasks. He too had to rock in his chair to build enough momentum to stand. When the phone rang, he couldn't see which button to push to activate the handset, and he cut off the caller by mistake. He couldn't make the remote control work until I turned the device in his hand,

aiming it at the TV instead of his belly. Despite everything, he was, it seemed, in good spirits.

Five days later Martha was discharged to a nursing home. It was never clear whether her problems were caused by damage from the first stroke, subsequent mild strokes, or by the medicines she was taking. It was clear, however, that without daily physical therapy, she would lose any chance of staying in the apartment. Thomas was not hopeful; he thought it likely that after a few weeks of therapy Martha would still need long-term care and that, at best, it would be possible for her and Papa to share a room in a decent facility. Things turned out differently.

Martha was asleep when I brought the fish sandwiches. It looked as if she'd been sitting on the edge of the bed one minute and then tipped over sideways and passed out. Her feet were still on the floor. Mr. Mason sat next to her in a wheelchair. He knew that someone had entered the room, but he didn't know it was me until I said hello. "Martha's asleep, Brother Mike," he said. "She was up and around earlier, then she fell asleep about, oh, thirty minutes ago."

We talked softly while Martha slept. He had taken the EZ Rider to the nursing home at noon, and planned to stay until 4:00. As usual, I'd drive him home. Martha woke and slowly pushed herself upright.

She was drooling and seemed dazed. "Brother Mike brought you a fish sandwich," Mr. Mason said. Martha managed a brief smile that looked as if it required a lot of energy and concentration. If she was getting better, after two weeks in the nursing home, it was not obvious. She sat with her arms out at each side, like support struts; her head sagged. "I need to use the bathroom," she said, and I went to fetch an aide. When I returned, Martha told the aide that she didn't need to use the bathroom.

Two well-scrubbed Mormon boys in white shirts and black ties came in and asked Martha if she would like to join in some singing. She looked at them, then at Matthew, then at me, not comprehending. They asked her again and she said nothing. "*Singing*, Miss Martha. Would you like to join in some *singing*?" the aide said, trying to force the question through the fog in Martha's head. "Thank you, but she doesn't want to," Mr. Mason said, and the boys and the aide left.

Martha perked up long enough to eat part of her sandwich, then keeled over again. Before she could fall asleep, Mr. Mason pulled up close to the bed and took her hand. "You're already sweet, Sugar. Now you *stay* sweet till I see you again, you understand?" he said. She mustered another faint smile and then her eyelids drooped. "I reckon we might as well go now," Mr. Mason said, and I wheeled him out, sandwich bag in his lap.

On the way out we passed the activity room. A middle-aged white man played "As the Saints Go Marching In" on the piano. Six people, four black and two white, sat in wheelchairs in a semi-circle around him. A few bobbed their heads in time with the music. Only the two Mormon boys were singing.

As I drove him home, I asked Mr. Mason if he'd thought more about moving into the nursing home with Martha. He said he'd decided to stay in the apartment and keep visiting her, as long as he could rely on the EZ Rider, cabs, Thomas, and me for transportation. I asked if he knew what they were doing for Martha at the nursing home. "They help her walk," he said. Beyond that, he wasn't sure. No one, as far as he could recall, had talked to him or Martha about the treatment she was receiving.

Martha was not happy. She hated the food, especially the Ensure they brought with every meal. The facility didn't provide comfortable diapers. It always took too long for an aide to come when she buzzed (the quickest response I observed was fifteen minutes, the longest, forty-five minutes). And on one occasion Martha was outraged because an aide tied her into bed to keep her from getting up at night and falling on her way to the bathroom.

Mr. Mason knew that Martha needed to be where she was, and that being there was no fun. He was determined, though, to make sure that Martha suffered as little as possible. If no one responded to Martha's buzz, he wheeled down the hall and pestered whomever he found at the nurses' station. His complaint about Martha being tied into bed got the practice stopped and the aide reprimanded.

Five weeks into her stay, there was no visible improvement. Martha experienced swelling in her legs, recurrent diarrhea, and periods of disorientation. Mr. Mason always told Martha that she was "looking better," but in the car on the way home he was less sanguine. Do you

really think she's getting better? "No, Martha's still not right," he said. But do you think she's getting *better*? "Not so's I can tell." I said that I didn't see any improvement either but that maybe it would just take a little longer.

The following week I was surprised to find Martha sitting up in a wheelchair, wearing a dress, her hair freshly braided. She was alert and lucid as she plucked one chocolate chip cookie after another out of a box that someone else must have brought her. I said she looked a lot like her old self. "This is the best I've felt since I've been here," she said. When the physical therapist came to walk her up and down the hall, she was eager to go. On the way home that day, we both agreed that Martha really did look better. "We sure are lucky folks," Mr. Mason said.

A few days later, Martha was trying to make her way to the bathroom in the middle of the night. About halfway there her legs gave out. As her eighty-year-old roommate told me, "You get out of bed and you're half asleep and you forget that your legs don't work like they used to, and down you go." The fall cracked Martha's femur. She was going to need surgery to pin the bone.

I was in Martha's room at the hospital when a nurse explained to Mr. Mason the nature of Martha's injury and the need for surgery. He sat in a wheelchair, looking intently at the nurse as she spoke. When she finished, Mr. Mason turned to me and said, "Did you get all that, Brother Mike?" The nurse then asked Mr. Mason to sign the permission form for the surgery. He said he didn't know what she meant. "I already signed it," Martha hollered from the bed.

After the surgery Martha returned to the nursing home. The pain made her irritable and the painkillers made her groggy. More than ever she wanted to be well and go home. "When I get out of here, I just pray I never have to come back," she said. By mid-April she was back on the upswing she'd been on before the fall.

As people moved into and out of the facility, Martha had a series of roommates. The third was a white woman in her mid-nineties. The first time I saw this woman, she was treating the Masons to a mean-spirited diatribe against people who didn't pay their rent on time, or who cohabited without marrying, or who received public aid. I sensed that, in another place, she would have added that a lot of the people of

whom she didn't approve were black. Martha introduced me as a professor at the university. "He brings me chicken nuggets and whatever else I need," Martha said. "He's writing a book on me," Mr. Mason said. The old woman didn't seem to know what to make of this and, blessedly, shut up. By the next week she was gone.

By the end of April 1997, Martha had improved considerably. She'd regained much of her strength and was now consistently clearheaded. She talked seriously about going home. Mr. Mason always encouraged her but privately told me that he worried about Martha coming home and falling again. I tried to assure him that they wouldn't discharge Martha until she was ready. "I s'pose that's right" is all he said.

The next time I saw Martha she was beaming. "I went *home* this morning!" she declared. She'd been accompanied by a social worker who evaluated the apartment and Martha's ability to navigate it. The verdict was favorable. With a few adjustments—an entry ramp, railings in the bathroom, a chair with higher arms—Martha could manage. The social worker would also arrange for the Masons to get a health aide five days a week. In mid-May Martha went home.

The aide cooked, cleaned, helped with bathing, steadied Martha when she walked, and occasionally picked up groceries. Despite the social worker's judgment that Martha could get around in the apartment, it seemed to me that, without the aide, the Masons could not have stayed there much longer. "We's *both* feeble now" was Martha's summary of the situation.

Before Martha's stay in the nursing home, the Masons didn't watch much TV. The set was rarely on when I visited. But in the nursing home Martha had gotten in the habit of watching the afternoon soap operas. She seemed to believe that what she was seeing was real. One time a plane crash on a soap coincided with the crash of a real plane, and Martha told me that the crash—on *The Guiding Light*—had been reported on the six o'clock news. What she then could not figure out was why the people on the show didn't know where Reva had crashed. Didn't they watch the news?

Mr. Mason ignored the soaps. He did side with me, though, on the occasion when I tried to explain that the shows were written and

acted. His discreet wink said that if Martha enjoyed believing in what she was seeing, we ought to leave it at that.

Things stabilized for the Masons throughout the fall of 1997 and the spring of 1998. No new health problems arose. The aides did chores around the apartment and made occasional grocery runs, as did Thomas and I. Thomas also deposited Social Security checks and paid bills. When I would ask Mr. Mason how he was doing, his standard reply was, "Pretty good. Pretty good. No *better* than that. And no *worse*, neither."

Other than for medical checkups, the Masons rarely went out. Martha had recovered sufficiently to *want* to go out. "These walls feel like they's closing in on me," Martha had once said, bemoaning the loss of mobility she and Matthew had enjoyed when they were younger. "We used to go all over," she said. "Matthew was a *driving* man!" But now Mr. Mason, who had only months before left the apartment every day to see Martha at the nursing home, did not want to go out at all.

In September, when Martha wanted to attend a small celebration for people in the apartment complex who had birthdays that month, Mr. Mason discouraged her. He said that she was not yet well and that he didn't want to listen to her whine later if she came home feeling sick and tired. He was right about Martha not being fully recovered, and I sympathized with his wish to avoid listening to Martha's complaints if she wore herself out at a party. Still, I was surprised at how strongly he resisted her going out, even for a little while. If anyone appreciated sociability, it was Mr. Mason.

The following spring Martha wanted to go to K & W Cafeteria for lunch on Mother's Day. She was by then easily able to handle such an outing. But Mr. Mason refused. When Martha brought up the issue while I was there, Mr. Mason told me that while he'd *like* to take Martha out, he couldn't do it because he had a heart condition and had been advised by his doctor to get lots of rest. Martha scoffed at the "heart condition" excuse—I didn't buy it either—and made the empty threat to take a cab and go by herself.

Because it happened gradually, it was hard to see the decline that made Mr. Mason reluctant to leave the apartment. His worsening cataracts had nearly blinded him. He refused to wear the hearing aid he needed (too uncomfortable, he said), and so he often had to ask people

to repeat themselves. His shuffle had further slowed and become more labored. And while it became more pronounced later, he was beginning to suffer from the dementia that led him to get badly disoriented—"turned around," as he and Martha called it—when he was not on familiar ground.

It helped that some services came right to their door. For years "the vegetable man," as he was locally known, brought a miniature farmer's market to the parking lot of the apartment complex. Every week during the growing season he sold apples, strawberries, sweet peas, potatoes, cabbage, collards, country ham, and side meat out of the back of his old pickup truck. One day I bought Martha two pounds of potatoes and two pounds of streak-o-lean for $5.50. The vegetable man threw in a few apples for free.

Insurance agents made monthly rounds to collect payments. Martha was at a doctor's appointment one afternoon when a life insurance agent came by. He was a tall, thin white man whose accent suggested Appalachian origins. At first glance, I was suspicious, but when he announced himself at the door, Mr. Mason immediately recognized him—or, rather, his voice—and invited him in.

Mr. Mason introduced me. "This here's Brother Mike," Mr. Mason said to the agent. "And pardon me, but I forget your name. I can't remember things like I used to." The agent said his name and we shook hands. "Is he a friend?" the agent asked Mr. Mason. "Oh, yeah. We been knowing Brother Mike a long time. He's a real nice man." The agent seemed relieved as he pumped my hand one last time and then fetched a chair from the dining area. "In that case, I guess we can do our business in the usual way," he said, pulling the chair up next to Mr. Mason.

The agent took a three-ring binder out of his briefcase and flipped through the pages. "Your payment this month is $83.99, Mr. Mason," the agent said. He then leaned over and plucked a box of checks out of a pile of bills, letters, and other papers that were stacked on the lower shelf of a small end table. Obviously he'd done this before. He tore off the top check and filled in the amount. No wonder he had qualms about my witnessing business as usual.

"I'll need you to sign this, Mr. Mason," he said. The agent put the check on top of his binder and set the binder in Mr. Mason's lap. He put

a pen into Mr. Mason's right hand. "Martha usually signs the checks," the agent said to me.

"It's gonna be a mess," Mr. Mason said, hesitating.

"That's okay, Mr. Mason. Just make your mark."

"What's that?"

"Just make your mark. As long as it's your hand, it's okay." The agent positioned Mr. Mason's hand above the check. "Start writing where your thumb is," the agent said. Mr. Mason made a squiggle that slashed diagonally across the signature line. "That's fine, Mr. Mason," the agent said, taking the check and the pen.

The episode with the insurance agent underscored for me the Masons' vulnerability. The Masons tended to be trusting and generous, and since they often had to rely on others for help, they could have been exploited by hucksters. If I hadn't been present, the insurance agent could have written in any figure he chose on Mr. Mason's check. As it was, we had to trust that $83.99 was correct.

Martha's apparent belief in the reality of soap operas coincided with other forms of misplaced belief. One time she answered the phone and heard a telemarketer ask, "Is this Mrs. Mason? How are you today?" Martha took the question as genuine and began to explain how she and Matthew were doing, including a detailed list of physical symptoms. When Martha paused and asked the telemarketer how she was doing, the poor woman barely slipped in a "fine, thank you" before Martha started again, this time reporting on her son's health. After a few minutes the telemarketer hung up. Martha looked at the silent handset with surprise. "I guess that woman don't want to talk," she said.

Religious books were often distributed free in the Masons' neighborhood (such books never showed up in our mailbox). "Isn't it nice they give us this for free? It's a *good* book, too. I read it cover to cover," Martha said one time, handing me a pulp paperback that explained how to obtain God's healing mercy through prayer. Martha had already filled out the order form at the back of the book. She was going to send for two more books in the series, at a cost of only a few dollars each. The form included a space for ordering prayers to be said for a sick loved one. Later, when Matthew came down with pneumonia, Martha bought prayers.

Dealing with bureaucracies could also be a trial. More than once I heard Martha try to reach a nurse or doctor to ask about her medication, or about Matthew, or about an upcoming appointment. Such calls often ended in frustration, as Martha either failed to reach anyone who could help, failed to ask her question in an understandable way, or failed to get a clear answer. Several times I took the phone and was able to get an answer, either by going up the administrative ladder or pressing for clarification.

Even after she had largely recovered from her stroke, Martha struggled to get out of her chair. It made me nervous to watch her shaky transition from sitting to standing to leaning on her walker. A neighbor recommended getting a lift chair, one that would bring Martha nearly to a standing position. This was a fine idea, except that a motorized lift chair, at about $600, was beyond the Masons' budget. When Martha heard that a display model was on sale at Wal-Mart for $350, she took that amount out of savings and asked me to buy the chair for her.

The sales clerk told me that Medicare might reimburse for the chair (I'd said it was for my grandmother) if a doctor deemed it medically necessary. As the clerk handed me a set of forms to fill out for reimbursement, she said, "It's probably a waste of time. They rarely pay for these chairs, and if they do, it's usually only part of the cost. They'll reject it if anything isn't filled out, and the doctor really has to emphasize that it's a necessity." I shared the clerk's pessimism as I looked at the forms. They reminded me of closing on a house.

I filled out the forms neatly and completely, following the instructions to the letter. Before I took the forms to the Masons' doctor, I attached a memo indicating the parts he needed to fill out and how they should be filled out. I followed-up with a phone call to make sure he'd sent them in. Four weeks later Martha received a check for nearly the full cost of the chair. I was glad the effort paid off, and the Masons were happy too. But I wondered about all the people who looked at those forms and gave up or who made some small, disqualifying error. Should it take a Ph.D. to deal with this system?

It wasn't that the Masons lacked all savvy when it came to dealing with medical and social service bureaucracies. The Masons had, in fact, been dealing with such bureaucracies for a long time and had developed

strategies for doing so. Mr. Mason's affability and tenacity served him well if he could plead his case (or Martha's) in person. And Martha, for her part, was certainly willing to get on the phone to complain or ask questions. But if detailed explanation or questioning was required, especially in writing, the Masons were seriously disadvantaged.

In mid-May of 1998 Martha began to have pains in her side and lower back. The pain was severe and persistent enough to keep her from sleeping. On a Friday afternoon she told me she'd been leaving messages for her doctor at UNC since Monday, asking him to call her. His call came before I left, and I heard Martha describe the pain in her side and back. "It's been hurting right terrible all week," she said, then asked to see him on Monday. When the doctor said he couldn't see her until the following week, Martha looked scared. Matthew coached from his adjacent chair: "Tell him that you want to see him on Monday, or you'll go to another doctor." Martha tried that and got nowhere. In desperation, she handed the phone to Matthew and said, "You talk to him."

Mr. Mason reiterated Martha's account of her pain. "My wife's been hurting all *week*," he said, "and she can't wait *another* week to see a doctor. That ain't right, is it?" Finally, the doctor said that Martha should come to the urgent care office on Monday at 10:30 A.M. and ask to have him paged. He'd try to get down there to see her if he could. For this, Mr. Mason thanked him several times before saying good-bye.

Mr. Mason had used the same strategy in the nursing home when he felt that Martha was being neglected. His sincere and unerring invocation of "what ain't right" often got him the help he needed. Mr. Mason pleaded from a position of weakness, but his rhetoric was strong and often worked, if it reached an audience with any compassion. And even if this rhetoric failed, as it sometimes did, it must have left a mark, I thought, on the conscience of anyone who chose to ignore it.

The doctor saw Martha on Monday. He thought her pain might be caused by a torn abdominal muscle. For this he prescribed Tylenol or coated aspirin. He also thought that the pain might be caused by heartburn. For this he prescribed an antacid and told Martha to eat smaller meals. Later that week Martha told me that her pain had subsided, though it didn't seem to be going away. She kept taking aspirin, which at least allowed her to sleep.

As Martha recounted the story of her visit to the doctor, Mr. Mason's head sagged and he began to doze in his chair. It was the first time he'd done it while I was visiting. Before, he'd always been alert and engaged when I came over. Now, as he neared his eighty-seventh birthday, he began to look like the tired old man he joked about being. "It looks like Matthew has drifted off," I said, interrupting Martha. "He does that all the time now," she said. At that, Mr. Mason's eyes popped open and he said, "Who? *Me?*"

That June, when Mr. Mason turned eighty-seven, the young fraternity boys did not take him to dinner for his birthday. He told me that he didn't want to go out and leave Martha alone. Martha told me that the boys had forgotten.

On days when his energy was high, Mr. Mason's wit and good humor belied his physical decline. He could always be made to laugh about *something*, and often he initiated a kind of banter that I imagined had served him well in the fraternity house. One day I brought him a bag of Hershey's Kisses (he loved chocolate) and a new pair of suspenders to replace the pair on which a snap had broken. Normally this would have elicited profuse thanks. But this time Mr. Mason seemed subdued, almost disappointed. I asked if anything was wrong.

"Well, Brother Mike," he said, looking sadly at the suspenders, "I was *hoping* you'd bring me a pint of liquor."

"A pint of *liquor?*" He'd caught me by surprise, and his act was so good that for a moment I thought he was serious.

"Or a gallon." Now I caught on.

"A *gallon?* But Mr. Mason, you told me you don't drink anymore."

"I don't?"

"No. No more toddies for your body. Not for a long time."

"A little toddy won't hurt nobody's body, but a lot of toddies will mess you up."

"That's right. So you didn't really want a pint of liquor, did you?"

"No, but I got to tell a lie *some*time, don't I?"

"But you told me that truth is the light of the world."

"It is. That's right."

"So how come you told a lie?"

"I got to stay in practice in case I need to tell one to Martha." Martha, who had been listening to all this, took her cue. "He can tell

all the lies he wants," she said, smiling, "but I always see the truth right on his face."

"Is that right, Mr. Mason?" I asked.

"I reckon it is, if Martha *says* it is." He managed to tweak us both, and I wished I could have seen him in his younger days.

A month later, when I was telling the Masons about my summer travel plans, which included driving to Wisconsin to see my family, Mr. Mason surprised me by saying, "Let's you and me go together. I need a break."

"You want to ride with me to Wisconsin?"

"Yeah, we'll get some liquor and pretty girls and let the good times roll."

"You think Martha would approve of that?" I asked.

"Makes no difference what Martha thinks, 'cause *she* ain't going with us."

"Maybe we should at least ask her before we leave."

Martha, who again had listened to the exchange, said, "You go," and turned back to the TV.

can't do like you used to

twater had it easy at Cat's. She fixed him small meals that he ate in his room on a folding TV table. He got at-home haircuts from an amateur barber who lived next door. He watched TV and slept irregular hours. As far as he needed to go from his room, on any regular basis, was two steps down the hall to the toilet. Atwater knew that for three hundred dollars a month it was a nice deal. "You talk about retired? I am into retired! These days I am the sitting-backest dude you ever saw in your life. I am enjoying it to death."

Occasionally an old friend would visit or call, but otherwise Atwater was cut off from sociability. Cable TV was his solace. "I'm addicted to that sucker," Atwater said. "I get to watching some old movie and I can't shut it off. Sometimes I watch it all night and sleep all morning." He especially liked history and nature shows. "I'm into a knowledge thing now, and that box is how I get it. I can't travel anymore because of my illness, but with this"—waving the remote control—"I can go any damn where I please, even under the ocean." His imagination, he said, compensated for the limits of traveling via television. "It's something about my mind. It's like everything I see on there is real to me. If I see a show about a storm in the desert, I have to wipe sand out of my eyes when it's over."

Atwater said he used to like to read, but that it had become too hard without prescription glasses. I bought him a small tape player and audio books I thought he might like: *The Autobiography of Malcolm X*

(Malcolm X with Alex Haley); *Oldest Living Confederate Widow Tells All* (Allan Gurganus); *Devil in a Blue Dress* (Walter Mosley); *A Red Death* (Walter Mosley); *White Butterfly* (Walter Mosley); *Downsize This!* (Michael Moore); *Black Boy* (Richard Wright). Of the latter, Atwater said, "That book was so damn true it made me cry." He didn't care for Michael Moore: "That's not much of a story—about how the government is run by rich white men and all fucked up. Ain't no news in that."

The strength of Atwater's addiction to tobacco continued to amaze me. I had told Atwater how my father, after a heart attack in 1993, had kept on smoking, though he was warned it would kill him. Atwater offered an interpretation. "How it is sometimes," he said, "is that you get to feeling that it would be more painful to quit than to die. It's like if you can't have one of the few pleasures you got left, then what's the point of living? Maybe that's how [your father] felt. That's how I feel sometimes, even though I know these suckers are killing me." The smoking issue had become even more loaded for me when my father, only a year older than Atwater, was diagnosed with lung cancer in the fall of 1996.

Atwater tried to cut down on the cigarettes. He asked Cat to ration him four a day, though he often wheedled extras. Several times he declared the cigarette in his hand to be his last—before taking a final drag and stubbing it out with a flourish. One time he sounded more serious than usual, and I grabbed my camera to record the moment. The next week I gave him a print. I said I was going to call it "Atwater's Last Cigarette," and that it was photographic proof that he'd quit smoking. He looked embarrassed. "If that's what you're gonna call it, you'll have to tear it up to keep it from lying," he said.

I tried to get Atwater out of the apartment for some air and a change of pace. Atwater had never seen a stage play and said he'd like to see one. Twice we made plans to go. Both times he canceled at the last minute, claiming to feel sick and offering profuse apologies. Later he admitted that he had not been sick but had feared running out of oxygen and, in a theater, not being able to get to the bathroom quickly enough. During his two years at Cat's, we had only two outings, one to the optometrist for glasses and one for ice cream.

Atwater with inhaler

Though quieter living eased the strain on Atwater's body, he wasn't exactly struggling to stave off decline. "I should get some exercise," he said. "Cat tries to get me out, but there's just nothing I feel like seeing or doing. My medication also makes me tired. So I sit here and watch TV and get weaker. The Bible says that young men have visions and old men have dreams. That's about all I got left is dreams. Dreams and TV. I'm too old for visions. That's hard to accept, old is. It sneaks up on you. One day you realize you can't do like you used to. And when you realize you can't even screw like you used to, then you feel old for damn sure."

In April 1998, Atwater began to complain of a roughness in his throat that made it hard to swallow pills. "My throat feels like a rusty old pipe," he said. He attributed the problem to smoking, to using his inhalers too often, and to a possible allergy to the medicine he used in the nebulizer. When the roughness persisted, be began to worry that

Atwater's last cigarette

maybe the laryngeal cancer had come back. Cat and I urged him to go the hospital and get it checked.

Atwater had never been shy about going to doctors, but this time he resisted our urging. When I pestered him about getting his throat checked, he said, "I hate to go to the doctor because it makes me feel like a fool to say, 'Doc, I smoked all my life and now my throat hurts, but I want you to fix me.'" Another time he said, "I have good days and bad days. On bad days I don't want to do anything, and on good days the last thing I want to do is go to the hospital."

By the end of May, when Atwater ate he had to take small bites, chew thoroughly, and wash each mouthful down with water. Cigarettes bothered his throat more and more. "I smoked as long as I got pleasure out of it, and now that I don't, I am done with them cocksuckers," he declared. When Atwater said this, I was skeptical, not only because of his history, but because there was a fresh pack on his TV table. He saw me glance at the pack. "I just keep that there to remind me that I quit," he said, invoking Atwater logic. When Atwater really did quit smoking, in June of 1998, I was worried.

On August 17 Atwater finally went to the ER to have his throat examined. The doctor who saw him suspected a tumor in Atwater's esophagus and scheduled a bronchoscopy for the following week. Before he went in to be scoped, Atwater told me, "I'm not exactly worried, but I am concerned about it being cancer. There's nothing I can do if it is. I don't believe in them cutting on old people. Anything in [my throat] will stay there. I'll go away with it. Surgery would just prolong the inevitable. When it's time to go, it's time to go. I just want some medicine for the pain." I couldn't tell if Atwater's fatalistic calm was genuine or a bluff.

The first bronchoscopy failed because they couldn't get the scope down Atwater's throat, so they scheduled another. This time they found a lump and took a piece for biopsy. The results were inconclusive, necessitating a replay of the whole procedure. A month after he'd first had his throat checked, the diagnosis was still uncertain. Atwater was suspicious of the repeated tests and unclear results. "People like us always get stuck with interns," he said, "and they like to diagnose stuff that isn't there, so they can practice on you." The sure thing was that Atwater's throat was closing and something had to be done.

At the end of September Atwater met with Dr. Jan Halle, an oncologist at UNC Hospital. She was going to give him the lowdown on his condition and recommend a course of treatment. Atwater asked me to come along.

Halle, a wiry, energetic white woman in her late thirties, was as unpretentious as the jeans she wore under her medical smock. She said the test results indicated cancer, which seemed to be confined to a marble-sized lump at the base of the throat. She recommended radiation combined with chemotherapy.

When Halle asked Atwater if he had any questions, he surprised me by saying, "Not really." Was he asking nothing because he was going to refuse treatment? Was there nothing else he wanted to know before making a decision? Moments passed and Atwater sat quietly, his usual garrulous self in hiding. Finally he looked at me and said, "Mike might have some questions." I thought maybe Atwater was overwhelmed and was passing me the ball. Halle turned to me.

I asked about radiation burns to the esophagus and what would happen if Atwater couldn't eat. She said it was possible that he would need a feeding tube through his stomach wall for a time. I asked about the possibility of scar tissue closing Atwater's throat and requiring endoscopy. She said that was a bridge to cross when and if one came to it, and hopefully we wouldn't. I asked about damage to the heart. She said that the lump was high enough that the heart would not be affected. I asked about necrosis because of Atwater's previous radiation treatment in the same area. She said that the area of overlap was small. I asked how Atwater's other conditions might affect his chances of survival. She acknowledged that he was a "high-risk patient" and had to be monitored with extra care.

Throughout this exchange, Atwater said nothing. When I had no more questions, we both turned back to Atwater. "It's true, Mr. Atwater," Halle said, "you're between a rock and a hard place. It's up to you how we proceed." She advised starting treatment the following week. Atwater promptly agreed.

Later I asked him why he had changed his mind about treatment. "If they said it had spread, I wouldn't let them do it. But they said it was just in my throat. The chemo doc said the treatment probably wouldn't cure the cancer. It could come back in six months and then there'd be nothing to do. So for now I'm just gonna let happen whatever is gonna happen and deal with it." If that answer made anything clear, it was only that Atwater wanted to live, more so than he let on. As Cat had said a few weeks earlier, "Popcorn talks tough, like he doesn't care if it's cancer and he's gonna let it take him. He talks that way, but really, Mike, he's scared and he doesn't want to admit it, to you or to himself."

The next week, Atwater was scanned, tattooed, and fitted with a piece of headgear to hold him still during radiation treatments ("it feels like I got a damn octopus on my face"). Depending on how fast the tumor shrank, he'd get four to six weeks of treatments, five days a week. He'd also get seven days of orally administered chemo at the beginning of his radiation and another seven days at the end. The process began in the second week of October.

Nausea from the chemo and soreness from the radiation made it hard for Atwater to eat. In two weeks he lost six pounds, and Halle

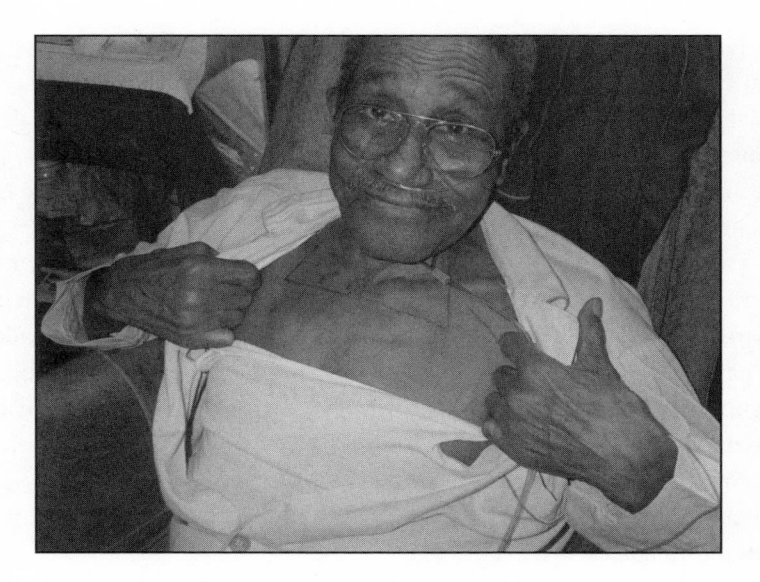

Atwater with radiation tattoos

ordered insertion of a g-tube—a direct pipeline from the outside world to Atwater's stomach. This required minor surgery and a few days in the hospital. "It's really no big deal," explained a chirpy nurse when I visited Atwater after the surgery. "It's very convenient. You can use it to inject nutrients and medication, or to drain." I almost wanted one myself. Atwater told her I was a professor and was writing a book about him. "Oh, and are you a special person, Mr. Atwater?" she chirped. "Yeah," he said, giving her the Atwater grin, "I'm tight with Colin Powell."

After she left, Atwater said he felt discouraged, even though Halle had said he was doing well. "I don't know, Mike, if I had known it would come to this"—he looked down at the tube—"I might not have gone for it. I'd rather have six months where I can eat and taste a steak than to have two years where they feed me through a tube." I pointed out that he hadn't lost his zest for talking trash with the nurses. "Now that's one reason I ain't ready to go away from here. It's wall-to-wall beaver in this place, like to drive a man crazy! When I don't care about that, you can pull the damn plug."

The plan was for Atwater to be discharged to Cat's care. She would learn how to feed him through the tube and how to clean it. Cat was leery about taking this on. She was already strained by weeks of daily trips to and from the hospital for Atwater's radiation. Atwater was strained too, of course, and he showed it by getting surly with Cat. She was tired of it.

There were other sources of tension. In mid-August, Cat; her husband, Sam; and Atwater had moved from South Roxboro to a nicer apartment. The new place was more expensive, and Atwater balked at paying more rent and a share of the moving expenses. He and Cat argued. He insulted her, and she would have put him out then, if not for the cancer diagnosis. The prospect of managing a feeding tube and cleaning up after Atwater when his liquid diet ran through him was too much. Cat said he should ask the hospital social workers to find him a different place to live.

And so Atwater stayed in the hospital for the duration of his treatment, while social workers tried to figure out where to put him afterwards. Since there was no suitable family placement ("I wouldn't live with anybody in my family nohow; they always try to dictate my shit"), and independent living was out of the question ("I know and they know that if I went back to an apartment I'd be dead in a month"), plans were made for Atwater to go to a nursing home. Atwater said he'd try the place for a month, let himself be taken care of while he recovered, and then decide whether or not to stay.

As it happened, the feeding tube fell out one night while Atwater was still in the hospital. His stomach wall healed so fast that the doctors decided against another surgery to reinstall the tube. Atwater happily went back to eating in small bites, chewing thoroughly, and washing everything down with lots of water.

In the third week of November Atwater received his last doses of radiation and chemo. Both treatments did what they were supposed to. The tumor withered under the onslaught, and Atwater had suffered minimal side effects in the process. His throat was sore and his tongue was swollen and he had some lingering nausea, but he was, in other regards and considering what he'd been through, doing well. Halle described Atwater's bodily resilience as "remarkable."

On November 25, 1998, Atwater was discharged to the nursing home. He was resting in bed when I saw him there a few days later. The last dose of chemo had left his mouth too sore for him to wear his dentures, and so he looked older than usual. "I'm in a junkpile now," he said, "where they throw things away." I thought Atwater's characterization of the place was apt, but I said he was the survivingest piece of junk I'd ever seen. He laughed at the Atwaterism and said, "Yeah, I spit out two cancers in the throat, and I ain't going away from here just yet. Maybe the Lord's keeping me around for a reason."

When I saw Atwater the next week, he was dressed and moving around his room, his oxygen tube draped over the back of a chair instead of the back of his ears. "I don't know what it is, Mike," he said, "but I feel so good it scares me. Maybe that radiation unclogged my breathing pipes."

At this point Atwater had been through two bouts with cancer, enduring two regimes of radiation and one of chemo. This on top of emphysema. Now he was looking, if not spry, at least rested and healed. When I saw him moving around his room, my father's final, bedridden days came to mind, and my amazement at Atwater's durability was, I realized, tinged with resentment. Eight months earlier, a week before Atwater told me that his throat felt like a rusty old pipe, my father, with family life still intact around him, had died of lung cancer.

With his admission to the nursing home, Atwater's life changed again. He had led a more solitary existence at Cat's place. Now he had a busy social world around him. It gave him a new set of people and problems to deal with. It also gave him resources with which to create problems.

For a while Atwater vacillated about his new location. One week he said, "This is a place for sick and old-ass people. I'd like to get out of here into a home-like atmosphere where people are more able to do for themselves." He also complained about the cheap bed linen (he had his cousin Lena bring him nicer sheets) and about his clothes being laundered along with those of people who had skin rashes. When I asked him if he went to any of the facility's social activities, he said, "I went to one thing they had going. It was six old white ladies making pizza. Now what the hell am I going to talk to them about?"

Several times he said he wanted to get out of the place as soon as he had his strength back and had saved a little money.

A week later he would sound satisfied and resigned. "I'm liking it here, Mike. I'm old now myself. This is my time to be here. It's about the best I can do. I can accept it, as long as they do what they're supposed to do and take care of me. This is my forty acres and a mule." As unpleasant as I found the place, I had to agree that it was about the best Atwater could do. I couldn't imagine him lasting long on his own or back in the company of the young women who knew him as Popcorn.

One thing that inclined Atwater to accept his situation was the chance it gave him to be Popcorn again. A few of the aides were women whom Atwater knew from his apartment days. Most were from low-income backgrounds and had little formal education. They were the audience that Atwater, as Popcorn, could impress. Before long, he was reporting on his sexual exploits. "The going rate in here is twenty dollars for head," he told me. "I got enough money to live like Bill Clinton—I won't have no 'sexual relationships,' but I'll get what I want." The aides were vulnerable not only to Atwater's charm but also, because of their low wages, to his money. He not only paid for services rendered, he made loans.

Atwater was not supposed to have extra money. Because of his low-income and lack of financial resources, Medicare paid the tab for Atwater's stay during his first twenty days in the nursing home. Later, Medicaid would pick up the bulk of the bill—all but a portion equal to the monthly income Atwater received from Social Security and from the VA. This income was his "payment liability," as the business office called it. Atwater was expected, in other words, either to pay up or sign his checks over to the facility (thirty dollars a month would go into an account he could tap for small purchases). When he first received a bill for nearly fourteen hundred dollars—based on a calculation of his payment liability for two months—Atwater was surprised and angry. "Maybe *somebody* owes them money," he said when he showed me the bill, "but it sure ain't me."

The bill prompted Atwater to consider leaving. He asked the in-house social worker to look into alternatives. He asked me to check out a place called Shepherd House, also in Chapel Hill. Atwater had heard

it was nice and, for some reason, thought he could afford it. Shepherd House, I discovered, was an upscale assisted-living facility far beyond Atwater's means. When I told him what it cost to live there, Atwater said, "That's the kind of place that rich folks like you can get into, but poor people are gonna end up right here. This is where my mother died. Right across the hall."

Atwater's miracle recovery was short. After a few weeks during which he said he felt good, he was back to breathing hard just going to and from the bathroom. In early February 1999, Atwater was moved to a wing that was occupied by long-term residents. He didn't like it. He said that the service was better on the short-term wing. His new roommate was an eighty-four-year-old man with a colostomy bag that sometimes leaked, causing the room to reek of shit. Atwater said this nauseated him and made it impossible for him to eat. He said he had asked for a fan to blow fresh air through the room, but so far his request had been ignored.

Because he was lucid and talkative, Atwater stood out among the other residents and got more attention from the aides and nurses. Atwater might complain about his Percocet being late, but when he buzzed for help, staff did not have to anticipate changing the befouled bed of a demented patient. I was there one day when a nurse brought Atwater his meds. She was stiff, and Atwater gave me a formal introduction: "This is Doctor Michael Schwalbe. He's in sociology at North Carolina State University. He's working on a project with me." The nurse just smiled and nodded, probably thinking Atwater was nuts. After she left I remarked on the formality of Atwater's introduction. He said, "Did I get it right? I want to practice getting that shit right, in case we get on Oprah."

One night, about a week after being moved to the long-term wing, Atwater was rushed to the hospital because of shortness of breath. His oxygen levels were so low that he was intubated and put on a respirator. Later tests revealed that he had also had a mild heart attack. Atwater spent several days in ICU before returning to the nursing home.

After this experience, Atwater seemed resigned to stay put. "I guess I'm here until the dying time," he said. Now he wanted to organize his remaining time well: "I'm trying to get my schedule right—watch a

little TV, read for a while, listen to my Bible tapes. I'm getting my shit together. I don't want to just sit here and stiffen up. When you're on the street doing your usual thing, age creeps up on you. In here, if you ain't doing nothing, it'll get on your ass fast." In addition to listening to Bible tapes, Atwater was reportedly doing other things to stay young.

Early on, Atwater had told me of his sexual exploits. It wasn't exactly high-energy stuff. "This one girl was helping me in the shower, and I asked if she could do a little something for me. She was gonna use her mouth, but she heard a noise in the hallway and stopped 'cause she got scared. But later she came to my room and took care of business." Another: "She climbed on top of me and was trying to make it work when she heard her supervisor in the hall. Man, did she jump off quick! If we'd got caught, we'd a both been out of here." Word got around, Atwater said, and one aide came by to marvel at his dick ("she didn't want to do nothing, just look").

A little sex—which Atwater insisted he did not have to pay for— was probably therapeutic, if risky. The real danger was smoke. I had heard that Atwater was bumming cigarettes. When I asked him about this, he reluctantly confessed. I suspected he was also partaking of another kind of smoke.

Although he never admitted it to me, Atwater told Cat of having aides blow crack smoke in his face so he could get high without irritating his throat. He told of reaping a profit by loaning aides money to buy and sell drugs. Why did Atwater, who had talked freely about crack parties in his old apartment, tell Cat and not me? I think he sensed my disappointment when I asked if he was smoking again. This backsliding dented the image he was trying to create for me of a man who had achieved wisdom and self-mastery in his old age. To admit messing around again with crack would have made an even bigger dent.

Atwater might also have been trying to protect the aides who abetted him, perhaps worrying that I might drop a word to the wrong person and get someone in trouble. It's more likely, though, that Atwater told Cat about his drug exploits as a way to make her feel guilty for putting him out. As if his backsliding were her fault.

Whereas the middle-class staff looked upon Atwater with bemusement (or irritation, or contempt), the aides, who were his class peers,

took him seriously. They appreciated Atwater's style, as well as the advice, loans, and pleasure he gave them as Popcorn. He also took them seriously. One aide brought in her eleven-year-old son for a birds-and-bees talk with Atwater, because she had no other adult male in her life to do it. Atwater comforted another aide who was distraught about losing custody of her children in a divorce. He loaned money to another to travel to her mother's funeral. He counseled another to quit the place, go back to school, and get a decent job.

One time I asked Atwater why the aides, other than those who were curious about his anatomy, liked to hang out with him. He laughed, then got serious. "Most of the time it ain't got nothing to do with John Henry, or anything else like some people think it does. Most of these women are starved for intelligent conversation. They don't have anybody to talk to who cares about anything but fucking. I listen to their troubles and give them a bit of the School of the PC. They appreciate that." Whatever his selfish motives might have been in some cases, he did reward his courtiers.

Not that Atwater was entirely happy with the place. He claimed that it took too long for help to arrive when he buzzed for it; that one old woman was left sitting naked in the hall for hours; that furniture left in the hall was a fire hazard; that the place substituted generic drugs for the name-brand drugs patients were supposed to get; that the showers were often broke; that they didn't give him an itemized bill; that no one explained why his medications had changed; and that ants came in through the window and crawled into his water pitcher.

I could verify only some of Atwater's complaints. Several times I saw it take over an hour for a patient's buzz to be answered. I never saw anyone left to sit naked in the hall, but other patients, some incoherent or staring blankly, did sit in the halls in wheelchairs. There was sometimes furniture in the halls, though I couldn't tell how long it had been there. Atwater's bills were indeed short on detail. As for the ants, they were no illusion. I once inadvertently drank a few.

The matter about which Atwater got loopy was his payment liability. For months, Atwater had ignored bills from the nursing home. Finally, when told that if he didn't pay, Medicaid would be cut off,

Atwater took money from the bank and paid part of his bill. In May of 1999 he signed a form allowing his Social Security check to go directly to the nursing home. His tab mounted, however, because his Social Security check did not meet his full liability, which included the two hundred dollars a month he got from the VA. Atwater claimed not to understand the bills.

In August 1999, I asked Atwater, after listening again to his rant about the bills, if he would like me to talk to the business manager on his behalf and see if I could get an explanation. "Sure," he said, "maybe she'll talk to you. When she sees me coming, she ducks into her office, or she talks to me like I'm an idiot." Maybe I didn't know much about the world Atwater created with the aides, but I figured I could help him deal with bureaucrats.

I sent the business manager a letter explaining my tie to Atwater and my interest in speaking to her about him. When I phoned a week later to arrange a meeting, she could not recall the letter. I explained it all again. We set up a meeting. When I showed up for the meeting, I had to remind her again who I was. I began to think that perhaps I hadn't given Atwater's account of dealing with her enough credence.

She was cordial but cool. Clearly I was an interruption, and being connected to Atwater did not win me any points. I said that I was not representing Mr. Atwater but was acting as a friend. I sought an explanation of his billing, I said, so that I could in turn explain it to him, to his satisfaction. I thus hoped that if Atwater was pestering her, she would see it as in her interest to give me the best possible lesson.

She gave me a more detailed version of what I had heard from the social worker months before when Atwater received his first bill. Since he was coming out of the hospital after a "qualifying stay," and since he met other eligibility criteria, Medicare paid his bill for the first twenty days. For the next eighty days, Medicare paid 80 percent, leaving a co-insurer—Medicaid, in Atwater's case—to pay the rest. After one hundred days, Atwater's stay was covered by Medicaid—minus his personal liability. The facility did not calculate this liability; rather, a Medicaid specialist in the county social service office investigated each case and told the facility how much to bill the patient. Atwater had a liability because he had income and no dependents.

What if Atwater didn't pay? One reason Atwater ignored the bills, he told me, was that he believed they couldn't put him out, whether he paid or not. The business manager said that she would continue to work with Mr. Atwater to arrange payment and that discharging him was not her decision. After she answered my questions, she added, "Mr. Atwater seems very comfortable here. He made friends quickly, and he's normally a pleasant man. But I think he resents not being in control." She had Atwater's number in more ways than one.

Before I saw Atwater again, I tried to find out more about Medicaid and about whether the facility could put him out for not paying his bill. I called the state Department on Aging and, after the usual search for the right person to answer my questions, found a helpful woman for whom these matters were second nature.

She explained that each facility billed Medicaid at a per day rate for each patient. The rate was set by Medicaid, based on the per patient cost of operating the facility. She said that in 1999 the average bill for a Medicaid patient in North Carolina was between twenty-six hundred and twenty-eight hundred dollars a month. (So, in Atwater's case, Medicaid was paying about two thousand dollars a month in addition to his seven-hundred-dollar-a-month personal liability.) She stressed that, from Medicaid's standpoint, they did not pay "instead of" a patient; they paid "in addition to" a patient—after a patient's resources were exhausted.

Could they put him out if he didn't pay? Yes, maybe, but they probably wouldn't. To get rid of him, they would have to give Atwater a thirty-day discharge notice. Atwater could appeal, but supposing that he didn't or that the facility prevailed, they still could not put him out without arranging a "safe and orderly discharge"—one that would not jeopardize his mental or physical health. However, if Atwater's condition improved such that he no longer required at least intermediate-level nursing care, he could be discharged in fourteen days, with no chance to appeal. Still, she said, "Generally, they do not put out Medicaid patients."

I also called the regional director of a state-funded agency that defended the rights of long-term nursing home residents. I explained Atwater's situation and asked more questions. She corroborated everything

I'd learned so far, adding a few details. I had done my homework and expected Atwater to be grateful when I reported back to him.

I started by relaying what I'd learned from the business manager. After I laid it out for him, he said, "I can see how you'd believe that." He was implying that I'd been duped. What are you saying? "Well, Mike, to you it probably seems true, what she said. I can see how you'd believe it." The subtext was clear: the white professor and the white accountant colluded in accepting lies that Atwater was clever enough to see through. I wanted to tell him he was slap-crazy.

"This is how the system works. Everyone else I talked to verified it. What part don't you believe?" I said, trying to maintain a teacherly calm.

"There are people here who don't pay anything."

"Right, but that's because they have dependents or have private insurance. You don't have either."

"That's what I'd expect them to tell you." Again with this!

"What you owe this place is calculated by a social worker using a formula that applies to everybody. That formula says you owe them your Social Security money *and* your VA money. That's why you keep getting billed."

"If they try to take that money too, I'm damn sure gonna go batshit on them. Start shooting some of these crazy-ass motherfuckers."

"But you understand *why* they are billing you for that money?"

"They can bill me all they want." Atwater could lose a thread sometimes when he told a story, but now it seemed that he was being willfully obtuse. I could see what Cat meant when she said that talking to him could be like talking to a wall.

"They will keep billing you, and they could throw you out for not paying."

"They can't throw me out. I know it."

"Actually, they could, but it would be a major production. They'd have to find another place to put you. But they *could* do it, even though you're right they probably won't." I summarized what I'd been told by the people at the Department of Aging and the advocacy agency. Atwater listened closely when I said that *if his care requirements were downgraded,* he could be put out in as few as fourteen days. This rattled him,

which at the moment pleased me, because I wanted to puncture his arrogance. Atwater nonetheless insisted that the nursing home managers would not throw him out, because he was a "moneymaker" for them.

"How do you figure that?"

"They charge the government the same for taking care of me as for taking care of these crazy people that need their diapers changed all the time, and I don't need any of that. They hardly do anything for me. That's how these greedy-ass people make their money."

I explained what I had learned about how nursing-home facilities bill Medicaid based on an independent determination of the per patient, per day costs of operation. Atwater listened doubtfully. All I wanted at this point was for him to abandon the idea that he was the target of a conspiracy.

"They should be giving me extra services," he said.

"What? Why extra?"

"Because they don't have to do for me like they do for these other people here, the ones that are too sick to do for themselves. What do they do for me anyway?"

"You get a place to live, meals, medicine. All that costs money."

"That's what I'm saying."

"What?"

"They're making money by charging the government for it."

"Of course! They try to get more back than it costs to run the place. That's how they make a profit. But that's not about you. It's business as usual."

"That's right, and it's crooked as hell because they charge the same for me as for these other people."

We were going in circles through Atwater logic: if he needed less care than someone else, then the place should charge the government less; if they charged the same, then he should get more services than he was now getting; if they charged the same and he didn't get more services, then the government was being ripped off.

"Look," I said, trying to find common ground, "I think everybody, no matter how much money they have, should be taken care of in their old age—and profit shouldn't have anything to do with it. But that's how the system works, and you're getting the same deal as everyone else."

"Ain't no way they're getting that VA money."

It seemed like a non sequitur, but this, I finally understood, was the real issue. Atwater wanted to keep that money and feel justified in doing so. Without the money, he couldn't sustain hope of moving out, because he wouldn't be able to afford it. Nor would he be able to dispense favors to the aides or buy extra things for himself. In his mind, keeping the money was justified, because he didn't need as much care as other patients. Therefore the place was not entitled to another two hundred dollars a month. Therefore he was not irresponsible for ignoring the bills.

Atwater was still agitated. Though he insisted that the place wouldn't put him out, he probably knew there was some risk, considering the suspicions about his behavior. I was irritated too. I felt I had failed as a teacher, and Atwater's accusation of gullibility stung. I wanted him to know that I was on his side and was not defending a corrupt system. So I asked if he'd like me to see if I could get someone from the state to look into his case. He said yes.

I called the Elder Rights and Long-Term Care Ombudsman's office. They were swamped, as I expected, but yes, they could help. "That's what we're here for," I was told. The advocate who reviewed Atwater's case was a white woman in her mid-twenties. She exuded a ferocity and determination that suited her role. I would have wanted her on my side, had I been in Atwater's shoes. She first talked to Atwater, then to the business manager. She knew what information to collect and how to interpret it.

"It was a little odd," she told me later, "the way they applied his check to his bill, but the balance is correct. I told Mr. Atwater that he would have to pay them monthly." She told him essentially what I had told him. She added that Mr. Atwater had listened carefully and seemed to grasp her explanation. When I next saw Atwater I asked him if he was now satisfied. He wore the same skeptical look he'd worn when he said he could see how I might believe what I'd been told. "I'm okay now. I decided not to let it worry me," he said.

Our conversations at the nursing home took both predictable and odd directions. I would ask Atwater about his symptoms, check details with

him regarding some story he'd told me, or ask what he'd seen on television lately or who had visited him during the week. Any of those openers could get us going. He surprised me one time by asking, apropos of nothing, how to get a Ph.D. in psychology. I explained the process. He jotted notes, asking how to spell "dissertation." Why do you want to know?

"I'm gonna tell a lie," he said, with a smile. I laughed. I didn't even ask for details. If he wanted to have some fun by bullshitting someone, it was fine with me. I was glad to get in on it.

"If you mention a dissertation, the first thing someone will ask is, 'what was it about?' You need an answer for that."

"What should I say?"

"You can say that you studied the coping strategies of street people."

"Man, I did that! That sounds good."

"Of course, someone will also ask where you went to school."

"I could say UNC."

"Better yet, you could say that you went through a nontraditional curriculum to become a folk doctor of psychology."

"Yeah! Damn right! That's what I did. If I said that, I wouldn't be lying."

He jotted more notes, and when he finished we talked about something else. I never followed up to see if he'd pulled off the scam, though on later occasions he joked, I presumed, about asking the place to knock a few bucks off his bill if he provided counseling services to other patients. "You could hang out a shingle and call your room 'The Head Shop of the PC,'" I said.

For the most part Atwater was in good spirits and doing well, or no worse than he had been for months. His throat was scratchy sometimes, but he was eating enough to have gained weight. He had outgrown the thirty-four-inch waist on his pants, which he now wore unbuttoned when he was in his room. He was up to 151 pounds, he said, more than he'd weighed in years. It was just past the one-year anniversary of his last radiation treatment and his move to the nursing home.

On December 6, 1999, I got a call from Lena saying that Shine had been taken to the hospital. "It's his breathing again," she said. It was

much the same as the previous episode, with Atwater ending up intubated in the respiratory ICU. (He had, in the meantime, clarified his
wishes regarding life support: "If it's just for a little while, I told 'em
that's okay. But I don't want to live like no vegetable on a machine. If
I had to be on a machine to stay alive, they can pull the damn plug.")
As before, Atwater pulled through, emerging tired and sore but in good
spirits.

Atwater spent another day in the hospital after he was released from
the ICU. I was visiting when a nurse brought him his meal. She saw
me taking notes and gave me a curious glance. Atwater introduced me
as a professor at NC State.

"I'm his sidekick," Atwater said to her. "We're like Sherlock Holmes
and that other guy. What's his name?"

"Dr. Watson," I said.

"Yeah, like those two," he said, pleased with himself. She seemed
amused but not sure what to make of it. "Well, that's nice," she said,
setting Atwater's meal tray in front of him. I wondered who Atwater
thought he was, Holmes or Watson.

getting turned around

On September 4, 1998, Martha fell on her way from the bedroom to the bathroom. Matthew called the rescue squad to help her up and take her to the ER. The X rays found no broken bones, but Martha complained of pain in the lower right part of her back—the same pain that had been nagging her for months—and of nausea. She was sent home with another prescription for painkillers. That day, at Matthew's request, I set up a bedside commode for Martha. In talking with Matthew, I mentioned that Martha would be eighty-two in less than two weeks. He was surprised to hear that. I was surprised that he didn't know what month it was.

A few days later, Martha couldn't get out of bed in the morning. The pain was worse now and running down the entire right side of her body. Matthew called the rescue squad again, and again Martha went to the hospital. This time the doctors discovered that one of her kidneys was abscessed and not functioning. She needed immediate dialysis and a heavy dose of antibiotics.

Martha was in the hospital all week, while Matthew managed at home with the help of the health aide. The aide usually arrived at 5:30 A.M. to fix breakfast. One morning a woman knocked at the back door at 5:00 A.M., claiming to be a substitute for the regular aide. Matthew told her to come around to the front door, where he let her in. "At first she was nice," Matthew said later. "Then she started talking foolish"— by which he meant that she demanded money. When Matthew refused, she knocked him down and took his wallet.

Masons in new bed

When the aide arrived half an hour later, she found Matthew on the living room floor, his empty wallet a few feet away. The aide called the police, who arrived in a few minutes and helped Matthew into his recliner. Matthew's vision was too far gone for there to be any chance of him identifying the thief. The main suspect, in Thomas's view, was a crack-addicted woman who sometimes hung out in another apartment in the complex, and who could have observed the aide's routine. But with no witnesses and no fingerprints, the police had nothing to go on (no one was ever caught). Matthew lost all of the one hundred dollars he typically kept in his wallet to buy groceries and sundries during the month.

Between Martha's falls and her kidney troubles, and the robbery, it seemed that life in the apartment was becoming untenable. While the health aide, who was present only during the day, could help with bathing and household chores, she couldn't keep Martha from falling

at night. Thomas also doubted that Martha would recover sufficiently to return to the apartment in any case. Matthew, however, rejected any notion that it was time to consider moving, insisting that he was going to bring his wife home as soon as she was well. Thomas was torn. The apartment situation was a problem, but independence meant a lot to his father. "I think going into a nursing home would kill him," Thomas said.

In late September, after spending her eighty-second birthday in the hospital, Martha was discharged and sent to the nursing home she'd been in previously. Antibiotics had cleared up the abscess, but her kidney function was still not normal and had to be monitored. She was also weak; shuffling fifteen feet down the hall, even using her walker, exhausted her. It wasn't clear how long she would need to convalesce. One nurse told me that the guideline, for an elderly person with kidney problems, was a week of rehabilitation for each day in the hospital.

Martha's troubles were not over. The kidney that had been infected was not draining properly, and she would need surgery to implant a tube to allow it to drain. This meant another five days in the hospital. When Martha returned to the nursing home, now equipped with a permanent in-dwelling catheter and a urine bag, she was weaker than ever. Thomas and Gloria continued to explore the possibility of placing Matthew and Martha in an assisted-living facility, if Martha recovered.

After the surgery, Martha's kidney function stabilized. But the hospital stays had caused her already weak legs to atrophy, and so she needed daily physical therapy to regain her strength. After a few weeks she was able to go up and down one hallway without having to rest in the wheelchair that the physical therapist pushed along behind her. Matthew settled back into the routine of visiting her every day, using cabs, the EZ Rider service, Thomas, or me for rides.

As she had before, Martha shared a room with a string of women who, like her, were elderly and recovering from hospitalization. Her room-mates often were, as Martha put it, "not right in the head," owing either to dementia or medication. When Matthew and I visited, the conversa-tions, freely joined by Martha's roommates, could be strange. One room-mate repeated over and again a sentence of which the only intelligible word was "Barbara." She was going on like this one day when Matthew

and I were trying to talk to Martha. "I think she's calling you," Matthew teased Martha, who was visibly irritated by the relentless babble. "No, she ain't," Martha snapped back, "she's praying for you."

Another roommate seemed more lucid, yet her talk was disjointed. One day I visited and brought Martha some Chicken McNuggets and Depends. Matthew was already there, having taken the EZ Rider. "This man here looks after us," Martha said, introducing me to her roommate, a gray-haired black woman, slightly darker than Martha, who looked to be in her seventies. The roommate looked at me, then at Martha, and said, "I don't know if I'd get married again."

"Do you have a husband?" Matthew asked.

"I hope so. I can't never tell. So much is going on," the roommate said.

"This is my wife and my sugar and my sweetheart," Matthew said, reaching out to touch Martha's hand.

"Somebody ought to write or do something," the roommate said.

"What did she say?" Martha asked.

"I wish I could get tired and go to sleep," the roommate said. "But I get tired and it doesn't help."

"I wish my son would call more often," Martha said, apparently picking up on the theme of wishes.

"It can take a long time but the things you do come back on you, only double," the roommate said.

The conversation, such as it was, was interrupted by a loud screech in the hall. I said it sounded like a bird. "That's that fella what dances down the hall," Martha explained. "He hollers all day and all night."

"Could you cut on the TV?" the roommate asked. I turned it on and the woman became absorbed, muttering to herself occasionally.

A few minutes later an obese white woman in a wheelchair rolled a few feet into the room, stopped abruptly, swung her gaze across Matthew, Martha, and me, and proclaimed, "It makes me happy to see you all here. I just wanted to stop by and say hello." Then she wheeled back out. I asked Martha who the woman was. "I don't know," Martha said. "She just goes up and down the hall. I reckon she talks to folks."

I remarked on the traffic in the halls. "There's a parade here everyday," Martha said. "You get to see everything. There's a woman with a teddy bear, a man who walks like he's dancing, and a six-hundred-pound

woman they have to put on wheels." Matthew had been quiet until Martha mentioned the heavy woman. "I ain't never heard of that," he said. I had seen the woman Martha was referring to. Martha's estimate was high, I guessed, by only two hundred pounds.

One day I took Matthew to visit Martha and we found her room empty. It wasn't the time of day for physical therapy, so it was clear that something was wrong. I left Matthew in his wheelchair in Martha's room and went to the nurses' station to ask what was going on. A nurse told me that Martha had gone to the hospital the day before, because she had a swollen leg and symptoms of a bladder infection. No one had called Mr. Mason to let him know.

On my way back down the hall I met the resident social worker, a thirty-something white woman. On previous occasions she'd been pleasant and helpful. I told her what had happened. She apologized for the failure to inform Mr. Mason, then smiled and said, "They're so cute together." Cute? She meant well, but under the circumstances her saccharine judgment irritated me. I silently wished upon her the infirmities and frustrations of old age, capped by the indignity of being treated, like a puppy or toddler, as "cute."

I told Mr. Mason that Martha was in the hospital, but that there was no emergency and she was fine. He was relieved, and justly irked. "They're supposed to call and tell the family if they're going to move someone," he said. "But didn't nobody call. And that ain't right, is it?" I said it wasn't right but that all we could do at the moment was to go see Martha in the hospital. At the hospital entrance I helped him out of the car and into his wheelchair. An entry aide offered to take Mr. Mason inside while I parked.

Ten minutes later I found Mr. Mason sitting twenty feet inside the main door, just out of the flow of foot traffic. He was wide-eyed but unseeing. He might have known, or known the families of, a third of the people moving past him, though he could no longer reach out to connect. "That you, Brother Mike?" he said when he heard my voice. "Sure is. Let's go see Martha." When we got to her room, I read Martha's chart and found that they'd done an ultrasound on her kidneys, suspected that a blood clot had caused her leg to swell, and that she had

a bladder infection. It looked like she would have to stay in the hospital a few more days.

We visited for an hour. On the way home from the hospital we passed the Phi Delta Theta House on South Columbia Street. When I told Mr. Mason where we were, he said, "How'd we get back in Chapel Hill so quick?" The question startled me. I knew that Mr. Mason couldn't *see* where he was, but still I thought he was aware of where he was. I said that we'd been in Chapel Hill, at UNC Hospital. "Oh, I thought we were in Durham," he said. It was the first time I'd seen him so turned around.

Martha spent another six weeks in the nursing home. Thomas had doubts about Martha's readiness to return to the apartment, but Matthew and Martha were adamant about it. "Anyone who didn't want me to come home should spend some time down there," she said later. With a higher level of in-home care, the social worker thought it would be doable. And so just before Christmas 1998, Martha came home. When she left the facility, her neighbor across the hall had been Anthony Atwater.

I saw the Masons on Christmas Eve. Martha told me her catheter had fallen out during the week but the nurse had come by right away to fix it. Matthew said that one of the older Phi's had given him a Christmas card with cash in it. "I'm a lucky old man to have someone drop by and give me a hundred dollars," he said. I said that I didn't have a hundred dollars for him but that I'd brought a cake and a basket of chocolates. "If you ain't got no liquor, that'll do," he said.

There were no more emergencies that spring. Mr. Mason sometimes reported feeling puny, a condition he attributed to old age and being worn out. He was nonetheless proud that he took only one pill a day (5 mg. of Ramipril), what he called his "heart pill." Martha took the same medication (2.5 mg. per day), though she called it, more accurately, her "high blood" medicine. But while Mr. Mason's body was not yet failing him, he was getting turned around more often.

It would happen in the apartment, Martha told me. Matthew would try to get from the living room to the bedroom, and he'd end up in the kitchen, not sure where he was, why he was there, or where he wanted

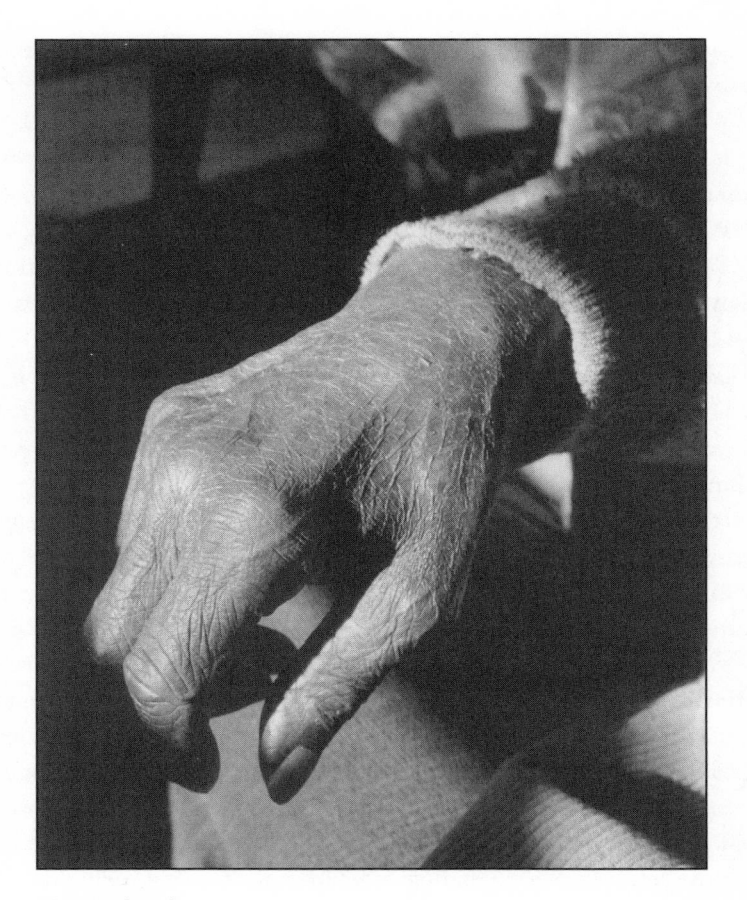

Mason's hand

to go. Then he'd holler for Martha, who would holler back, coaching him on which way to turn and telling him to follow her voice. Part of the problem was Matthew's nearly complete blindness, which meant that he literally couldn't see where he was. He also began to get turned around in other ways.

Sometimes Martha would ask me to bring in the mail, if she'd seen the carrier come by before I arrived. It was June 3, 1999, the day before Matthew's eighty-eighth birthday. As usual, their Social Security checks arrived on the third. I handed the familiar envelopes to Martha

and said, "There you go. The eagle has flown. You got your Social Security check, Mr. Mason. Kind of like an early birthday present."

"What's that?" he said.

"It's your Social Security checks," I said, louder, thinking that he hadn't heard me.

"What?"

"Your Social Security checks," louder still. "Today is the third of the month. You always get your checks on the third. Tomorrow is your birthday, so these are sort of like an early birthday present." I felt foolish trying to explain a remark that wasn't all that funny to begin with. Usually when this happened Mr. Mason would eventually get the explanation, say, "Oh, yeah," and then generously offer a laugh.

But now he said, "Social Security?"

"It's your *Social Security* check," Martha interjected. "You been getting it since you's sixty-two years old."

"Oh, oh, yeah. Social Security," Matthew said. "I know what that is now. I just forgot for a minute. Ain't that something?"

On an earlier occasion a fraternity member who graduated in the sixties came by to say hello to the Masons (and to urge them to vote for his wife, who was running for lieutenant governor). Mr. Mason introduced me as a younger member of the fraternity. I quickly reintroduced myself, indicating that I did not belong to the fraternity. Mr. Mason must have noticed my reaction to being misidentified, because, after the alum left, Mr. Mason apologized. "I know you ain't a Phi," he said. "I don't know why I said that. I guess I thought you was someone else. My mind don't work good all the time anymore."

On his eighty-eighth birthday I brought him a bag of Hershey's Kisses. Mr. Mason looked confused when I wished him happy birthday. "It's your birthday? Well, happy birthday," he replied, reaching out to shake my hand. I told him it was *his* birthday, and that he was eighty-eight. He eagerly accepted my offer of some chocolate to sweeten him up. I opened the bag and gave him one of the Kisses. He nearly had it in his mouth before I reached across the arm of the recliner and stopped him. "You'll have to unwrap it for him," Martha said.

It was still only occasionally that Mr. Mason got turned around. Most of the time his mind worked just fine. A month before his

birthday, when I asked how it felt to be coming up on eighty-eight years old, he declared, "I'm eighty-seven now. On June the fourth I'll be eighty-eight. After that, I'll be getting up to ninety. When I'm ninety, that'll *sound* old, but I won't *be* old. I'm gonna act like a teenager and let the good times roll." He was also aware, as implied by the remark about his mind not working so good, that his memory was failing. One time when I confessed to forgetting the tangerines that Martha asked me to pick up at the grocery store, Mr. Mason said, "You must be catching that from me."

The television soap operas, which Mr. Mason wisely ignored, sometimes inspired me to ask a question. When a character on *The Guiding Light* mused about her wishes, I asked Mr. Mason what he wished for. "Some whiskey," he said, smiling. I asked if he wished for anything he could actually have. "No, it doesn't matter," he said. "What's gonna happen will happen. Wishes don't make no difference." In some ways, he could still see perfectly clearly.

When I visited, Mr. Mason never failed to ask how my family was doing. But he was becoming quieter, less likely to initiate conversation. Now, if our talk lagged for a few minutes, he dozed off. That summer he reported feeling puny most of the time, and said he hadn't felt right since his birthday. I noticed, too, that he no longer set out a chair for me next to his recliner, as he'd done for years (he used to move it from the dining room right before I'd arrive—one hand on his cane, one hand pushing the chair). It was a characteristic act of hospitality that he would have performed if he still could.

For the health aides, the toughest part of the job was dealing with Martha. The cooking, cleaning, and help they gave with bathing took only about half the time they spent in the apartment on any given day. The rest of the time they napped, read, or watched TV, a situation that bothered Martha. Even though she wasn't paying their wages, Martha thought the aides ought to keep busy.

And so the aides ran for groceries, took Martha to Wal-Mart, sorted old clothes in the closets, moved furniture, trimmed nails, pruned plants and weeded Martha's tiny tomato patch, picked up prescriptions, brought things to and from other people in the complex, and carried

trash to the street. The problem wasn't so much that these extra tasks were not part of the aides' prescribed duties—the rules were often bent, as a practical matter and a matter of kindness—but the way that Martha ordered them done.

Each aide enjoyed a honeymoon period. At first the aide would get along splendidly with the Masons, showering them with affection. Martha would praise the aide, saying how much nicer she was than the one who preceded her. The aide would cheerfully do whatever Martha asked. But then, after several weeks in some cases, months in others, there would be a blow-up and the aide would quit.

At first these episodes baffled me. One week it seemed that the aide was doing fine and getting along well with Martha. The next week the aide would be gone and Martha would tell me that the aide had "blessed her out for no reason" and stomped out the door. What on earth was going on? Why these dramatic reversals of sentiment?

The first clue came when I heard Martha say to one of her neighbors, speaking on the phone, "I'll have my girl come over and fetch that"—referring to the aide, who was sitting a few feet away. I began to see how Martha was treating the aides: like her gofers. The picture was filled in on another occasion when Martha referred to an aide as "our maid." Eventually she went through six of them, nearly exhausting the agency's pool of aides who would work with the Masons.

Perhaps because the aides were supposed to cook and clean, and because they didn't wear nursing uniforms, it was easy for Martha to see them as maids. And perhaps Martha, having done domestic work for decades, never asked them to do anything she hadn't once been asked to do herself. She might even have thought that, after years of cleaning up other people's messes, she was now entitled to a maid.

For his part, Mr. Mason sided with Martha. When things were going smoothly with the aides, Mr. Mason was his usual genial self. He would thank the aides profusely for whatever help they gave him. But then if he heard angry voices he would jump in and defend Martha, as if she were being attacked. It didn't matter who was right or wrong; his loyalty to Martha was unwavering.

Martha could also be fussy about food. The seventy-five-cent weekday lunches brought by meals-on-wheels were rarely up to Martha's

standards. "Today we got the sorriest dinner [lunch] I ever seen," she said one time. "It was some kind of meat and massacred potatoes. I didn't even eat it. I had the Africa girl [an aide who was originally from Sierra Leone] open me a can of sardines, and I ate that instead." Another time the main item was fish that "didn't look or taste like no kind of fish I ever seen."

Martha's efforts at control extended, of course, to Matthew, though with mixed results. One time she told Matthew that he could not go alone to the eye doctor because he couldn't see well enough to get there. When Matthew insisted that he was going to go by himself anyway, Martha said, "Then at least let me buy you some new pants. Otherwise people are gonna look hard at you because you're old." Matthew laughed and shook his head. "Help me out, Brother Mike," he said, giving me an imploring nod and a conspiratorial wink. "Tell Martha I don't need no more pants."

He didn't. In the closet behind him were two pairs of corduroy slacks that Martha had given him for his birthday. When I pointed this out, Martha said, "It's too hot for them pants. He needs some light slacks." Of which kind there were also two nearly new pairs in the closet, though I bit my tongue. "She just wants me to look sporty," Matthew said, giving Martha one more tweak.

Martha, annoyed at Matthew's stubbornness and my unwillingness to gang up on him, went to the bedroom to lie down. Knowing that she could hear him perfectly well, Matthew said, "Does your wife boss you, Brother Mike? My wife bosses me." I said that we didn't bother trying to boss each other, because it didn't work anyway. "That's right," he said. "Me and Martha got a good arrangement just like that. She don't listen to me and I don't listen to her."

It was tempting to see Martha as controlling. Certainly she liked to have things her way, and complained if she couldn't. Then again, being in control was hardly the main condition of her life. In fact, the apartment was probably the only place where she had been able to cook what she wanted, clean the way she wanted, stock the groceries she wanted, and generally do what she wanted. Now she couldn't. Which led me to see her bossiness less as an enduring flaw than as a sign of frustration over the loss of what little control she'd once enjoyed.

Matthew suffered from insomnia, as he had for years. He would wake up at night, sit in his recliner for a few hours, then go back to bed. One night in early October 1999, Matthew woke up just before midnight and couldn't get back to sleep, so he went to sit in his recliner. When he tried to go back to bed, he couldn't get up. He was stuck in the chair until the aide arrived the next morning. The experience convinced him that he needed a lift chair like Martha's. The fraternity paid for it, and I arranged to have it delivered.

With so much sitting and so little movement, Matthew was getting shakier on his feet. His doctor's advice to walk for exercise went unheeded. By way of excuse, Matthew told the cautionary tale of man who, after a heart attack, had taken his doctor's advice to do a lot of walking. "He walked everywhere. All over town. You understand? He was in the middle of the street one day and had a heart attack and died. Just like that. So you know what I'm going to do? I'm going to sit here and take it easy and cool it." Which is exactly what he did.

In November, Mr. Mason's oldest daughter, Gloria, came down with severe bronchitis. By Thanksgiving she was in the intensive respiratory care unit at UNC Hospital. The antibiotics she'd been given were not working and her lungs were filling with fluid. On December 3, 1999, Gloria Mason Williams died at the age of sixty-five. It was a shock to the family and the community.

Though Mr. Mason tried not to show it, Gloria's death hit him hard. He was, Martha told me the next week, alternately grouchy or withdrawn when they were alone together. "It was her time," she said about Gloria, perhaps hoping that Matthew could accept this. "God don't make no mistakes." Years later, another time when Martha and I talked about how Gloria's death had affected Matthew, she said, "You ain't supposed to love one child more than another, but Gloria was his favorite. She would do anything for him. When she passed, that took him way down."

Mr. Mason's sense of humor nonetheless remained intact. One day, about a week before Christmas, I arrived just after the aide had given Mr. Mason a shave. "It smells like a barbershop in here," I said to Mr. Mason. "A barbershop? You say you're going to start a barbershop here?" Mr. Mason said, eyes wide, as if surprised by this news. "Does that mean me and Martha got to move out?" For a moment I thought

he was serious, then he grinned. He'd gotten me again. "No, you can stay," I said. "But you got to help people let the good times roll when they come in for a haircut, so they'll keep coming back." Then he let out the laugh he'd been planning all along.

When I remarked on the absence of a Christmas tree, Martha said, "Them boys ain't brought us nothing for a while," referring to the young Phi's. "I reckon they don't think they need to bring us anything anymore." I said maybe they were too young to understand what they owed Matthew. "I think that's right," Martha said. Matthew nodded as if to agree, but stayed quiet. Martha and I waited, knowing that in a moment he would come to their defense. "As long as they pay the rent," he said, two beats later, "that's a lot."

On Christmas Eve Matthew told me that he'd fallen the day before. Martha had called the rescue squad to help him get up. Matthew insisted that he was okay and didn't want to go to the hospital. When I said that this was the second time he'd fallen (the previous occasion that I knew of was in May) in the apartment, Matthew corrected me. "I've fallen *five* times in this apartment," he said. He was proud, it seemed, of miraculously never having seriously hurt himself.

When I visited I often asked, as I parked my bag on the floor and sat down on the small sofa nearest to Mr. Mason's recliner, what was new. "Ain't nothing new here," Mr. Mason would say. "Everything here is *old*." Or he'd say, "If there's anything new here, they ain't told me about it." Sometimes I would ask if it had been a quiet week, which usually cued Martha to say that it had been "*too* quiet, child." One day in January 2000, I got a different answer.

"I reckon it was quiet," Martha said, "except for Matthew hollering at that girl [the aide], and her hollering back." She sounded faintly disgusted. I asked what the hollering was about. "Ask Matthew. Something about where to put his hands when she was giving him a bath." I asked Mr. Mason what had happened, and Martha turned to the TV as he started talking.

"Brother Mike, she got to hollering at me and I liked to slap her down," he said. "How much you reckon it would cost me if I slapped her down?" His tone was playful, but whatever had happened was nothing that Martha found amusing.

"You'd get in a whole lot of trouble," I said.

"A hundred dollars?" he said.

"I said you'd get in a lot of *trouble*."

Martha turned back to him. "It would be just you and me here and no help," she said sharply, clarifying one form of trouble.

"Oh, well, then I reckon I won't do it," Matthew said.

"You have to be patient with young people," I said.

"Young people? Young people are supposed to be patient with *old* people," he said.

"I try to be patient with you," I said.

"They ain't many like you," he said.

"It might be harder to be patient if I had to give you a bath," I said.

"We got a man what comes in," he said.

"Who you talking about?" Martha snapped again, turning away from the TV.

"He gave me a bath this morning," Matthew said.

"That was the *aide*. She's a *woman*. She ain't no man just because she wears pants!" Martha said, exasperated.

"Oh, that's right," he said, now sounding more contrite than playful. "I got confused. I get things mixed up. Martha, you got to keep me straightened out."

"I do the best I can," she said.

The details of Matthew's bathtub episode with the aide weren't clear. But it wasn't hard to imagine what might have happened. When he wasn't sure where he was or what was happening, Matthew got frustrated and ornery.

I witnessed this later, after Matthew became weaker and needed help to get from the living room to the bedroom. I would walk along beside him and give directions: "you're doing fine; just keep going straight," or "okay, now turn a little to the right." Usually, he complied without hesitation. But sometimes he would angrily insist that he couldn't turn because his foot was stuck or the wall was in front of him—when neither was true. He also got scared when he had to trust others to keep him from falling, because he couldn't see where they were or what they were doing. And so I could picture him, in a moment of helplessness and confusion, lashing out at the aide who was trying to help him get into the tub.

Mason being fed

In the late winter and early spring of 2000, Matthew reported feeling punier than usual. Martha was concerned and wanted him to go to the doctor. Matthew refused, saying that *he* knew if he needed to go to the doctor or not. The aide thought his weakness was caused by dehydration, so she tried to get him to drink more water and fruit juice. Matthew realized that he was losing strength. "Me and you," he said one day, "are gonna have to go out and let the good times roll, before I get too old."

In late February, Matthew got a wheelchair to use when making trips out of the apartment. He might not have used it for months, if the EZ Rider drivers had not insisted (Matthew was too wobbly on his feet to get in and out of the van safely). Matthew's appetite was also declining. In mid-March he began eating nothing but a small can of fruit cocktail for supper. He lost a few pounds—his waist size shrank from forty-six to forty-two inches—but then his weight stabilized.

I guessed that half of his caloric intake came from the hard candy and sugary cough drops he ate day and night.

Martha, who had been in bad shape during her months in the nursing home, was now the more physically able of the two. She worried about Matthew's bouts of confusion and his blindness. She kept hope that a miracle would restore his sight. One day Martha received a call from someone soliciting donations to a fund for the blind. She listened to the pitch and then asked, "Can you help my husband's eyes? He's got glaucoma and cataracts, and he goes to the eye hospital but they can't do nothing for him." Martha was starting another sentence when I heard the click. "She done hung up," Martha announced, staring at the silent handset. Matthew, who heard more than he let on, said, "If they hung up, it ain't nobody. Nobody to help, anyway."

On March 23, 2000, Martha called at 8:20 A.M. Between sobs she told me that Matthew's left knee was red and swollen and he could barely walk. Would I take him to the doctor? I said I would, then asked to talk to the aide, who confirmed Martha's report. The aide didn't think the situation was an emergency, so we agreed that she would have Matthew ready to go in two hours.

We checked in at the ER entry station and again at the billing counter. It was a little after 11:00 A.M. Mr. Mason was in his wheelchair. We waited thirty-five minutes in the outer waiting room before being called back to the smaller waiting room of the urgent care clinic.

We shared the second waiting room with two elderly black women, one middle-aged black man, and one young black woman. After twenty minutes we were taken to an examining room and seen by a nurse. She took Matthew's temperature and blood pressure and jotted notes as we described his symptoms. "The doctor will be in shortly," she said, then ducked out. Shortly turned out to be forty-five minutes.

The doctor, a white man in his late twenties, asked the same questions the nurse had asked. We were both surprised when Matthew began talking about his arm. "Your *arm*?" I said. "Mr. Mason, I thought it was your *knee* that was hurting." Mr. Mason thought for a moment, then corrected himself. It was his knee, though he wasn't sure which one. The doctor examined both knees, noting that the left was slightly

swollen. Since the knee didn't feel warm, he thought that the problem was accumulated fluid, rather than infection.

After offering his diagnosis, the doctor rose to leave—he'd been with us for six minutes—but said he'd be right back. I thought perhaps he was going to consult with a joint specialist, order an X ray, or grab a prescription pad. Twenty-three minutes later Mr. Mason's patience was wearing thin. "You know, this place puts a lot of pressure against your health," he said. You mean seeing all these different people and having to wait so much? "That's it. That's exactly right," he said.

My patience wore out at thirty-six minutes. I went to the desk and said that Mr. Mason and I had been waiting nearly forty minutes for a doctor who said he'd be "right back." The receptionist, a young black woman, apologized for the delay. She was polite and sympathetic, but conveyed a feeling of helplessness about the situation. "Would you please ask the attending physician to see us in the examining room?" I said. She nodded and smiled ambiguously. I wondered if her expression meant, *"fat chance that will do any good,"* or *"it's about time somebody complained,"* or *"too bad, buddy, you have to wait like everyone else."*

Complaining seemed to help. In less than five minutes we had two white male doctors in the examining room, the second doctor clearly older than the first. They both reviewed Mr. Mason's symptoms and checked his knees, agreeing that the problem was osteoarthritis. The doctor who'd seen us first offered Mr. Mason a cortisone shot to reduce the inflammation. Mr. Mason said that if he didn't *need* a shot, he'd just as soon not have one. We left at 2:00 P.M. with a prescription for over-the-counter Tylenol.

When we were sitting in the examining room, Mr. Mason told me how the previous aide (one that had quit) said that he and Martha ought to be in a nursing home. Mr. Mason said again that he was willing to go to a nursing home if he *had* to, but he wasn't ready for that yet. I wondered, as I helped him make the painful, slow-motion transition from the wheelchair into my car, what he would consider compelling circumstances.

Back at the apartment I gave Martha a report on our trip. She was relieved that the problem with Matthew's knee wasn't serious but seemed skeptical that Tylenol was going to help. I told her that the

doctors had said that this sort of problem could come and go and that Matthew would probably feel better in a few days. I went to the drug store for the Tylenol, choosing the "arthritis formula" in hopes that the label would enhance the placebo effect. When I got back, the aide was hanging clothes on the lines behind the apartment. We talked for a few minutes about Matthew's condition. At one point she glanced at the back door of the apartment, as if to make sure that Martha wasn't there, then said, in a voice just above a whisper, "He's going to need twenty-four-hour care before very long."

A week after I took Matthew to the ER, Martha began talking about going to see Shepherd House, an assisted-living facility on the southern edge of town. I was surprised by her sudden willingness, with Matthew's apparent consent, to consider moving. I also wondered where Martha got the idea that Shepherd House was an option. About a year and a half earlier I had looked into the place for Atwater. At that time (1998), the cheapest unit, a 322-square foot semi-private room with bath, cost $1,750 per person per month. A 675-square foot bedroom suite with private bath and kitchenette cost $4,995 per person per month. The place was way beyond the Masons' economic reach.

It turned out that Martha thought Shepherd House was a possibility because another elderly black couple from the complex had moved there. It wasn't clear how this other couple could afford it, unless they had family members who were paying, or the facility admitted people on Medicaid. I told Martha I would call to see what I could find out, and, if possible, arrange a visit.

I called Shepherd House and talked to the admissions manager. Prices had gone up. A unit for the Masons, presuming they didn't need special care, would cost $3,675 per month. That was nearly $3,000 more than the Masons' combined monthly income from Social Security, so I asked if Shepherd House admitted people who needed Medicaid to supplement their payments. I was told no. I was also told that a "pre-admission financial assessment" required prospective residents to show, up front, that they had the resources to pay at least four years' worth of monthly fees.

In view of the financial barrier, there didn't seem to be much point in taking the Masons to look at Shepherd House. On the other hand, Martha was excited about going, and I thought that seeing the place might prompt the Masons to think more seriously about getting out of the apartment. And despite my question about Medicaid, the admissions manager had said to come by anytime for a tour.

At first Mr. Mason didn't want to use his wheelchair. I told him that Shepherd House was a big place, and that to see it all would require more walking than he could manage with just his stick. Martha told him not to be foolish and to get in the wheelchair. To my relief, he quickly agreed. Martha was in her wheelchair and ready to go.

I rolled Mr. Mason to the car, opened the door, and positioned him to get out of the chair. "You have to lift up out of your chair now," I said, getting myself in place to steady him. "I do?" he asked. "I never had to do that before." He was thinking of the EZ Rider van, in which he could stay in the wheelchair. "This is my car, Mr. Mason," I said. "You've ridden in it lots of times. You have to get out of the wheelchair and into the front seat." At that moment, he couldn't remember ever having ridden in my car, but he consented to following my instructions as to how to get in.

At Shepherd House, the receptionist, a young black woman, helped me get Matthew and Martha out of the car and into their wheelchairs. The same woman narrated the tour while pushing Martha. I pushed Matthew. We saw the dining room, the activity room, and peered from the hallway into an apartment. Martha's response in each case was, "It's nice, real nice." She was right. The place was modern, elegantly furnished, and spotless.

As we rolled by what looked like a nurses' station, the receptionist said that the facility handled prescriptions for residents. Mr. Mason, who had been silent until then, asked if someone brought medicine to you. "No, usually you get your medicine at breakfast," she said. Then added, "They like you to do as much for yourself as you can. This is *assisted* living." I took her emphasis on "assisted" as conveying skepticism about the Masons' fitness for the place. Though several of the residents we saw used walkers, none was in a wheelchair.

We visited the couple who had lived in the same apartment complex as the Masons. Other than the receptionist and two janitors, they were the only black folks we saw during the tour. Both the color imbalance—"too much salt and not enough pepper," as Martha put it later—and the social class gap were glaring. Even if there were resources to allow the Masons to live here, it seemed unlikely that they would fit in socially. The woman of the couple we visited nonetheless avowed, echoing Martha, that the place was "real nice" and they got along fine with everybody.

Back at the front desk we picked up a cost sheet and waited for the admissions manager, who reviewed the application process with us. Martha, who had eyed the cost sheet, now realized how expensive the place was and began to tell the manager how Matthew had worked for the Phi Delta Theta fraternity for sixty years and maybe those boys would pay the bill. At mention of the five-hundred-dollar reservation fee, Matthew said, "Five hundred a month?" astonished at such a high figure. The manager seemed taken aback by Matthew's incomprehension. I jumped in: "Mr. Mason, that's like a fee for moving in. We can talk more about that when we get home."

The admissions manager thanked the Masons for their interest in Shepherd House, then gave them each a friendly, parting handshake. I pulled the car into the drive-up and got Martha in first. The receptionist watched the process of getting Matthew into the car, then, as I was stuffing the folded wheelchairs into the cargo space, she asked if I was a social worker. I told her that I was a professor writing a book about Mr. Mason. "What's he done that makes him of interest?" she asked.

Her tone implied no disrespect. But perhaps it was her bluntness, combined with the rejection implicit in the cost sheet that Martha had neatly folded and put in her purse, that made me want to tell a lie. Would she be interested in hearing about Blind Boy Matthew, the once-famous but now forgotten blues musician whose songs were stolen in the 1940s by unscrupulous white record producers, and who ended up penniless and living in public housing in Chapel Hill? Or would she be interested in the life of Matthew "Reet" Mason, one of the southern black folk poets whose material was exploited by the well-known playwright Paul Green?

I made up no such story, and instead gave her the standard blurb.

She listened intently as I explained. The badge on her lapel bore a sur-name that was shared by many blacks and whites in the area. It would have been a safe bet that her family history included stories much like Mr. Mason's. I added that I had also been intrigued by the challenge of trying to understand Mr. Mason's life. "I can imagine," she said, smiling and raising an eyebrow. What I imagined was her wondering how much I could ever understand about such a life, the life of, say, her great-grandfather.

Back at the apartment Matthew thanked me several times for taking him and Martha to see Shepherd House. He asked if they could move in right away if they decided to go. I said that to move would require a lot of arranging, and that they should talk to Thomas, or to a social worker, to find out what had to be done. Martha said nothing.

The next week, when I asked if they'd thought more about moving, Martha assumed that I meant moving to Shepherd House. "That place is too rich for our blood, child," she said, sounding more amused than disappointed. So are you going to stay here? "I reckon we are. The helper girl we got now treats us real nice." Matthew seconded Martha's praise: "She's the best one we've had," he said.

mudslide

When Atwater left the hospital after his episode of respiratory failure in December 1999, he insisted on getting a list of his medications. The list included Flovent, Serevent, Atrovent, albuterol, Isordil, Zoloft, Colace, aspirin, Cardizem, Synthroid, Prilosec, Megace, levofloxacin, nitroglycerin, and iron sulfate. "That's why I have to stay here now," he said, referring to the list. "I could never keep track of all that shit on my own." He did, however, keep track of the inhalers and the nitro, both of which were always within reach. Painkillers were also never far from his mind. "My throat is still in raggedy-ass shape," he said, "and those Percocets cool down the pain. If I take two, then I'm sure enough gonna mellow on out. It's like how I used to smoke cigarettes to help me relax."

At the nursing home, Atwater was put in a room on the short-term wing. He was glad for the change. "The service is better on this side, more professional. On that other [long-term] wing, the aides were as crazy as the patients. And here I don't have that shitbag smell making me sick all the time." Atwater had been sent back to the nursing home with a pressure-support ventilator—a smaller, simpler version of the machine that had kept him alive in the ICU. Using the machine meant wearing a tight-fitting plastic mask over his nose and mouth while he slept.

Atwater had used the machine for three nights in the hospital before he was discharged. "I was so uncomfortable at first I was gonna take it off and tell 'em to let me die. But by the third night I kind of learned to

Atwater in nursing home

blend in with it, match my breathing to what the machine was doing. Once I stopped fighting it, it was all right." Atwater said the machine helped him sleep better and wake up feeling rested. Are you using it now? I asked when I saw Atwater in the new room. "Not yet. First they said there was a piece missing. Then they said they didn't have nobody that knew how to set it up. The service is better on this side, but it's still kind of a pitiful-assed place." By the next week, Atwater had gotten a different machine, one that was easier to set up and operate, and was using it nightly.

Atwater shared the room with a man who lay silently in his bed, staring at the ceiling. In response to a greeting, the man would offer a barely

perceptible nod. One time, when the man was out of the room to receive a bath, Atwater said, "He's quiet, but that's all right. I don't care. He gets up in the middle of the night and sits on the edge of his bed. I asked him what he was doing and he said he was waiting for somebody to take him home. He sits there for hours and then goes back to sleep." One day when I visited, the man was gone. Atwater said that whoever the man was waiting for had finally come to get him.

It wasn't clear if Atwater was going to stay put. He badly wanted to, believing that the care was better on the short-term wing. "I'd go back on the street before I'd go back to that other side," he said. "It'll take a damn act of Congress to get me out of this room." At the time, Atwater had the room to himself, something of a rarity. Would he get a new roommate? "I don't know. They don't tell me nothing. I just know I don't want to be moved around anymore. I don't care about a roommate. I'll take the devil for a roommate; just don't give me one of those crazy shit-spreaders." As it turned out, Atwater kept the room to himself.

As he had a year before, in the first month following his cancer treatment, Atwater went through a period of feeling good. Using the ventilator at night seemed to help. He also enjoyed a new color TV that he had had Lena buy for him. A departing patient gave Atwater an old recliner, which he parked in front of the TV, as he had done at Cat's. Sometimes he dozed in the chair while listening to classical music on a beat-up boom box. No doubt having the room to himself contributed to Atwater's ease. So did the Percocet.

Atwater boasted about his recovery. "How many people do you know who had two cancers in the throat? The doctors call it cancer; I call it 'inconvenience.' I got that shit beat, 'cause I know how to tap into the part of the brain you can heal yourself with." But then he might, a few minutes later, say that he was not so sure of victory. "Dr. Halle never gave me a complete okay. She says I'm doing fine, but when my throat gets sore, I get scared to death. The first thing I think is that that cancer is working on me again." The healing and fearing parts of his brain, Atwater might have said, were pulling against each other.

Atwater finally settled the billing matter, if not his outstanding bill. "I'm gonna sign the papers making me a permanent resident," he told me. "They'll get my VA money, but I don't care. I was tired of them

pestering me. Besides, now I got a right to stay in this room." He didn't mind them getting the VA money, he said, because he had enough salted away with Lena to pay for his cremation.

Despite the effort six months earlier to explain his bill to him, Atwater still ranted occasionally about the place overcharging the government for his care. But in a few weeks the rants subsided, and Atwater resigned himself to looking after his day-to-day comfort. "I'm here now for the final mudslide," he said one day. Mudslide? "Yeah, Mike, the final mudslide. I'm gonna ride it down easy until it's time to cross that bridge and see what's on the other side." I imagined Atwater on his haunches, riding downhill on a wave of mud that deposited him, magically clean in his pajamas and bathrobe, at one end of a golden bridge. "I just hope it happens with no fuss," he said.

For Christmas I gave Atwater a book called *If . . . (Questions for the Game of Life)*. The book contained hundreds of if-you-could or if-you-had-to questions, some ridiculous (If you had to be the underwear of someone famous, who would you choose to wear you?) and some serious (If you could teach your children only one lesson in life, what would it be?). I thought Atwater would enjoy the book, and that it might spark some fresh conversations. One time I pitched him a handful of questions more or less at random.

If you could talk to a famous historical figure, who would it be? "Napoleon," Atwater said, "because every great person has got some insane shit inside him, and I'd like to know what was going on in that dude's head."

If you could enact a law of the land? "Everybody would have to do at least one thing every day for someone else."

If you could change one thing about your parents? "That they got along better and weren't always pulling against each other."

If you could be a great writer from history? "Mark Twain. Not because he was white, but because he did a lot of good and entertained a lot of people. *Huckleberry Finn* is my favorite book."

If you could go back and fix a great mistake in your life? "I'd go to Officers Candidate School. Not doing that when I had the chance was a big mistake."

If you could tattoo someone? "I'd put a tattoo of a scorpion on my ex-wife's ass."

One question asked, If you could make someone else live one moment from your own life, who would you select, and what moment? I expected something glib, but Atwater surprised me: "I'd want Bernard to know how I felt when Dot told me she was pregnant with him and I claimed him as my own. I'd want him to know how much I was look-ing forward to playing some ball with that boy. I don't think he ever understood that, and after his stroke we couldn't really talk about it, so now he'll never know." Until then I hadn't fully appreciated the depth of Atwater's regret.

I asked a variation on the same question. What moments from your life would you want *me* to live, to understand you better? Atwater named three, without hesitation: "I'd want you to know what it was like to see that sign on the fence around the swimming pool that said 'no nig-gers or dogs allowed.' I'd want you to know what it was like to see your momma pee on herself because they wouldn't let her use a restroom in a gas station. I'd want you to hear that racist Georgia shit I heard in the army and feel like you never wanted to be around no white people ever again." After hundreds of conversations about what it was like to be Atwater, that gap remained. It wasn't about drinking, fighting, drugs, work, money, politics, religion, or sex. On those matters we could find common ground. The gap was between what he had felt as a black man in a white supremacist society and what I had not felt and never could.

Over the years we had, in fact, talked a lot about race. In the spring of 2000 we had occasion to talk more, as I was then teaching a course called "Race and Ethnic Relations." Perhaps never having taken the course in school was to Atwater's advantage. This meant that he had not learned to mince words.

When I told him that in my class we were reading about how Euro-pean settlers took land from Native Americans, Atwater said, "That's always been the European thing: look for someplace to move to where you can take other people's shit. The Europeans did that to each other for a thousand years, then they started doing it to the rest of the world." This account of history was, to many of my students, new and disturb-ing. To Atwater it was pedestrian.

One time I mentioned an article in which it was said that 75 percent of African Americans had at least one European ancestor. "I don't doubt it," Atwater said. "But I'll tell you, I'd rather be a dead nigger than any part of white. When I was a little boy I wanted to be white. When I saw them in the nice swimming pool and I had to go through brambles and snakes to swim in a creek, I wanted to be white. But that was before I knew what went into getting that swimming pool. I couldn't live with that—knowing it came out of holding other people down."

Atwater understood that a great deal of white wealth, especially in the South, derived from exploited black labor. To Atwater, this was a fact that required no fancy research for verification; all he had to do was to look over his shoulders and the shoulders of his forebears. Yet I found that many white students failed to grasp this fact after a semester's worth of reading and discussion. I wondered which form of denial, the psychological kind that Atwater practiced, or the mass kind practiced by my white students, was more damaging.

We also talked about the so-called achievement gap in school—that is, black kids not doing as well in school, on average, as white kids.

I told Atwater that many white students attributed the problem to black kids' failure to work hard. I could guess what Atwater would say to this, but I wanted to hear him say it: "A lot of black kids, they seen their grandaddies and granmommas work hard; they seen their daddies and mommas work hard; they seen every damn black body around them work hard—and not get ahead. So if you tell him 'work hard and you'll do all right,' he knows your ass is lying and he ain't gonna listen." What would you tell him? "The truth. Then he *might* listen to what else you got to say about school giving him *some* advantage."

What if all the black kids started doing well in school? Atwater laughed. "Whitey for damn sure would still have to find somebody to do his flunky jobs or things would blow all to hell!" On the final exam, Atwater might have lost points for lack of nuance, but he'd have earned them back for lack of bullshit.

Atwater was of the generation that peopled the civil rights movement. But he was uninvolved. "I never marched against segregation," he said. "I figured that if Charlie didn't want my money, to hell with him. I'd spend it somewhere else." I told Atwater I was surprised, given

his grasp of racial politics, that he didn't participate. He said, "Well, Mike, I was pretty fucked up in those years. There was a lot going on that I didn't even know about. I was wide open and didn't give a damn about Chapel Hill or the South." Given Atwater's knack for turning a phrase, I wondered what part he might have played, if he'd had his head together. He'd once been Shine. Malcolm had once been Detroit Red.

I gave Atwater a copy of W. E. B. DuBois's *The Souls of Black Folk*. Atwater was moved by the book and talked about it more excitedly than anything else I gave him to read or listen to on tape. A week or so after I gave him the book I asked how he was liking it. "Man, his essays are like poems," Atwater said. "It makes you feel like he's talking right to you, and I can identify with what he's saying. He says that you *gotta* be black—you can't do anything about it, because it's put on you. Then you end up living one way and feeling another. That's me. That's how my life has been. Like a double man. Living one way and feeling another."

He went on: "If I'd read that book thirty years ago, maybe my life wouldn't have been so rocky. He's saying that not all whites are bad and that *greed* is the source of the problem. Most black folks can't see that. All they can see is whitey. They don't see how greed can make black folks act just like white. If I'd understood that, maybe I could've slapped that hate off sooner."

Atwater jumped to thoughts of school: "Another reason I lost interest in school is that I wanted to talk about philosophy and psychology and shit like that, and it was a slack place in those departments. They didn't give us books like [*The Souls of Black Folk*] when I was in school. All they wanted you to be was a farmer or a mechanic. Or if you wanted to go to college, they wanted you to be a teacher, and I didn't want that. I went into the army thinking that if I fought for whitey, he'd let me get a decent education and the kind of job I wanted. But when I came out of the army I was not in a smooth relationship with myself and couldn't get my shit together. I was too young to know how to handle my emotions."

"Maybe this book would've made a difference," Atwater continued. "If I'd read it a long time ago maybe I wouldn't've been such a dumb ass and wasted all those years. Really, Mike, all those years—when I was

in school and in the army and on the street—all I wanted was to feel like a man. Part of me was trying to live the way whitey wants you to live, and another part was trying to get the rest of my shit together in a way I was comfortable with. But I could never get those pieces together, and I thought it was my fault and that I wasn't gonna amount to shit. So I gave up on myself. Now I see why that was wrong—to blame myself and give up."

Atwater had said some of this before, and much had been there between the lines, but DuBois's book brought it out. Much of the blame Atwater had laid on his mother and ex-wife, Atwater confessed, was a smokescreen. All those years he wasn't angry at his mother or his ex-wife so much as he was angry at himself. It wasn't as if Atwater hadn't known that whitey was an obstacle to the realization if his dreams. But still he absorbed the message that, as a man, failure was his and his alone. Atwater's anger was, then, largely anger at what he had believed to be his own weakness and unworthiness. Maybe, too, Atwater had thought—hating the thought and himself for thinking it—that whitey was right about black men.

Atwater's dilemma was bigger even than this. The white world set a standard for manhood that it would do little to help Atwater meet. In fact, the white world was happy, or at least willing, to let Atwater stumble and fall short. When he did, the women in his life tried to protect and comfort him. Knowing what he faced as a black man, they went further and forgave his sins against them. But their forgiveness could not validate Atwater's manhood. Rather, it only underscored his weakness, hence the anger he perversely vented at those who loved him. The kind of validation Atwater had sought, and loathed himself for wanting, was from the audience least likely to give it: whitey. This is what DuBois helped Atwater understand. And perhaps, finally, what DuBois did was to help Atwater forgive himself.

Atwater was also a man who could laugh, a capacity that had helped him survive a multitude of pains. One time when a conversation about the future of race relations had left us both feeling depressed, Atwater suddenly flashed a grin and adopted the pose of a fire-and-brimstone preacher. He sat on the edge of his bed, leaned over his meal table, pointed a finger at the sky, and said, "I'm gonna lay some prophecy on

you now, Mike. Listen to me. No *lotion*, no *screen*, no *oil* is gonna make it safe for white people to be out in the sun—not once the ozone layer is gone. Then only the mixed people and Africans will be able to be out there getting things done." He brought his finger down and tapped the back of his hand. "*This*, this pigment, will become the key to life, and it's something the white man can't make. I tell you, brother, the white man has done fucked up the ozone to put dollars in his pocket, and for that he will fry his own ass."

Three days after his sixty-seventh birthday a nurse called to say that Atwater was going to the hospital. His red blood cell count was low, making it hard for him to stay oxygenated. A transfusion might be necessary. They were also going to do a colonoscopy to try to find out why there was blood in his stool. If all went well, she said, Atwater would be back the next day. This time, he was. Atwater did not need a transfusion, and the colonoscopy found only hemorrhoids. Was anything else wrong? "I don't know," Atwater said later. "No one told me the results of the tests they did. I think they're back to experimenting on me."

For a while, things stabilized. As usual, our conversations rambled. Atwater told me of a job he'd once had putting new covers on worn-out mattress springs. "They'd make 'em look like new, then sell 'em to poor folks as if it was a bargain." He told me of a time he cleaned blinds in a D.C. hotel. "One time I did the room where Nixon and his wife stayed. Before I left, I crawled into the sheets for a minute, so I could say I was in the same bed as the president's wife." He remarked on the Elian Gonzalez affair: "That's damn ridiculous. They should have given that boy back to his daddy right away. Anyone could see that the uncle was crazy as shit. It's all a publicity thing to make Cuba look bad." About a proposed lottery in North Carolina: "That's like playing numbers— a damn waste of money. When I was on the street I'd rather drink my money up than play the numbers. But some people, man, they had all kinds of systems. That's all they'd think about was playing numbers, and they'd spend their last dollar doing it."

On a warm day in late April, as I was getting ready to leave, Atwater and I stood at his window looking out at the blossoming trees. The window was open and the breeze that wafted in carried the scent of lawnmower exhaust and freshly cut grass. We watched a dark-skinned

young woman in tight jeans walk across the parking lot. As she passed out of sight, Atwater turned to me and asked, "Mike, you ever had any black pussy?" He was indeed back to normal.

Months earlier, Atwater had talked about making audiotapes for his family. At his request, I bought him a cassette recorder and a package of blank tapes. What do you want to say? I asked. "I need to tell my family some things so they'll understand why I did the things I did. I need to lay some truth on them. They've never heard my side of the story." It was his sons he wanted to speak to.

For months Atwater said he was trying to get his thoughts organized and to get up the energy to make the tapes. After a while, when it seemed clear that Atwater wasn't going to manage it on his own, I offered to videotape him if he wanted to make a statement to his family. "Ooowee! Wouldn't that be something!" he said. "I'd be dead as hell and *still* talking to them, apologizing for whatever I done to fuck their heads up." That was the only time I heard him mention an apology.

Talk about making tapes for his family fed my doubts about how well I'd really come to know Atwater. Through hundreds of conversations, through interviews with others, by digging up records, and by observing what he did, I had, in many ways, come to know him very well. Did Boswell know Johnson any better? As Atwater once said, surprised at some piece of information I'd found, "Mike, you got more shit on me than I got on myself." I suppose I did, inasmuch as I found out things he'd forgotten or chose not to remember. Still, I wondered what remained unsaid.

Atwater's sexuality was more complex than the image of the everready hetero stud that he fashioned for himself. His sexual voracity was a consistent theme. But here too, he was, it seems, a double man.

He dropped hints, such as a story of an encounter with a transvestite. "Years ago I had to do it to one up in Connecticut. I picked her up and later found a little penis down there. I did it to her anyhow. She was pretty; had titties and everything." Such as a comment on how men become HIV-positive: "It might be drugs or it might be sex. You never know. They might go one way [sexually] for a long time, then another. It ain't as set as it seems." Such as a comment on the body: "The asshole is sensitive. Sometimes a man explores his body and finds out he's got some woman in him." Such as a casual remark in the context of

talking about sexual adventures in his apartment: "I like to try every-thing once."

I had heard from others that Atwater was for a time the paid com-panion of a rich bisexual man in Washington, D.C. Atwater never vol-unteered the story. And never seeming to find the right moment, I didn't ask him to confirm it. For all his heterosexual brag, I didn't find it hard to imagine Atwater—in his years as a barely employable, hard-core alcoholic—playing this role, selling his dick. If the story is true, and Atwater chose not to mention it, I suspect this had as much to do with not wanting to appear submissive and dependent as with not wanting to appear gay.

In an early interview, Atwater told me that he was once charged with a crime against nature. This happened in the late 1950s when Atwater was back in Chapel Hill after getting out of the army. Atwater said he had been "sort of playing around" at a party with a young gay man and that the charge—which Atwater insisted was false and which was later dropped—arose out of a dispute over a stolen jacket. The sec-ond time Atwater told me the story, while he was living at Cat's, he said, "Man, I run off at the mouth sometimes," implying that he'd just offered a special revelation. I said that he had told me the same story before. "I did? Well, shit. I guess now you know every damn thing about me." Not really, but much of the rest was guessable.

The biographer wanted Atwater to remove his masks. The friend, the part of me that felt affection for Atwater and liked to spend time with him—lies, tales, wit, masks, and all—left some things unasked. I'm not sure why. Perhaps because I felt that Atwater had given enough. Perhaps I also dreaded the finality implied by saying, "Well, that's it. No need to talk anymore. Now I really do know everything about you."

In early June I read Atwater a draft of the chapter on his childhood. I pulled a chair up next to his bed. He laid back and listened. When I finished, he said, "That's accurate as hell—right down the damn alley. I like it. Makes me feel like a big shot, lying here putting my stamp of approval on what you wrote." I flipped back through the pages and got Atwater to clarify a few details. As I tucked the manuscript into my bag, he said, "You know, Mike, if you can get two damn words out of all this that will help somebody understand another person or another culture,

or get off the bottle or the smoke and get their shit together, then it's worth it." I damn sure hoped he was right.

Every night before bed Atwater rigged his ventilator. This entailed switching his oxygen tube from the machine to a tank and then, when he had it ready, to the ventilator. Atwater got it down to a routine, though it made him nervous. "It isn't hard, Mike. You could probably do it in ten minutes. But it takes me thirty minutes, sometimes an hour, 'cause I have to rest and stay calm. Just the *idea* of having to rush can trigger my shit and I start having breathing trouble." Atwater said he had asked for help with the ventilator but was told that he should continue to set it up himself as long as he was able.

I saw Atwater in early July, after a two-week vacation. While I was gone, he had acquired an electric scooter, something he'd been wanting for a long time. He bought it used for $250 from a guy that Dr. Halle had put him in touch with. The scooter was candy apple red with black trim. On a label below the handlebars was the model name: *Celebrity*. Perfect for Atwater.

Also new were Atwater's swollen ankles. When I pointed this out, he said his ankles didn't hurt and he had no idea what was causing the problem. I suggested he see a doctor about it (Lena noticed the swelling and made the same suggestion). Later, when I looked up from jotting notes, I noticed another first. For over four years, no matter how tired he might be, Atwater had always been alert and tuned-in when I saw him. Now he dozed off.

A week later the ankles were still swollen. Atwater had not seen anyone about them. He was also using an oxygen tank instead of the machine. When I asked why, he said the machine wasn't working right and that he wanted "good strong oxygen" from the tank instead of the "broken down shit that comes out of the machine." He also said he'd stopped using his ventilator at night because he didn't have the energy to hook it up. He said he'd asked Lena to look into getting him help with the ventilator.

Atwater was barely coherent as he ranted about the oxygen machine and the lack of help with the ventilator, so I wasn't sure how to judge his complaint. It worried me that he seemed addled, because if there was

one thing Atwater was normally good at, even if his logic was quirky, it was speaking plainly. I sat and jotted notes as Atwater strapped on the nebulizer mask to take a breathing treatment. Afterwards, he was relaxed and clearheaded. I thought perhaps his earlier muddle was attributable to a low oxygen level in his blood.

We joked that day about how he had taken over the entire room and now had a "one-bedroom suite with garage." Atwater mentioned some risqué show he'd seen on TV (he'd gotten cable), and I proposed that he show one of his raunchy videos in the activity room and lead a discussion on sexuality for seniors. He laughed. "Yeah, lock the doors and let the old folks get naked! Hah!" I said that the people who ran the place might disapprove of geriatric orgies. "Hell, Mike, one look at all that sagging flesh and no one would want to do nothing nohow."

On July 27 I went to see Atwater and found his door closed. I knocked, got no reply, and pushed the door open gently. He wasn't in the bathroom either. When I inquired at the nurses' station, I was told that Atwater had gone to the hospital earlier in the week because of chest pains. I wanted to give someone chest pains.

When I found Atwater at the hospital, he was dozing between bites of lunch. He told me that he'd gone to the hospital because his chest pains didn't go away when he took nitro. Now he was feeling fine and was set to be discharged. He told me he'd asked the people at the nursing home to call me (Lena hadn't been called, either, as it turned out). I said that we ought to tape my phone number to his wrist, otherwise the last paragraph of the book might have to say that I went to see him at the nursing home on Friday and found out he'd croaked on Monday.

Atwater laughed at the morbid joke, but the possibility of his suddenly being gone brought me up short. I recalled what he had said after one of his previous trips to the ER: "No matter what happens, I always think I've got a little longer to live. But one day it's gonna be alley oops!—I'm gone." I knew he was right; it could happen exactly that way. Even so, I hoped that when the time came, I'd have a chance to be there and say good-bye.

We were interrupted by a visibly pregnant social worker with a clipboard. She asked Atwater if he understood that he was being discharged to the nursing home. "I ain't got no place else to go," he said. When

she finished, a nurse with the same standard-issue clipboard came in and asked Atwater to sign a form. It seemed innocuous, but Atwater politely said no. Later I asked Atwater why he'd refused to sign. "I don't sign no papers in the hospital," he said.

Atwater returned to the nursing home and I saw him again on August 10. He told me he couldn't charge the battery on his scooter. I looked at the scooter but couldn't figure out what was wrong. "For $250," he said, "I didn't get no owner's manual." I said I'd try to get one from a dealer. I noticed that he had a new ventilator. Atwater said he'd brought it back from the hospital, but hadn't used it yet, because he couldn't get anyone to help him set it up.

I asked if he'd thought more about making tapes for his family. He said he'd thought about it but couldn't get up the energy. "I'm a lazy ass, Mike. I sit here and look at myself and wonder why I don't do nothing. I've got to get into *something*, some reading and straightening shit out. Back in my apartment I sort of thought I'd kill myself, in a nice way—smoking and fucking. Then you came along and gave me this book thing to do, but I still can't seem to do much on my own." Does that make your days here drag? "No, time flies. That's the funny thing. I don't do nothing, but my days go by fast."

On the evening of Wednesday, August 16, I returned from a conference in Washington, D.C. After five days of meetings and a five-hour drive, I wanted to eat, read for a while, and sleep in my own bed. I would see Atwater and Mason the next day. The phone rang at 6:10 A.M. It took me a moment to recognize Lena's voice. She was calling from the nursing home. "Anthony passed," she said. "I thought you'd want to see him before the funeral home people take the body away."

I met Lena at the nurses' station on Atwater's wing. The duty nurse said she'd found Atwater on the bathroom floor at 4:30 A.M. He had apparently suffered a heart attack while using the toilet. They used the lift to put him back in bed, which is where he was when I went to his room. His face was puffy and had begun to lose color. The oxygen tube was gone. The other half of the room looked as if it was being set up for a new resident. I wondered if the prospect of a roommate had upset Atwater.

Lena said that when her phone rang at 5:00 A.M., she thought it meant either that Shine had gone to the ER again or that he had died. She called me as soon as she found my number on a slip of paper in his dresser. I said something about Shine's death not being a surprise and about him wanting to go without fuss. We agreed that he had managed to do that.

Atwater's son and ex-wife arrived. I exchanged hellos with Chris and nods with Dorothy. There was talk of cremation, a memorial service, a will (Atwater did not have one), and what to do with Atwater's belongings. I kept expecting Atwater to sit up and offer an opinion. At a little after 7:00 A.M. two people from the funeral home arrived. We left the room while they moved the body from the bed to a folding gurney. In a few minutes, they and the body were gone.

The expectation, as Lena understood, was that Atwater's belongings would be cleared out right away. Lena and I went to scrounge for boxes and plastic trash bags. When we returned to the room, I said we could load everything into my car, and that I'd give Chris a ride home, so Dorothy left. Lena, Chris, and I packed. "This is the last thing I expected to be doing today," Chris said. "When the time came, I thought it would be Bernard doing this." It took less than an hour to sort and pack it all.

We filled the back of my small station wagon, which had held all of Atwater's belongings once before, when he moved out of Cat's place. On the way home, Chris said he wasn't sure what he was supposed to do next. I wanted to offer some soothing advice, but I had none. I said that nobody knows what to do when a parent dies, but that the people at the funeral home, where he would meet Lena later, would have a checklist of things that needed to be taken care of. We spent the rest of the short ride talking about shopping for school supplies for his kids.

At the house we put the bags and boxes on the front porch. Chris said he would figure out what to do with it all later. He offered me another chance to take anything I wanted. I said I'd gotten my stuff, the books and tapes I had loaned Atwater, while we were packing. We stared silently at his father's belongings. I saw, or thought I did, in Chris's expression a feeling of loss that surprised me, considering the estrangement between him and his father.

"I know you didn't have a great relationship with him," I said, looking for a way to acknowledge what he seemed to be feeling, "but still it's upsetting when a father dies."

"No, it wasn't a great relationship," he said. "But he was who he was."

It was an ambiguous assessment, but all its possible meanings seemed apt: *he was who he was*—my father—and whatever his flaws, I loved him; *he was who he was* and now he's gone, so there's no point in bemoaning what we didn't have; and *he was who he was*, and no one could change him, for better or worse. Yes, he was who he was, I thought, and under other conditions he could have been more.

Atwater was sixty-seven years, five months, and fourteen days old when he died on August 17, 2000. Right before his sixty-sixth birthday, he'd told me, "Everything past sixty-five is bonus time, 'cause I done enough already to kill myself." I said that he'd already beaten the odds. He knew what I meant: that he'd exceeded the average life span for a black man in the United States. "Yeah," he said, "I've always refused to be statistical damn categorized." For which I was glad.

Before I left the nursing home on the morning Atwater died, I asked Lena to call me and let me know about the funeral. She didn't call, and when I tried to reach her the next day, she was out. I was upset by Atwater's death and not thinking clearly. Which may be why I began to imagine that I was being excluded. It was as if all the time Atwater and I had spent together, all the effort to document and make sense of his life, counted for nothing. "Whatever he was," I imagined I was being told silently, "he was one of us, a member of *this* community, and he's ours again now, not yours, so stay away."

On Friday evening I called Cat. Her husband Sam answered. Cat was at work, he said. He also told me that Atwater had died and that the funeral was tomorrow at 11:00 at Jones Funeral Home. Welcome or not, I decided to go.

Lena called the next morning at 9:00. "I suppose you saw the obituary," she said. I hadn't. It had run in Friday's edition of the Chapel Hill paper, which I hadn't seen. Lena confirmed what Sam had told me. Is Jones the small place on Roberson? I asked. Out of reflex—perhaps assuming that *of course everyone knows where Jones Funeral Home is*—she said yes. But I was thinking of the wrong place.

It was 10:50 A.M. when I parked on west Franklin Street, near its intersection with Roberson. I walked from there to the funeral home: *Knott's*

Funeral Home. When I realized my mistake, I felt beaten. I was saddened by Atwater's death, angry and disappointed about what I perceived as exclusion, worried about how welcome I'd be at the service, and, with only five minutes left before the service was to start, lost. I had no idea where Jones Funeral Home was.

I started back to my car. As I turned the corner onto Franklin Street, I saw a mail carrier, a tall black man, my rescuer I hoped, emerge from between two buildings. When I asked him for directions, he smiled, as if I'd asked how to get to Chapel Hill. "It's on Graham, right over there," he said, pointing. It was less than a block away. I ran, tie flapping.

The sign on the front of the small white building announced the service. It was not for Anthony Atwater, as I expected, but for William B. Atwater, Jr. It was a symbolic reclaiming. His family had given him back the name he bore when he was still his mother's sweet boy, full of promise. I thought of the name on the sign as an encrypted biography, readable by those who knew both "William B. Atwater, Jr." and Burness, Shine, Popcorn, or Anthony. Even in death, Atwater was a double man.

I made it with a few minutes to spare. I filed in behind a pair of older men and sat in a back row. I counted sixty faces, mine the palest in the room. Chris, standing up front with his family, had seen me come in, and now he came back up the aisle toward me. I tried to read his expression.

"I'm glad you could make it," Chris said, reaching out to shake my hand. "There'll be a chance to say a few words later, if you'd like to do that." It was as if I'd been falling and now an invisible parachute opened. I was relieved, embarrassed by my paranoia, and nonplussed.

Of course I should do it, I thought. Who was in a better position to eulogize Atwater? Chris's invitation was a compassionate acknowledgment of this position, and I wanted to say yes, to rise to the occasion. But I had gathered no thoughts, and did not feel confident about speaking off the cuff. I told Chris that I wasn't prepared to say anything. "Think about it and I'll check with you again later," Chris said, then returned to the front to sit with his family.

The service began with "Amazing Grace." The officiating reverend read Ecclesiastes 3:1–8, reminding us that there is a time for all things. Cat's son Ira testified that Atwater had, two years earlier, asked the

Lord for forgiveness. The Reverend Marie Mann (Mr. Mason's niece) offered words of comfort. She stressed repentence, letting bygones be bygones, and getting right with God. She said, "God does not judge the way that man judges," and everyone knew why she said it.

Atwater, it seemed, was serving as two kinds of cautionary tale. He had done plenty, as many of the assembled well knew, to incur the need for forgiveness, and it would behoove us all to avoid getting so far into spiritual debt. One also would be wise, the Lord's boundless mercy notwithstanding, to seek forgiveness sooner rather than later. But then the second lesson: whatever the apparent misdeeds, it is not our place to judge. To dwell overly much on the sins of a neighbor is to court pride and to risk blindness to the beam in one's own eye. Good points, with which Atwater would have concurred.

The time came for members of the gathering to speak. Chris walked back and asked me again. I demurred, feeling unable to do justice to Atwater or to the occasion. There were no other statements, only mention that the family had received cards of sympathy, one of which was read aloud. Listening to those impersonal lines that had nothing to do with Atwater, I regretted my silence. Here, then, too late, is what I might have said:

> The man I knew for the past four and a half years as Anthony Atwater—the man many of you knew as Burness or Shine, and some of you knew as Popcorn—once told me what he wanted said, and not said, at his funeral. "They could say," he told me, " 'Anthony tried to be a good person'—and that's it; that's all they need to say. I don't want a preacher making up stories about me. They can't say I accomplished a whole lot in life. I wasn't a good husband or a good father."
>
> Strange as it might seem, it comforts me to recall those words and the honest self-appraisal they contain. Anthony knew what it meant to be a good person, and I think that's what he wanted to be. His failures in this regard, failures of which he was well aware, grew out of ordinary human weakness combined with conditions of life that capitalized on those weaknesses.
>
> In *Notes of a Native Son*, James Baldwin writes about his father's funeral. In speaking about his father and other black men in Harlem,

Baldwin says, "it was better not to judge the man who had gone down under an impossible burden. It was better to remember: Thou knowest this man's fall; but thou knowest not his wrassling." And so it was with Anthony. We know his falls but not the inner struggles he went through before and after. I believe he did struggle, precisely because there was inside him a good man, if not the best wrestler.

When Anthony said he didn't want a preacher telling stories about him, making him sound better than he was, I believe that was the good man inside him speaking. I took him to mean it this way: If, when I am gone, you want to get some value out of my life, then tell the truth about me; otherwise, how can you learn from what I did or didn't do? A lesser man might not have cared or might have preferred to anticipate sugar-coated stories.

How Anthony wanted the story of his life told is important to me, because I am writing about his life. I met Anthony while I was inter-viewing men for a book about fathers and sons. As he told me about himself and his life, I began to wonder how he'd come to his circum-stances at that time and how he made sense of his life. I thought maybe there was something valuable to be learned by answering those ques-tions. And so I asked if I could write about him, and he agreed.

Biographies are usually written about people whose lives are full of accomplishment. Anthony did not fit that pattern. He was not a hero, nor am I trying to turn him into one. I wanted to understand him as a man who, for better or worse, played the hand he was dealt. I believed then, when I met him, and believe more strongly now, that we can learn more about the times we live in by studying how ordinary folks deal with life than by creating characters who are larger than life.

To my mind, it was accidental that I met Anthony. But that's not how he saw it. He said it was God, or, as Anthony called him, the Boss, who had brought me around. "He knew I still had something to say," Anthony once told me, "that's why he let me survive that throat cancer and brought you around—so you could get it all down." There's no doubt that Anthony liked the attention and liked the idea of being written about. But I think he also saw it as a chance for redemption, a way to make his life count for more than it had.

A few months ago Anthony told me that if I got only two words out of his life that would help people understand each other better, or help someone get off the bottle or off the smoke, then our project was worth doing. I believe that Anthony's life holds lessons that can help people understand each other better and avoid the traps in which he got caught. If I can draw those lessons out, perhaps Anthony's life will yield more than any of us can now imagine.

I know it would provide comfort on this occasion to say that Anthony had gotten right with God before he died. While none of us can know what was in Anthony's heart before he passed, I can share with you something he wrote not long ago. It's a poem to which Anthony gave the title "Who Am I Today? A Thankful One." It goes like this:

O God! I want to thank you this day for making
me to rise with such feelings of joy.
My friends have been wonderful to
me. And this in itself is a blessing of
great value to me. Oh, how much I thank you.

O God! I have in my heart a message for
my friends. A message I can't seem to
bring out in words I feel would reveal
the full extent of my expression, and
the expression that must come from
within the depth of my bowel to maintain
its special beauty.

Please God! In the presence of my friends, allow me to
pull back, to peel, so to speak, each layer of
my being and expose the core of my soul,
for it is here where my special kind of thank-you's live.

I don't know if this poem proves that Anthony had gotten *right* with God, in the way that's usually meant. But it seems to me that he couldn't have written this poem, which is also a prayer, if he hadn't at least smoothed things out with God. Anthony tells us that the part of him

from which his gratitude arises is deep inside and not easy to open up. This is his insight into himself. But is this not true of men more generally? In our fear of making ourselves vulnerable, do we not often keep our feelings of love hidden inside? So perhaps Anthony's poem is addressed not only to God but to us all. The message being that we should not wait to share the love we feel for others. We should tell it, show it, as often as possible. I see this poem as a window to the goodness that was inside Anthony, goodness that was often trumped by the weakness of his flesh. In this regard he was like us all, and so we all might learn from his struggles. And perhaps in the long run that will be the gift of Anthony's life: a little more understanding of what it means to be human and to try, win or lose, to be good. It might seem odd, or against all odds, that this result should come of Anthony's troubled life. But as Anthony once said, paraphrasing a familiar line, "The Boss works in mysterious ways."

Out of respect for the solemnity of the occasion I would have left out Atwater's pithy summary of his own life, this one cribbed from Julius Caesar. "The story of my life," Atwater once said, "is, 'I came, I saw, and it conquered my ass.'" It was not great wit, but coming from Atwater it was honest and fitting. And, like his poem, it offered another lesson: we should be sure to laugh sometimes at our own pretensions.

The service ended, and I found myself walking next to Cat as we filed out. "It was Popcorn's time," she said, tears welling in her eyes. "He was suffering so bad, the way his breathing was. The last time I saw him, last week Sunday, I gave him a kiss on the forehead before I left. And he said, 'Oooh, keep going.' I just said, 'You won't never give up, will you?' And he said, 'I won't stop wanting it 'til I'm dead.' That's how he was. That was Popcorn." It was. Part of him, anyway.

Three months later I called Cat to arrange lunch. She told me she had run into Chris at the hospital. They both had laughed at the irony when he told her that Atwater's ashes were on the shelf in Dorothy's house. "Popcorn always wanted to get back with Dorothy," Cat said to me. "He said he hated her, but he really didn't. He didn't want anybody to know how he felt. He loved them and they loved him. They just couldn't get along." Nor he with himself.

two old birds holding on

About twenty women were gathered around four rectangular folding tables that had been set up on the shaded green next to the apartment complex. The tables were littered with frosted plastic cups, empty two-liter soda bottles, paper plates, plastic forks, and remnants of cake. None of which seemed to interest the women as they talked in twos and threes. The party, put on by the housing authority and the residents' council, was for everyone in the complex who had a birthday in September.

Martha, who was turning eighty-four, sat in her wheelchair at one end of the table nearest the parking lot. I gave her a birthday kiss and showed her the presents I'd brought: peaches and pickled okra. Matthew was not there. "He's in the apartment," Martha said. "He said he was feeling too puny to come out."

Matthew was dozing in his recliner when I rapped on the outer door. He snapped awake and hollered for me to come in. As soon as I cracked the door I said hello, loudly, so he'd know who was there.

I sat down in Martha's recliner and asked him what he was thinking about. Usually he denied thinking about anything, but this time he said, "I was thinking about how I used to let the good times roll, and about how I can't do that anymore." I asked if he was feeling sick. He said no, that he "just didn't feel like going out there," though I hadn't mentioned the party.

Joann from the residents' council popped in to say hello. She complimented Mr. Mason on his new haircut and said that it made him

look ten years younger. "Thank you," he said. "Just hearing you say that makes me *feel* ten years younger." Mr. Mason had long since forgotten that Joann introduced me to him—almost five years earlier—so now he introduced me to her: "This here is my friend, Brother Mike Schwable," reversing the *l* and the *b*, as he often did. "He's kept me out of a lot of trouble. If I get off track, he says, 'Now, Dr. Reet, don't you go doin' that.'"

Joann was leaving as Martha rolled up the ramp. She held the door open for Martha and stayed to talk for a few more minutes. After Joann left, I helped Martha get into her recliner. I asked if she'd had a good time at the party. She said she did, adding that Matthew should have come out, too. "I told you I felt *puny*," he said, sounding irritated. "And don't you complain tomorrow if you're sick because you were out there all day." That was as clear an indication as Matthew ever gave, in front of me, that he was angry at Martha for leaving him alone.

I suspected that Martha had given Matthew a hard time about coming to the birthday party because she was worried about him. His decline was gradual and, over a short period of time, barely noticeable. But Martha could see that Matthew was looking different and no longer doing things he used to.

One day, near the end of October 2000, I remarked to Matthew, who had been dozing in his recliner, that he seemed sleepier than usual. "Just old is all," he said, coming around a bit. "Old and tired." That was true, but he was either a notch below normal, or normal had slipped a notch. Martha knew it too.

"Matthew looks pitiful," she said. "He needs to get outside and walk; that's what the doctor told him." This woke him up.

"I'm ninety years old," he came back at her. "I can't be running around out there like a baby."

"You ain't no *ninety*!" Martha said, slapping her hand on the arm of her chair. "I sure wish you'd stop rushing it along. You're only eighty-nine!"

Matthew declined to rebut. He tucked his chin into his chest, seemingly beaten, then leaned his head back and resumed dozing. Martha stared at him for a second, then turned her attention to the TV. "I don't believe in that, either—" she said, nodding to indicate a holiday commercial on the screen, "bringing Christmas here before it comes."

For months Martha had talked about getting a new bed. The double bed on which they'd slept for years was shot. One end of the box spring was broken and propped up by bricks and boards. The headboard and frame had nearly fallen apart when I once moved the bed to look for a missing pair of Martha's shoes. What Martha wanted was a queen-sized bed, with wooden head- and footboards.

The room was already cramped. With Martha's dresser on one side, and Matthew's dresser and armoire on the other, there were only narrow passages between the bed and the walls. It didn't help that the walls were lined with boxes of old clothes. Still, the Masons managed to get in and out with no problems. Everything had been in place for years, and Matthew knew—once he was in the bedroom—how to find his way to his familiar spot on the mattress.

I suggested that a queen-sized bed might be too big, and that a double would fit better. Matthew didn't want a new bed at all. But Martha was determined, and fixed on a queen. And so she had the aide take her to a furniture store, where she picked out a new bed, box spring, and mattress.

The phone rang at 5:45 A.M. the day after the bed was delivered. It was Martha, in tears. Matthew couldn't get off the bed. "He can't get his feet on the floor," she said. "He's been like that since 2:30." I asked to speak to Matthew. I tried to coach him to pull himself toward the edge of the bed, but it wasn't working. "I can't understand what he's saying," I heard him say, as he handed the phone back to Martha.

Fifteen minutes later I saw the problem. Matthew's knees were at the edge of the bed, his feet dangling four inches above the floor. He was in his usual house clothes: a loose pair of old gray pants, a gray knit sweater over a plaid flannel shirt, and his black vinyl slippers.

Martha said he'd been trying to get up to use the bathroom when he got stuck. "I been *trying* to get to the bathroom," Matthew affirmed from his helpless position. I pulled him toward the edge of the bed until his feet reached the floor, then I got behind him on the bed and pushed him to a sitting position. When he got his feet under him, I slid off the bed and helped him stand.

I was behind him, my arms around his chest, nudging his feet forward with mine. There was so little space between the side of the bed and the dresser that we couldn't have turned if we wanted to; all we

could do was to go straight ahead. We were nearly to the end of the bed, about six feet from the bathroom, and I thought we were home free, when Matthew said, "I can't hold it any more. Can you get me something?"

There was no room to go around him, so I climbed across the bed and over the footboard, looking for something that would spare Mr. Mason a further indignity. I grabbed a large plastic cup on Martha's dresser, dumped out the earrings it held, and told Mr. Mason to hold on another second. I undid his belt and zipper and told him to pull himself out. I held the cup where he couldn't miss.

He tucked himself in and redid his pants. For the moment he was stable, steadying himself on the walnut footboard of the big bed, so I went to fetch his wheelchair. When I got him to the living room, he couldn't get out of the wheelchair by himself. Even with help, moving from the wheelchair to the recliner tired him. I'd never seen him so weak.

Matthew thanked me when I brought him a glass of water. Martha, who was next to him in her recliner, said she was glad that I was able to come over. Matthew thanked me again and said he was pleased to meet me. "That's Mr. Mike," Martha said, trying not to sound like she was scolding him. "You been knowing him a long time."

"I have?" he said. "Oh, yeah. That's right. I just got turned around there."

"He *really* got turned around," Martha said to me.

I went back to look at the bed. Whereas the old bed had been set up perpendicular to the doorway, they'd had to turn this one 90 degrees to make it fit. I tried to imagine how to arrange things so Matthew could get around. A lot of stuff would simply have to go.

The Masons were settled in their recliners when I left at 7:00 A.M. The weekend aide would arrive in an hour. Martha had no objection when I told her that the bedroom had to be rearranged.

I called later to see how Matthew was doing. "A whole lot better now than this morning," Martha said. The aide had put him to bed at 4:00 P.M. before she left, so that he wouldn't have to walk by himself from the recliner to the bedroom. "He was turned around pretty good this morning," Martha went on. "I just hope and pray that he don't get

turned around no worse. Matthew will do anything so he don't have to go into no nursing home."

A month later Matthew came down with bronchitis that turned into mild pneumonia, weakening him further and leading to a fall in the bathroom. Though he maintained his miraculous record of no serious injury, he did spend a few days in the hospital. When he got home, he was too weak to walk on his own, and so he spent the hours from 4:00 P.M., when the aide left, until the next morning, in bed. This necessitated the wearing of Depends and, for a time, a condom catheter.

Being sick dulled his appetite. For years, his usual breakfast was two eggs, two slices of toast, a piece of sausage, juice, and coffee. Now he was down to half a slice of toast, a bit of egg, and some juice. In the afternoon, the aide spoon-fed him his fruit cocktail while he sat in his recliner, a bath towel serving as a bib. He'd lost enough weight for his gums to shrink, causing his upper dentures to keep falling loose.

The denture problem added to his disinclination to eat. He also tried to avoid having to pee so often by drinking too little water (despite the aide's urgings). And so, on top of everything else, he was getting dehydrated, which further weakened him.

In mid-December Thomas contacted a social worker in the county's department on aging. The social worker came to the apartment and met with Thomas, Matthew, and Martha to discuss options. Martha seemed to understand that Matthew needed more care than he could get at home. But a place like Shepherd House wasn't an option, the social worker explained, unless Matthew was able to do more for himself. The only option, then, besides staying in the apartment, was what Matthew and Martha thought of as a nursing home.

The Masons listened, and it seemed that Martha was swayed toward moving. But Matthew had figured out that, if they left the apartment, there was no coming back, even if he regained his strength. I visited him the next day.

"You still feeling puny?" I asked Mr. Mason, who was in his recliner. "I sure am. That's the truth. I am feeling puny," he said. When I asked Martha about the meeting with the social worker, Matthew jumped in before she could answer: "I ain't going to no nursing home."

"Sometimes you got to do what you don't want to do," Martha said to him. Turning to me she said, "He can be so *contrary* sometimes!"

This was a minefield, so I teased. "Matthew? Contrary? Is that true, Mr. Mason?"

"Honey," he said, "can't nobody boss *me* around." Mr. Mason indeed refused to be bossed, or persuaded, and so after a week there was no more talk of moving.

Martha tried to find someone to help during the evenings. This would mean paying out of pocket, since the Masons were at the limit of their social service benefits for in-home care. Though Martha said she found someone who would work for nine dollars an hour (the usual rate was fifteen dollars), even this was beyond the Masons' means. So she tried the church. As it turned out, there was a volunteer available, someone with experience as a nursing assistant, to provide a few hours of help a week. Martha told me that the volunteer was a "Miss Lena," who was the sister of Reverend John Atwater. That's Burness's cousin, I told her.

By Christmas, Mr. Mason was strong enough to use the bedside commode (a vertical wall railing had been installed so he could steady himself). He was also able, using a walker, to shuffle around the apartment. But he was still unsteady and couldn't get up from his recliner without help. And so the weekday aide continued to put him to bed at 4:00. The weekend aide would have had to put him to bed at 1:00, when she left, but since the semester was over I was able, for the next few weeks, to come over at 5:00 and help Mr. Mason to bed.

Sometimes Mr. Mason's refusal to be bossed made it hard to give him the help he needed. It was a little after 5:00 P.M. on the day before Christmas Eve, when I said, "Okay, Mr. Mason. We should probably start moving you toward bed." (I was dismayed at how easily I'd fallen into using that patronizing "we.") Matthew and Martha were both in their recliners. I had just finished cleaning up after feeding him his fruit cocktail.

"Martha can go to bed if she wants to," he said, "but I'll stay out here a while." He might as well have proposed walking to the grocery store for a sack of potatoes.

"Matthew," Martha said, with a pinching tone, "you *know* you can't go all that way by yourself. Mr. Mike come over to help you get into bed."

"Mr. Mason, I know that your legs are getting stronger—"

"That's right," he said.

"—but it would be *safer* if you walked to bed while I'm here, because you're not back to 100 percent yet."

"That's right," Martha said to me. "He's *not* back to 100 percent. He's still weak."

"I can walk," Matthew said.

"Then you *show* him. Get yourself up out of that chair and *show* him you can walk," Martha said. She was just goading him to move, but I didn't want Mr. Mason to think that I expected him to prove anything to me.

"It'll be safer," I said, appealing to good judgment, "if you do it while I'm here to help, *if* you need it."

"All right. All right," he said, and started trying to stand. He rose about six inches before settling back down. I set his walker in front of him and helped him up. Halfway through the dining area his pajama bottoms fell to the floor. I pulled them up and guided him the rest of the way to the bedroom, one hand holding the back of the waistband.

"Where's Martha?" he asked, as I swung his feet onto the bed. She had been right behind us and was now making her way past the foot of the bed. "I'm coming, Sugar," she said. "The old lady is here." Before I left, I stocked Martha's nightstand with candy and cough drops for Matthew, a fresh bottle of Sprite, and a roll of toilet paper. I shut off the light in the kitchen, drew the blind in the living room, shut off the TV, locked the door, and left the key in the mailbox. I wondered how long things could go on this way.

A bit longer, it turned out, because Matthew amazed us by rebounding. By late January he could walk using only his cane, and his appetite picked up. For the first time in almost two months he could get from the bedroom to the recliner on his own. In another week he was able to get out of the recliner and to the bedroom by himself. By April, he and Martha were managing nearly as well as they had six months earlier.

For the most part, his mind was intact. One day he asked me if I'd been doing a lot of partying lately. I said no, not much at at all. "How come?" he asked. "You young! When I was your age I used to let the good times roll, child!" I told him that I used to do that, but

that I'd slowed down about twenty years ago. "You slowed down too early," he said.

His memory, though, betrayed him more and more often. One day he couldn't remember my name.

"Who's writing a book about you?" I asked him.

"You," he said, without hesitation. Then, perhaps because his brain wasn't giving him my name, he said, "Did I ask how your wife's doing?"

"Yes, you did. She's doing fine. How's *your* wife doing?"

"She's kind of frisky." That got Martha's attention and drew a laugh. "I'm too old to be frisky," she said.

"What do you mean by 'frisky'?" I asked Mr. Mason.

"Oh, you know. Getting kind of fast and giving me liquor." Martha laughed again.

"She's just trying to keep you young," I said.

"That's right. I reckon so," he said.

Forty-five minutes later I asked if he remembered my name. "Brother Mike Schwable," he said firmly.

"When you first started coming over here," Martha said, "he could remember better than me." Mr. Mason, who had prided himself on his memory, was apologetic: "Brother Mike, I done so much, worked so many jobs and knowed so many people, that I just can't keep up with myself anymore."

Often the first thing Martha did when I got to the apartment was to tell me about some curious piece of Matthew's behavior. One time she told me he'd cussed her out for no reason at all. "He called me everything but child of God," she said. Matthew, sitting next to her in his recliner, looked embarrassed. "Now, Martha, you know that ain't true," he said. "I ain't never called you anything but honey and sweetheart."

Another time she told me how Matthew had said, in bed the night before, that he loved her: "He told me, he said, 'You been a good wife to me and I could kiss you all the time.' I just cried when he said that." She cried when she told me too.

Matthew still liked to tease. I asked him one day, shortly before his ninetieth birthday, if there was anything I could do to make him more comfortable. "You could get me a fifth of liquor," he said, matter-of-factly.

Matthew Mason's ninetieth birthday

"What kind do you want?" I asked, just as plainly.

"Scotch," he said.

"I'll look in my bag and see if I've got some," I said.

The aide, who had been listening to the exchange, was astounded. "Are you *serious*?" she said to me, her eyes wide. I knew Mr. Mason would be delighted by her gullibility. I picked up my shoulder bag and pretended to search its depths.

"Mr. Mason, I'm looking in my bag, and I'm sorry, but I don't see a fifth of Scotch," I said.

"A *pint* will be okay," he said. I poked around in the bag some more.

"I don't seem to have *any*. Can you get by without?"

"Yeah, I reckon I can," he said. "For a little while."

"But it won't be easy, right?"

"Right boy!" he said, tipping his head back for a big laugh. It was good to see him do that. He hadn't done it in months.

On Mr. Mason's ninetieth birthday Martha gave him ninety dollars. He laughed when I said he shouldn't spend it, because he was going to

have to give her back eighty-five dollars in a few months. I took a picture as Martha handed him the money. The next week I showed Martha the photograph. She studied it for a minute, then tapped her finger on the picture and said, "Them's us—just two old birds holding on."

When I first met Mr. Mason, he would tell me about the sayings and toasts that he had used to entertain the fraternity boys, implicitly distinguishing himself from those bits of Dr. Reet shtick. But over the last year, those bits had come to fill a larger part of his conversation. It was if they were pieces of a script etched deeply in his mind, impervious to age. The slightest cue could elicit *Right, boy!* or his favorite toast: *Makes no difference whether you're young or old, let's get together and let the good times roll, because, don'tcha know?, when you're dead, you're done.*

And so I wondered what it meant when even the part of his mind that held the toast seemed to fail him. "Did I ever tell you this?" Mr. Mason began. "What's that?" I played along, though I knew what came next.

"Makes no difference whether you're young or old, let's get together and let the good times roll." I waited for him to finish. After a few seconds, I tried to cue him: "Because, don'tcha know. . . . " He didn't pick it up.

"Don't know what?" he said.

"Because, when you're dead . . . ," I tried again. He just stared vacantly.

"Say it again, Mr. Mason. Your toast. Say the whole thing."

He started over, again ending with "roll." Again I tried to cue him to finish, but he couldn't. He was stuck. Finally I said, "Because, don'tcha know? When you're dead, you're done. Right?"

"Right, boy!" he affirmed, with the usual exaggerated nasal twang.

I wondered if he was really unable to remember the whole toast, or if his infirmity had reached the point where the truth of the last line was unbearable. A few weeks later he gave the whole toast, with zest from start to finish, like he always had. It was the last time.

Martha told me that Matthew was getting turned around more often. He would try to get to the bedroom or bathroom and end up lost in the kitchen. Calling to him didn't work anymore; she had to go get him.

Masons at fraternity house, October 2001

One day she said Matthew was feeling weak (though he wouldn't admit it) and asked me to help him get to the bedroom. He still got turned around, once angrily insisting that the bedroom was to the left when it was to the right, and then wanting to rest on a stool that wasn't there.

I steered him into the bedroom, helped him use the commode, then got him into bed. His mind cleared for moment: "I'm an old man, you know. Thank you for everything, you hear?"

On October 13, 2001, a crisp football Saturday, Mr. Mason made his last appearance at the Phi Delta Theta fraternity house. Several alums had undertaken to raise $600,000 to help endow a Phi Delta Theta/Matthew Mason professorship at UNC, and they wanted Matthew there to hear the speeches and inspire contributions.

Matthew wore his dark blue fraternity blazer, shirt and tie, hat, dark slacks, white socks, and house slippers (to accommodate his swollen ankles). Martha, too, was decked out. She thought they were naming a building after Matthew.

The Masons sat in their wheelchairs in the shade of the porch. It was mostly older members, some decades past graduation, who talked to Matthew and Martha. Matthew rose to the occasion, reeling off his signature phrases and asking the alums how they and their families were doing. Several asked him for a little salt and pepper. He obliged by holding up a hand and allowing them to hook a finger around one of his.

After two hours Matthew was exhausted. The speeches had been made and the Phi's, old and young, were leaving for the stadium. As I wheeled Matthew through the maze of cars parked tightly behind the fraternity house, we skirted a small group of beer-drinking men who looked to be in their mid-fifties. As we passed, one of them glanced at us and said, "My God. Dr. Reet. That man is a living legend."

Back at the apartment we got Matthew out of his jacket and tie and into his recliner. "Martha, when can we go home?" he asked.

Mr. Mason's body was weakening, but he was still capable of snappy exchanges and, when he wanted to, of capping Martha's hectoring. One day I brought Mr. Mason some chocolate. As I unwrapped a piece for him, Martha remarked, "Matthew used to always get me chocolate on my birthday, or any day." I said that he must have been trying to keep her sweet.

"Now I have to keep *him* sweet," she said.

"How do you do that?" I asked. She turned to Matthew.

"Mr. Mike wants to know what I have to do to keep you sweet," she said.

"I'm too old to be sweet," Matthew replied. "Ain't nothing you can do anymore."

"It sure ain't easy, that's for sure," she said.

Before I left, Martha wanted me to help Matthew to the bedroom. He hesitated, mostly for show. "Get up!" she finally hollered at him.

"I don't need any help," he said. "I'm too frisky for that."

"You ain't *frisky*. You's old. Now get up," she ordered.

"We's *both* old," he reminded her, consenting then to be helped out of his recliner.

Another afternoon later that month Matthew was, apropos of nothing in particular, reprising his toast. "Makes no difference whether

you're young or old, let's get together and let the good times roll," he said, ending there, as he now did.

"How should we do that?" I asked.

"Get us some liquor and music, and then cut up," he said.

"Okay, you start," I said, evoking his laugh.

"Well, I don't know," he said. "I reckon Martha might not like it."

Martha jumped in: "He'd be even worse if he was drinking. He used to holler when he'd get drunk."

"Who, me? I don't remember that," Matthew said.

"You don't remember nothing," Martha said.

"Nothing I don't *want* to," he said.

On December 23 Martha called at 10:00 P.M. to say that Matthew had fallen in the bathroom and that the rescue squad was on the way. Matthew's younger brother David and his wife, Emma, were there. Martha was upset and not speaking clearly, so I asked for Emma. "Matthew's on the floor in the bathroom," she said. "He doesn't seem to be hurt. He's laughing and saying 'let the good times roll.' " Even so, they were going to send him to the hospital when the rescue squad arrived.

Matthew came home the next day. The EZ Rider wasn't running, so they had to send him home in an ambulance. By 6:00 P.M. on Christmas Eve the crew had Matthew back in the big bed in the apartment. "They was in and out of here in five minutes," Martha told me. Not surprising, on Christmas Eve.

On Christmas Day I took Martha a box of tangerines and Matthew some chocolate. Soon after I arrived Martha asked me to help Matthew use the bathroom. He had a cold, she said, and was still a little turned around from his trip to the hospital. I used the wheelchair to get him to the bedroom, then stood him next to the commode. He had to pee so badly that he started before I could get the diaper down and his pajamas clear. The front of his pajamas got soaked.

When he finished at the commode, I sat him on the bed and said that I would get him some fresh clothes. He showed none of his usual reluctance to be helped. He cooperated but stayed quiet as I put a fresh diaper and pajama bottoms on him. As always, he thanked me. But there was now a resignation in his voice that I hadn't heard before.

The aide wasn't working on Christmas, and there was a good chance Matthew hadn't eaten. So when I wheeled him out of the bedroom I asked if he'd had lunch. He didn't know, but Martha said he hadn't. There were two lunches in styrofoam clamshells on the dining area table. Martha had eaten half of her meal. Matthew's was untouched. I pushed him up to the table.

"Would you like some of the chicken?" I asked. He said he would, so I cut the bits into smaller bits and fed him. It didn't work. His upper dentures were so loose that he couldn't chew even small pieces. He had to spit them out. I opened a can of fruit cocktail, and he ate about a third of it. Then I gave him the longest drink of water I could get him to take.

"Matthew's medicine they gave him is on the table there," Martha said. She always invited me to look at his prescriptions, perhaps to verify that he had medicine and was thus destined to get better. Under the pill bottle was the hospital discharge sheet, with scribbled notes that read: "pt. blind, confused, hostile, unable to grasp discharge instructions."

As I cleaned up the table, Matthew said he wanted to get into his wheelchair so he could lay back. I said he was already in his wheelchair. He insisted on getting into his "lay-back wheelchair."

"You's already *in* your wheelchair," Martha shouted from her recliner.

"Do you want to get into your recliner? Your layback chair next to Martha's chair in the living room?" I asked him.

"No, it's a chair just like this one," he insisted. "It lays back. It's here. I been in it. It sleeps real good." He must have been thinking of his recliner.

"There ain't no other chair to go to. It's time for bed, anyway," Martha said.

I took Matthew back to the bedroom. I put my hip against the foot-board and nudged the bed six inches toward Martha's side to make room for the wheelchair. As he made the transition to the bed, Matthew seemed to be terrified of falling and moved more haltingly than usual. At one point, trying to maneuver in the slim space between the bed and the wall, I leaned against his hand and he let out a painful "oooh." I apologized twice and stifled an impulse to kick the damn bed.

Matthew sat on the bed and laid back, then I swung his feet up and pivoted him until his head was above the pillow. I held his shoulders and lowered him gently. "Are you comfortable now, Mr. Mason?" I asked.

"I'll be comfortable when I pass," he said, startling me.

"You ain't gone yet, so we might as well make you as comfortable as possible, *if* you don't mind," I said. He was lucid enough to recognize that I was tweaking him, sounding like he would have sounded if he'd been in my shoes. He laughed and then startled me again: "What are you gonna do when I'm gone?" he said. I wasn't sure what he wanted me to say.

"I'll miss you and I'll never forget you," I said. He was quiet after that. I wondered what else I could have said to comfort him. That I would look after Martha?

I pulled the bed back to the center of the room, then went to the kitchen and rinsed out the fruit cocktail can, washed the silverware, and bagged some garbage. It took about four minutes. When I peered into the bedroom, Matthew was asleep.

Martha was still in her recliner. "The Lord sent you right on time today," she said. "I didn't know how he was gonna get to the bathroom. Rosetta's son was here, but he's sick and he couldn't help." I remembered the card that my mother had sent for the Masons. I took it from my jacket pocket and gave it to Martha. She opened it and read the inscription aloud, as she always did when she got a card. "Merry Christmas," she ended.

On January 4, Martha called from the hospital. She had been admitted a few days earlier with severe abdominal pain (Thomas and David had taken turns staying in the apartment with Matthew). "It was like a toothache at the top of my stomach," she said, attributing the pain to a bad egg she'd eaten on New Year's Day. I asked what they had done for her at the hospital. "They worked me *hard*," she said, referring to the battery of tests they'd run. "They even put me in a big barrel that spins around you." The problem, as it turned out, was not food poisoning but pancreatitis.

She came home late that afternoon. I came by the next day and made a grocery run for them. To make room to put things away, I had to clean out the refrigerator. I filled a large trash bag with meals-on-wheels

leftovers that had gone bad. I fed Matthew diced peaches and brought Martha strawberry Jello in a coffee cup. She said her stomach felt better, but she was sticking to Jello for a while. Neither of them got out of bed while I was there. "Thank you a thousand million times," Martha said as I left.

Thomas had gotten a social worker to talk to Martha during Matthew's recent stay in the hospital. During that conversation she agreed that Matthew needed more care than he could get in the apartment and that a rest home would be better for him. She told the social worker to look into rest home placement for the two of them but later reneged and told the social worker she wasn't ready to move. Convincing Martha was the key, because Matthew had said if she was willing to move, he would go along with no fuss.

Within a week, the balance began to tip irreversibly toward moving. An allergic reaction to her medication forced Martha to spend a day in the hospital. When she came home, she was haggard and weak. "My stomach still ain't right," she said, resting her head on the dining area table, next to an untouched meals-on-wheels lunch pack. Now Thomas and the social worker persuaded her that she too needed extra care, and that, in the event of an emergency, Matthew would need more help than she could provide.

Lena took another step. She asked two people from the rest home where she worked to come talk to Martha. The administrators made their pitch, emphasizing the services their facility offered, and making clear that it was a *rest* home, not a nursing home like Martha had been in before. Martha listened but wouldn't make any commitments.

Then Matthew fell again. It was the morning of January 16, before the aide arrived, while he was using the commode. Martha called the rescue squad to get him up. Although he hadn't been hurt and had refused to go to the hospital, Martha seemed to recognize that Matthew's fall was a sign that their time in the apartment was near an end. "I reckon we's gonna have to move," she said, "on account of Matthew." He fell again, in the same way, on the morning of the eighteenth. Three days later, Martha agreed, finally, to move.

It wasn't clear how well Matthew understood the situation. Martha thought he knew, at least part of the time, that they were going to

move. She wasn't sure if he understood that they wouldn't be coming back to the apartment.

Matthew now spent the day in bed, in his pajamas. One day, shortly after the decision to move had been made, I went to the bedroom to visit with him. He sat up and we sat side by side on the edge of the bed. Perhaps as a distraction, perhaps because I wanted to project him farther into the future than his condition implied, I said, "Mr. Mason, you've got a birthday coming up. On June the fourth you'll be ninety-one."

"That's right," he said. "I was born June the fourth, 1911."

I recounted his early life. I said that he'd been born in the southwest corner of Durham County, on his Grampa Dick's farm; that his family had worked halves on the Tom Mason place in Chatham County; that he'd plowed a mule when he was eight and worked in a sawmill when he was ten; that he'd worked at the tobacco factory in Durham for a year when he was twelve; that he'd come to Chapel Hill in 1924 when he was thirteen; that he'd done yard work for a while and then worked at Harry's Grill; and that he'd started at the Phi Delta Theta fraternity on the Monday after Mother's Day in 1934.

As I offered each piece of his biography, he nodded his head, smiled, and said, "That's right." When I brought him up to 1934 and his start with the fraternity, he said, "You sure do remember good. I didn't know you was that old."

"I only know it because you told me," I said. "I was born in 1956."

"1956?" he said.

"Yeah. April 1956. You were forty-four then."

"Forty-four?"

"I bet I can tell you the name of Tom Mason's mule," I said.

"Sure enough?"

"Rhodie," I said. At that he smiled and tipped his head back and laughed.

"That's right!" he said with amazement. "Rhodie. That's sure enough right."

It was as if he had given me a set of keys to hold, so that I could help him access memories that were now locked away in his mind. I reached down to clasp his hand as I said good-bye. "Thanks for coming by. I sure have enjoyed you," he said.

There was a double room available immediately in a nice rest home in Hillsborough, but this place was too far away for David and Emma to visit easily. Martha was also sold on the place where Lena worked. It was a comparable facility on the southwest edge of town, within range of the EZ Rider. A suitable room could be ready in a week or two.

That it was time to move was clear. In fact, once the decision had been made, it seemed long overdue. Someone meeting the Masons for the first time, even a year earlier, might have found it easy to declare that they belonged in a rest home.

But those of us who saw them all along, who saw gradual decline and thus normalized each stage of lesser functioning, who saw them get through one day after another—and still laugh—could not be so certain. Knowing what it meant to them to stay in the apartment, and knowing Mr. Mason's dread of nursing homes, also made it hard to pressure them to move. As one geriatric social worker told me, "A lot of old folks will tell you that they'd rather fall and die on the floor of their own place than to spend one day in a nursing home." To which Mr. Mason might have said, "That's right. That's exactly right."

On February 8, 2002, the apartment was coming apart. The walls and shelves had been emptied of photographs and plaques. Empty cardboard boxes, awaiting filling, were stacked in corners. Other boxes had been pulled from closets so their contents could be reviewed and then kept, discarded, or given away. Martha was in her recliner, directing the aide to go through this or that box, or to pull another one out of the closet. Matthew was lying in bed, seemingly oblivious to the shambles. The Masons would move to the rest home the next morning.

I visited with Matthew for a while. When I asked how he was doing, he said, "Makes no difference whether you're young or old"—and stopped there, shortening his toast even further. I finished the next line, which elicited a strong "Right, boy!" He asked, every few minutes, how my family was doing. I assured him that we were all doing fine, then said I was going to see if Martha needed any help in the living room.

Martha was making phone calls. When she got an answering machine, she left a short message: "I just called to tell you we got to go out there

tomorrow. Maykatie [Matthew's daughter Mary] is here to help. We're going to the rest home tomorrow. Bye."

I asked her if she thought Matthew knew they were moving. "I don't know if he understands it or not," she said. "But he has to wear pants out there. They say he has to wear pants and go to the dining room. I reckon that'll be good."

The next morning, Thomas, Mary, two of Martha's grandnieces and two of their male friends, Lena, and I helped make the move. Matthew and Martha were taken first. Everything else—the TV, their recliners, a table lamp, the commode, a few boxes of clothes, three Bibles, a portable radio, and some of their pictures and knick knacks—fit in the bed of a pickup truck and the back of my Civic. The Masons' new living space was 9-by-12 feet, with a bathroom (toilet and sink, no shower or tub), and a small closet. Which meant that most of their possessions could not go with them.

There was no joy at the apartment as things were sorted, bagged, boxed, junked, or distributed according to Martha's wishes and the claims of family members. The sorting and cleaning distracted from the questions that hung over the situation: Would Matthew and Martha be okay in the rest home? Would they get proper care? Would they really be *better off* now? "It's a decent place," Thomas had reassuringly asserted earlier. "You just have to keep an eye on them—make sure they're treating Papa and Martha right." We'd all nodded, wanting to agree.

At the rest home, the Masons got separate, single beds on opposite ends of the room. Matthew lay quietly dazed in his bed, the wall on one side and a raised safety railing on the other, while Martha sat on the edge of her bed, which was next to the door. She complained about the room being small and about having to leave so much behind. She made a list of things for Thomas to do: get TV cable hooked up, call phone company, contact housing authority. She asked me to get her some crackers from the vending machine. I gave Matthew a piece of candy and said I'd be back later to check on him.

As I left, I passed several aides in the hall. They all smiled and returned my hello. The hall was clean and the air was free of the smell of urine and bodily decay that permeates the air in badly run nursing

homes. I remembered, too, that this was a rest home, not a nursing home, and the residents were, on the average, in better shape than the place where Martha had stayed before. So while it wasn't Shepherd House, it was by no means the reeking house of neglect that Mr. Mason had feared.

The next afternoon when I came by, Martha was in her wheelchair, wearing a nice dress and a hat and looking ready to go out. It was Sunday, and she told me that there was a church service in the dining room at 3:00. She and Matthew wanted to go. Matthew was dressed and in his recliner. "Is that you, Brother Mike?" he said when he heard me say hello to Martha. He was lucid, and being dressed and sitting up he looked better than he had during the last month in the apartment. I took it as a sign that this place really was going to be better for them.

The intercom announced that the service would begin in ten minutes. Since no aide had come to get them, I told Martha that I'd roll her to the dining room and then come back for Matthew. In the hallway Martha said hello to another resident, an elderly black woman, who gave us a friendly toothless smile and asked her if I was her son.

I asked Martha if she thought Matthew was doing okay. It was good, she said, that they helped him get dressed and get into his chair. She, too, was pleased to see him look more like he used to, as if the calendar had been turned back a few months. Does he know where he is? "Matthew knows we ain't in the apartment no more," she told me. "He hollered last night and said he wanted to go home. But I told him there ain't no more home to go to. This is it."

About twenty people were scattered around the tables in the dining room. Elderly white women in wheelchairs made up the largest category. Most sat alone, speaking to no one. Two college-age white men stood in the front of the room and paged through hymnals. They wore white shirts, black ties, and crew cuts. Two older men, one black and one white, stood nearby, next to a portable lectern. They consulted over a Bible held open by the white man. Behind them a large screen TV with the volume off showed the face of a famous sportscaster. I parked Martha at an empty table and went to get Matthew.

He understood that I was going to take him to the dining room so he could be with Martha during the service. I helped him get out of the recliner and pivot into the wheelchair. There wasn't much of the

maneuver that he could do by himself anymore, and it struck me how fully dependent he now was.

On the way to the service Martha told me that Matthew hadn't wanted to stay in the dining room for any of the meals they'd been served so far. She said he ate very little and wanted to go back to their room right away. Having to be fed in his own home was bad enough, I supposed. Here he was being fed in front of a roomful of people. I wondered if he could accept that. Can every indignity of old age be normalized? And if not, what then?

As we moved down the hall, I told him I thought that he and Martha would be safer now and better taken care of. There would be someone around all the time, if they needed help. And they wouldn't have to worry about whether the aides were easy to get along with. He nodded slightly but didn't say anything, and so I went on to say how it might take some time to adjust to the new place. "I reckon that's right" was all he said.

By the time I got Matthew to the dining room, the preacher, the white man who'd been holding the Bible, had started. We paused for a moment at the door. The preacher talked of *abiding* with Jesus, *trusting* in Jesus, *standing fast* with Jesus. "Satan is the god of the flesh, and the god of all that is against God," he said, as if scoring a debating point. I missed the segue, but then heard him quote the Epistle of James: "A double-minded man is unstable in all his ways." I thought of Atwater.

When there was a break for a hymn, I pushed Matthew to the table where Martha sat. "You're right by Martha now, Mr. Mason," I said, leaning over to speak into his ear.

"Is that you, Martha?" he said.

"I's here," she replied, turning to look at Matthew.

She had already turned back toward the boys, who had begun the hymn, when Matthew lifted his arm from the wheelchair and reached in the direction of her voice. He made it only halfway across the gap between them, and there wasn't room to move his chair any closer to hers. I cleared my throat and tapped the wheel of Martha's chair with my foot. She turned back toward me and then saw Matthew's extended hand. She reached out and covered it with hers.

"I's here, Sweetie," she said. "I's here."

epilogue

On April 14 Matthew Mason had no desire to eat. His brother David was visiting and wanted Matthew to eat *something*, so he wheeled him to the dining room for lunch. After a few small bites, Matthew was done. Martha called the next morning. "Matthew wouldn't eat nothing for supper or breakfast," she told me. "He was breathing funny, too, like he had fleem [phlegm] in his throat. He wasn't looking very good." The rest home had sent Matthew to the hospital after breakfast.

It was pneumonia again. Matthew was also dehydrated and his kidneys were failing. On Monday and Tuesday the word from the hospital was that Matthew was stable and they were "closely monitoring his condition." Thomas called from the hospital at 7:15 P.M. on Wednesday. "If you want to see him alive," he said, "you'd better come down now." Fifteen minutes later I met Thomas in Matthew's room.

Mr. Mason looked small and wasted in the bed, his forehead glistening with sweat. Though he was unable to carry on a conversation, he smiled faintly and nodded when we spoke to him up close. His breaths were shallow and ragged. As Thomas and I sat at the foot of the bed and talked, Matthew's voice, a raspy whisper, filled the space between our sentences. "Right, boy. Right, boy. Right, boy," he said.

When the nurse came to check the IV and monitor, I asked about Matthew's condition. She said that he was on antibiotics for the pneumonia (methicillin-resistant staphylococcus aureus), but, because he was so weak, there was a chance that the infection would spread to his blood. He was being rehydrated to improve his kidney function, she said, but this posed the risk of causing fluid to build up in his lungs. I asked about the ragged breathing. She said that Mr. Mason had resisted efforts to aspirate him and clear the fluid.

"It seems," she said, "that he doesn't want us to do anything for him."

The next day things were much the same. Martha told me that she and Thomas had instructed the hospital not to put Matthew on life support if his condition worsened. "I asked the Lord to touch him and help him," she said. "That's all I could do."

Martha called the hospital at 7:00 every morning that week. On Friday she was told that Matthew was having a hard time breathing and needed more oxygen. "He was worser today," she said when she called me after talking to the nurse. "They talked like it was pretty bad." She said that she'd woken up at midnight and couldn't get back to sleep. "That must have been about the time he started going down," she said. I told her that I would go to the hospital and check on Matthew.

I spoke with the doctor and with a geriatric nurse specialist. They said that Matthew's kidneys were failing, fluid had built up around his lungs, and the infection had spread to his bloodstream. It was also clear, they said, that Matthew did not want to be treated. From the time he was admitted, the doctor said, Matthew had verbally or physically resisted intervention. The nurse specialist said that she hoped to hold a family conference that afternoon to discuss the hospice option.

It was a little after 1:00 when I got Martha back to Matthew's hospital room. Thomas, David, and Emma were already there. A short white woman on the far side of middle age stood next to the bed. She introduced herself to Martha and me as a hospital chaplain, then had us form a circle around Matthew and join hands. He was weaker now but calmer, and, as the chaplain prayed, he looked toward her voice and seemed to know we were there.

After the prayer, we moved down the hall to a conference room. The doctor, the nurse specialist, the chaplain, a social worker, Martha, Thomas, David, Emma, and I sat at two round tables that had been pushed together into a figure 8. The doctor reviewed Matthew's condition. He spoke frankly, saying that more antibiotics would not change the outcome, and that Matthew had communicated, as clearly as he could, that he did not want anything done to him or for him.

The nurse explained that in hospice Matthew would be made as comfortable as possible and could have visitors twenty-four hours a day. Martha could stay there, too, if she wished. The social worker

said that Medicare would cover the cost, except for ambulance transportation. A bed was available at an excellent facility in Hillsborough, she said. Matthew could be moved there later that afternoon, if the family agreed. Agreeing meant giving Matthew no more antibiotics or nutrients. It also meant that Matthew would have, by the doctor's estimate, only a few more days.

After nearly ninety-one years of life, Matthew Mason's body was failing and there was nothing left to do. Matthew had also indicated that he was ready to rest. It was obvious, too, that it would be easier for all if Matthew's final days were spent in a small, quiet place rather than on the eighth floor of a busy hospital. Martha, Thomas, David, and Emma all agreed to moving Matthew to hospice care.

The next day I took Martha and her grandniece to see Matthew. The hospice was located on the grounds of an old farm east of town. It was a modern, six-bed facility built next to the original farmhouse, which had been converted to offices and a bereavement center. Other than the adjustable bed, Matthew's room had none of the cold mechanical trappings of a hospital. Two patio-style glass doors gave a wide view of a green field and a small pond.

Matthew had been put on morphine and was not responsive that day. But he was breathing easier and slept more calmly than he had in the hospital. A nurse explained to Martha what was being done for Matthew. She said that Martha could stay as long as she liked or call at any time. Before we left, we got the nurse's name and two phone numbers for the main desk. Martha called early the next morning, Sunday, and the nurse told her that Matthew had slept peacefully through the night. "I'm glad of that," Martha told me later. "They's taking good care of him."

I visited Matthew that afternoon. I thought it might be my last chance to be alone with him. He was the same as he'd been the day before—in and out of sleep and too weak to respond, though the nurse said he could hear me. I sat down next to the bed and spoke to him. Thank you, Mr. Mason, I said, for everything you've given me. His eyes opened for a moment then closed again, and I hoped that the nurse was right.

Nothing changed on Monday. When I called to ask how he was doing, the nurse said, "About the same." When Martha called on Tuesday

morning, the nurse told her that Matthew had woken up and was "a bit more responsive," then went back to sleep. Martha called me later and asked if I would take her to see Matthew. We got there about 3:00 P.M.

Matthew looked the same as he had since arriving at the hospice, though his breathing was shallower and a beat slower. I wheeled Martha to the side of his bed, where she held his hand and talked to him. "How you doing?" she asked. "Mr. Mike brought me up to see you. They said you was doing a little better." His face twitched when Martha first spoke, but then gave no further sign of response.

When we were ready to leave, I stood next to Martha and leaned over Matthew's bed. "Good-bye, Mr. Mason," I said. "I'll see you 'round like an orange." His faced twitched again. Martha caught it. "See that?" she said. "He smiled when you said 'see you 'round like an orange.' He knows your voice. He knows we're here." She looked at me, looked back at Matthew, and then pulled herself a few inches closer to the bed. "I've been praying for you," she said to him. "Maybe the Lord will lift you up again. I love you, Sugar. I'll always love you and think about you."

I got home from campus at about 7:45 P.M. the next day, April 24. There was a message from Thomas on my machine asking me to call him back. I called and got his machine, then tried Martha. Her line was busy. In a few minutes she called and said that Matthew had just passed. We agreed that he had died peacefully and with the most comfort possible. David, Thomas, and his wife, Sarah, had been with Matthew. "It was the Lord got them up there in time," Martha said, "so Matthew wouldn't be alone."

The funeral service for Matthew Mason was held on Sunday, April 28, 2002, at the First Baptist Church in Chapel Hill. Pastor J. R. Manley officiated and delivered the eulogy. The Reverend Marie Mann, Mr. Mason's niece, read the Scripture selection. Remarks were made by Richard Vinroot, Phi Delta Theta brother, ex-mayor of Charlotte, and Republican candidate for governor of North Carolina; and by Shoff Allison, Phi Delta Theta brother and chief fund-raiser for the Matthew Mason/Phi Delta Theta professorship. I said a few words. Following the service Mr. Mason was buried with Masonic rites at the Chapel Hill Cemetery. On May 29, 2002, Martha Mason left Chapel Hill to live closer to her relatives in Rockingham, North Carolina.

A few months after my father died, my sister told me of overhearing him being interviewed for a research project. It had been years earlier, when she was an undergraduate. Home from school during the week, she found a young man with a briefcase and clipboard asking our father questions at the kitchen table. She heard the young man ask my father if he was satisfied with his life. There was no way to avoid hearing his answer: a distinct "no."

My father was in his fifties then and had long since lost the zest he once had for hunting and fishing. Other than my uncle, he had no close friends. He often seemed depressed and even mildly agoraphobic. Except to go to work or to buy cigarettes or gas, he rarely left the territory comprising the house, the yard, and the garage. In the evening, after a few beers, he might loosen up a bit, but there were no other visible expressions of joy in his life. A disinterested observer might have said it was obvious that he was unhappy.

Still, it disturbed me to think of my father as having somehow failed, which is what his answer seemed to imply. I wanted to see my father, a figure of power in my imagination, as *capable*, as having gotten what he wanted out of life. It also saddened me to think that he might have seen himself as a failure.

No less troubling was the possibility that perhaps we had failed him. Was he dissatisfied with his children? Whatever else he had or hadn't done, couldn't he see us as evidence of meaningful accomplishment? For forty years he had amply provided for a large family, and we wouldn't have been there without him. I suppose we thought, with the egocentricity of children, that pride in us should have overridden all other considerations.

But perhaps what disturbed me the most was the mystery: not really knowing what my father thought and felt about his life, or why. As far as we knew, he was not one to talk of such things—to anyone. Yet he shared his feelings, some that were unfamiliar to us, with a stranger. That seemed unfair. If anyone deserved to know what was going on inside him, wasn't it those closest to him and most profoundly affected by him?

The stranger had advantages. My father had no stake in upholding for him an impression of being satisfied with his life. Nor was the

stranger invested in embracing any such illusion; there was nothing about my father's state of mind or biography that the stranger needed to believe for the sake of his own comfort. These are conditions under which, as bartenders and cab drivers know, people will sometimes reveal intimate details of their lives. Strangers with clipboards and tape recorders can learn things that insiders might never know.

These thoughts about my father and the interviewer came to mind when I worried about my ability to understand Mason and Atwater. In one view, the gap was too wide: no white man in a privileged class position could understand the life of a working-class black man in the South. The partial truth of this is undeniable. Even if I have at times, coming from working-class origins, been excluded and disrespected, such experiences, at the hands of a dominant group, were never my daily grind or the unrelenting forecast for my future. And so I could never fully know what it *felt like* to live in black skin in a white society.

How, then, to measure what I was learning about lives that were different from my own? Sheer information, though it was thin in places and didn't always come easily, was there to be found. It came from Atwater and Mason themselves, from people who knew them, from written records, and from observing. But the more I learned, the more it bothered me that I would never know everything, that I would never know the truth about past events (or even be sure they had actually occurred). It remains that people who were close to Atwater and Mason know things that only they will ever know.

To know everything, however, is impossible. In writing about the culture of biography, Justin Kaplan cites Julian Barnes's notion that biography is like a net: "a collection of holes tied together with strings." Kaplan goes on to say that those holes contain "half-truths, untruths, evasions, and incongruities. The reality of the life slips away like a greased piglet, a flown bird."[1] Which is to suggest that biographers often end up with, at best, an engaging story that holds a few of the thicker truths of a life.

---

1. Justin Kaplan, "A Culture of Biography," in *The Best Writing on Writing*, vol. 2, ed. by Jack Heffron (Cincinnati: Story Press, 1995), 131–43.

On the other hand, if biography is seen as a kind of micro anthropology, there is some hope to be taken from Clifford Geertz's description of what the task should be about. The aim of studying different others, Geertz says, is not to try to inhabit their souls through feats of imagination but to "figure out what the devil they think they are up to."[2] One might still never be sure even of this. Yet there is a good chance, when biography can portray its subjects in word and deed, over time, that it will become apparent, as the story unfolds, what the devil people think they are up to. And, as Geertz also says, it is not necessary to know everything to understand something.

What I knew about Matthew Mason and Anthony Atwater was not everything that had happened to them, not even during the years I spent with them. Nor did I understand what it felt like to be them, perhaps no more than I understood what it felt like to be my father. But I did know the outlines of their lives, the social landscape in which those lives played out, and many of the details of their endtimes. I knew the stories of their lives and the stories they told about their lives. What I think I understood, in the end, was what they desired and what mattered to them.

Atwater and Mason wanted respect as men. As southern black men, they had to contend with forms of racism that made it difficult to achieve this respect in equal proportion to white men of lesser caliber. They adapted, as they had to, using the resources they possessed. In part this meant creating personas—Shine/Popcorn and Dr. Reet. It also meant acting, being double men, and suffering a chronic self-doubt because of it. The search for respect thus brought with it a psychic pain that had to be repressed, or assuaged with alcohol.

Atwater and Mason wanted a measure of control over their lives, and their personas helped them get it. Shine/Popcorn and Dr. Reet elicited predictable reactions, and so the control thereby achieved, though slight, was not imaginary. Unfortunately, what worked with some audiences created trouble with others. That trouble highlighted the contradiction in which both men were caught: striving for control, in the way

2. Clifford Geertz, *Local Knowledge: Further Essays in Interpretive Anthropology* (New York: Basic Books, 1983).

white society allowed, unraveled other parts of their lives. When the contradiction became too much to bear, there was, again, the escape afforded by alcohol, and with it more unraveling.

To say that Matthew Mason and Anthony Atwater wanted respect and control does not mark them as unusual. It is nearly a truism, in fact, to say that men—given what men are taught to be in our culture—desire respect and control. In this regard Mason and Atwater were men like most others. Likewise in forging masks and stories to deal with their fears and vulnerabilities they were like most men. We all learn to call upon myth to rescue us when the world resists control and the self falls short.

Yet for Mason and Atwater there were extra burdens. As *men* they were supposed to command respect and achieve control—or not be counted as men at all. But as *black* men and as *working-class* men, they were hindered in their quest for the masculine ideal. Frustration and anger were natural results. It seems no wonder, then, that at times both men, despite the goodness they harbored, lashed out at vulnerable people around them, and at themselves as well.

The dilemma faced by Mason and Atwater is by now familiar. It can be no surprise to anyone who has thought seriously about the meaning of manhood in America. Or about our national contradiction: an ideology of fairness and opportunity butted against the enduring realities of racism and inequality.

Less familiar is how black men, and working-class men like my father, wrestle with the dilemma and how the struggle shapes them. The result is not only suffering, but, on the other side of trouble, wit, invention, humor, and resilience. We can see in the lives of Mason and Atwater this duality in which mind and spirit resisted limitation and tried, with mixed success, to turn suffering into insight and compassion. But I am wary of such a high-toned generalization, even about so few as two men. For it is in grasping the particulars, the flesh and bone of experience, that we find our way to common ground.

acknowledgments

I am indebted to a great many people who provided information for this book. First and foremost I want to thank the friends and family members of Matthew Mason and Anthony Atwater for sharing with me their time, stories, and insights. Without their help, this book would not have been possible.

On the Mason side of the ledger, I owe special thanks to Mary (Mason) Boyd, Bertha Brown, Arnita Davis, Wayne Durham, Alma Jones, Jesse Lassiter, Marie Mann, Allen Mason, Bettie Mason, David Mason, Doretha Mason, Emma Mason, Herman Mason, Martha Mason, Matthew Mason Jr., Thomas Mason, Georgia Barbee McCallum, James Nunn Jr., Rashii Purefoy, Martha Summers, and Gloria (Mason) Williams. On the Atwater side, I am especially grateful for help from Ella Atwater, Chris Atwater, Cleavon Atwater, Dorothy Atwater, John Atwater, William T. Bass, Catherine Foushee, Lena Paylor, and William Williams.

Others who provided valuable information or assistance include Bill Allen, Helen Allen, Harold Baldwin, Rosetta Barbee, Willis Barbee, Wade Barber Jr., Kate Barrett, Lou Bilionis, J. E. Booth, E. I. Brown, Ed Caldwell Jr., Hilliard Caldwell, Rebecca Clark, Ada Council, John Edwards, Renee Gledhill-Earley, Cleo Ferguson, Bryan Freidel, Susan Freidel, Dr. Jan Halle, Frances Hargraves, Sarah Harrington, Ollie Jenkins, Kim Lassiter, Thomas Little, Rev. J. R. Manley, Joshua Mann, Wallace Markham, B. L. Mason, Ronnie Mason, Lee Mazaras, Esther McCauley, Flo Miller, Kirk Obsborn, Linda Perry, Adolph Reed Jr., John Shelton Reed, Randall Roden, Barbara Roth, Kristie Russ, Collie Mack Sears, Jasmer Sears, Thomas Sears, Elizabeth Scott, H. Clay Scott, Walter Shackelford, Joann Shirer-Mitchell, Susan Simone, R. D. Smith, Hugh Stevens, Robert Teer, Patricia Thomas, Jean Triplett,

Ruel Tyson, Roberta Vereen, Phyllis Wall, Chris Walsh, William Webb, Harold Wolfe, and David Zonderman.

Although I don't suppose that all members of Phi Delta Theta will agree with my assessment of Mr. Mason's relationship with the fraternity, I could not have arrived at that assessment without the help of many of the brothers. My thanks, then, to the fraternity members who sent letters or spoke to me by phone: John Acee, Marshall Acee, Rick Adams, Chuck Anderson, Lawrence Austin, Clinton Benbow, Mac Boxley, Paul Burroughs, Tom Butler, Larry Cahall, Peter Callahan, John Calvert, Tom Cannon, Marcus Cherry, Rhodes Corbett, William Dunlap, Whitney Durand, James Durham, Bob Eaves, Jack English, James Epps, Ray Farris, Sam Froelich, Charles Gilmore, Joseph Grier Jr., Robert Grubb, Henry Harris, George Henderson, Richard Hendrickson, Ed Huffman, Tom Jones, Eli Joyner, McKibben Lane, John Lindsay, Al Long, Jim Martin, John Medlin, Eugene McDaniel, Robert McGimsey, Ed McLaughlin, Frank McSwain, Allen Merrill, Don Millen, Rolfe Neill, Bob Page, Bill Pittman, Gray Poole, Mark Pope, Ramsay Potts, Edward Pleasants, Riley Pleasants, Inman Reed, James Reston Jr., Tom Rogers, Sherrod Salsbury, Bert Smith, Ralph Strayhorn, Irvin Tucker, Billy Urquhart, Cutler Watkins, Harold Wells, Joe Webb, J. Cross Williams, Robert Williams, Stuart Woodman, and Thomas Worth.

Several colleagues commented on parts of the manuscript. Maxine Thompson, Kecia Johnson, and Michelle Wolkomir helped me keep faith that there was a story here worth telling. An early version of what became chapter 1 ("Room to Be Human") benefited from comments by Phillip Lopate, Paul Wilkes, and Jean Florman. Craig Gill of University Press of Mississippi showed an enthusiasm for the manuscript that helped me get through the last tough stages of editing. My thanks to you all.

Writing is hard enough when you have the time to do it, and even harder when it has to be squeezed in between regular teaching duties. And so I am grateful to North Carolina State University for providing me with a leave during the spring of 2001 to help me move things along. Those few months made a huge difference.

The decision to write a biography was risky, and I doubt that I would have made such a decision without the support of my life partner,

Sherryl Kleinman, who saw, before I did, that I had to write about Mason and Atwater. Along the way, she provided essential advice, modeled a soul-saving disregard for academic convention, helped me befriend the Masons, and nurtured the love that makes good work possible.

I regret that Matthew Mason and Anthony Atwater did not live to see themselves in these pages. It's to them that I owe the greatest debt. I can only hope that the time we spent together gave them as much pleasure as it gave me, and that the results of this book will honor their lives.